STAR WARS
THE RISE OF
KYLO REN

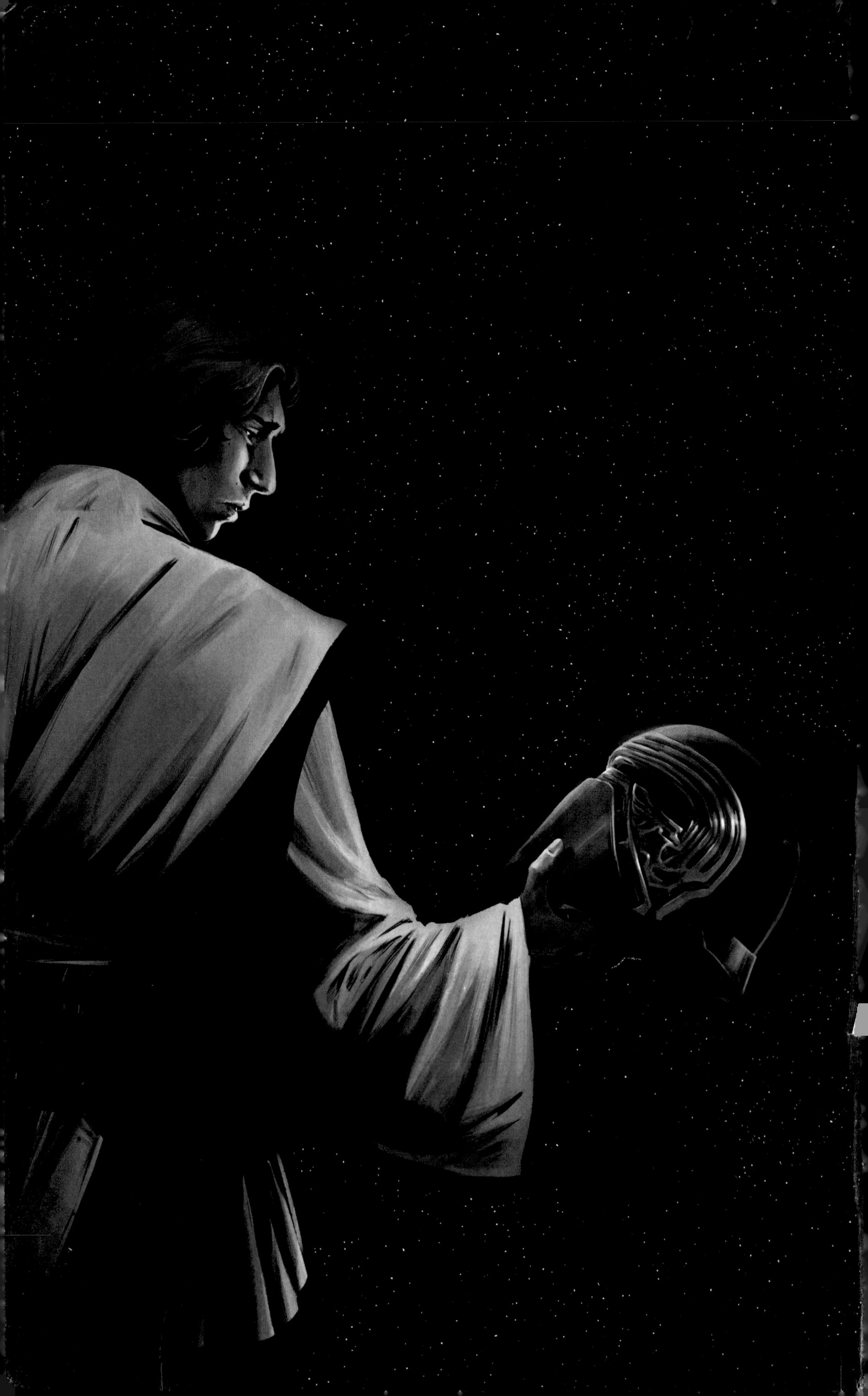

THE RISE OF KYLO REN

Writer CHARLES SOULE
Artist WILL SLINEY
Color Artist GURU-eFX
Letterer VC's TRAVIS LANHAM
Cover Art CLAYTON CRAIN

Assistant Editor TOM GRONEMAN
Editor MARK PANICCIA

Special thanks to J.J. ABRAMS

Collection Editor JENNIFER GRÜNWALD
Assistant Managing Editor MAIA LOY
Assistant Managing Editor LISA MONTALBANO
Editor, Special Projects MARK D. BEAZLEY
VP Production & Special Projects JEFF YOUNGQUIST
Book Designer ADAM DEL RE
SVP Print, Sales & Marketing DAVID GABRIEL
Editor In Chief C.B. CEBULSKI

FOR LUCASFILM:

Senior Editor ROBERT SIMPSON
Creative Director MICHAEL SIGLAIN
Lucasfilm Story Group MATT MARTIN
PABLO HIDALGO
EMILY SHKOUKANI
JAMES WAUGH
Lucasfilm Art Department PHIL SZOSTAK

STAR WARS: THE RISE OF KYLO REN. Contains material originally published in magazine form as STAR WARS: THE RISE OF KYLO REN (2019) #1-4. Second printing 2020. ISBN 978-1-302-92418-8. Published by MARVEL WORLDWIDE, INC., a subsidiary of MARVEL ENTERTAINMENT, LLC. OFFICE OF PUBLICATION: 1290 Avenue of the Americas, New York, NY 10104.

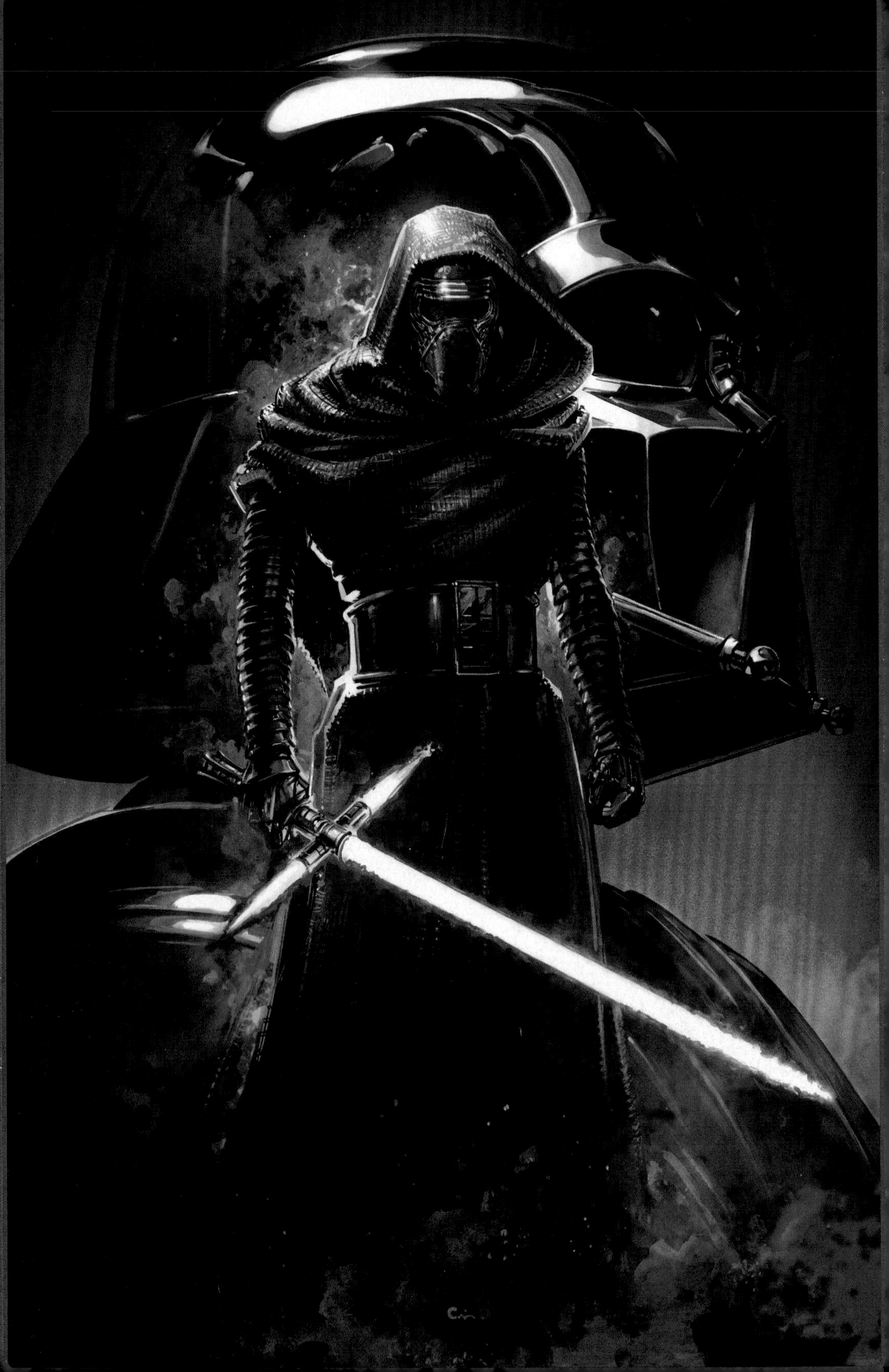

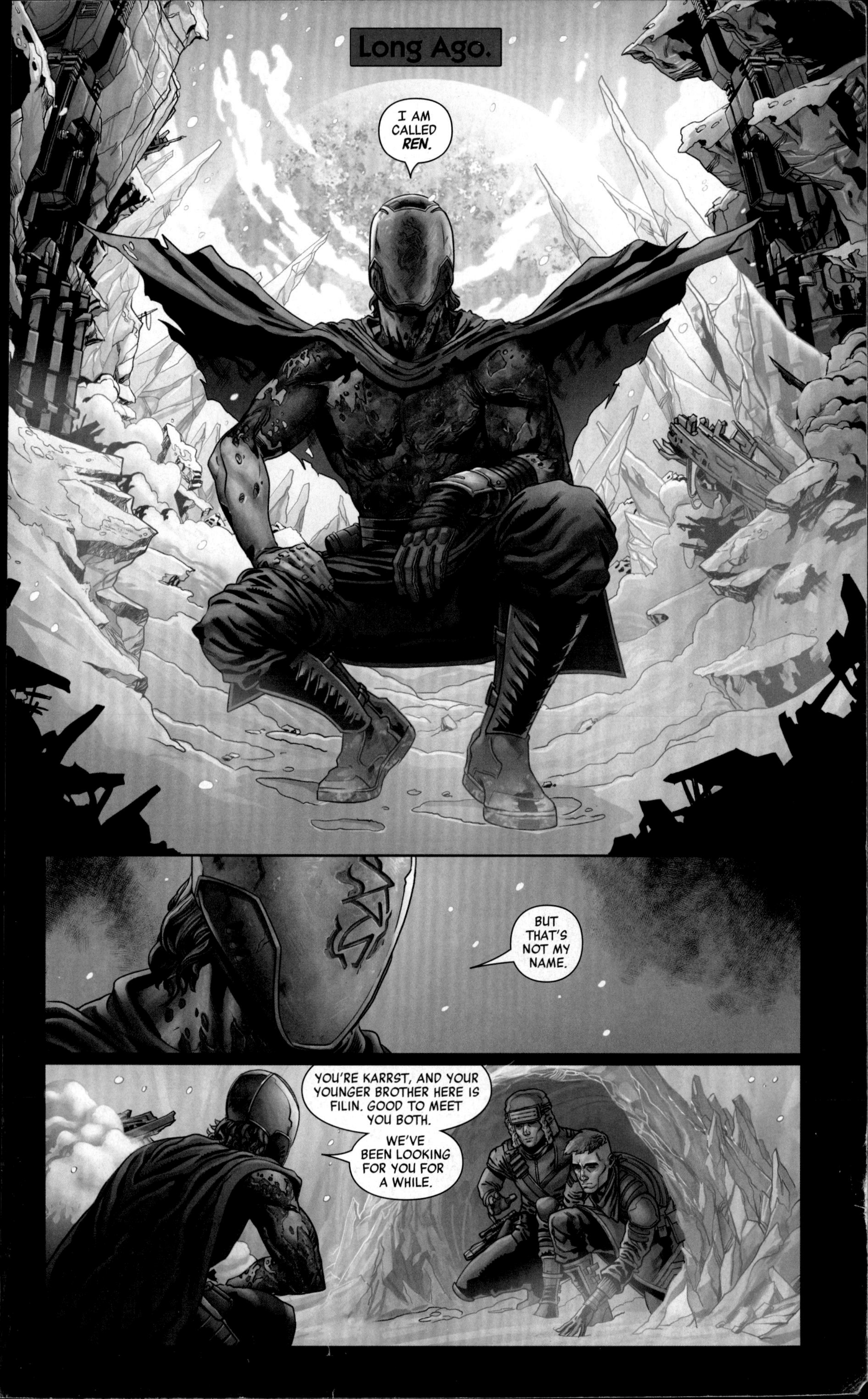
Long Ago.
I AM CALLED REN.
BUT THAT'S NOT MY NAME.
YOU'RE KARRST, AND YOUR YOUNGER BROTHER HERE IS FILIN. GOOD TO MEET YOU BOTH.
WE'VE BEEN LOOKING FOR YOU FOR A WHILE.

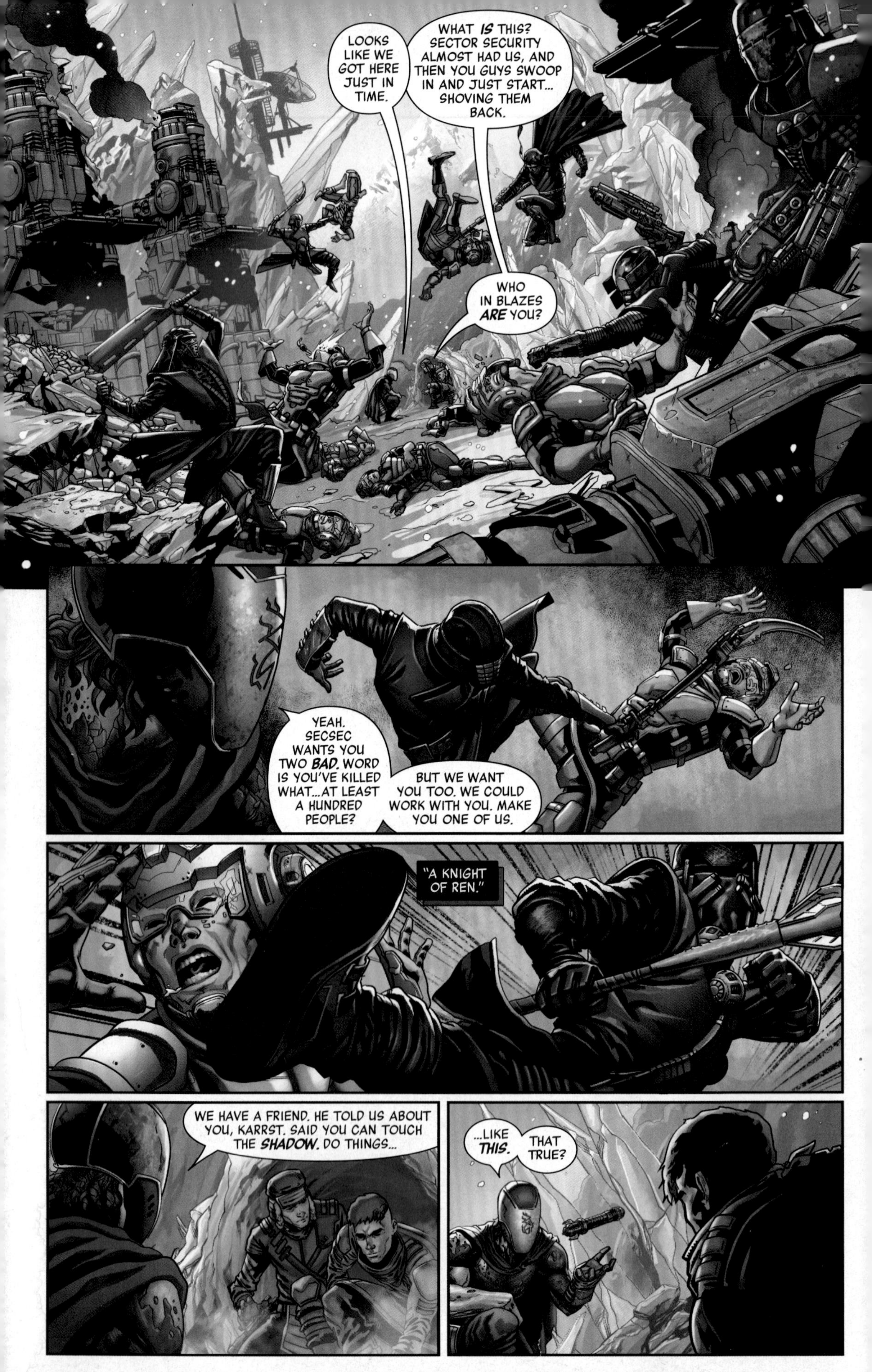
LOOKS LIKE WE GOT HERE JUST IN TIME.
WHAT IS THIS? SECTOR SECURITY ALMOST HAD US, AND THEN YOU GUYS SWOOP IN AND JUST START... SHOVING THEM BACK.
WHO IN BLAZES ARE YOU?
YEAH. SECSEC WANTS YOU TWO BAD. WORD IS YOU'VE KILLED WHAT...AT LEAST A HUNDRED PEOPLE?
BUT WE WANT YOU TOO. WE COULD WORK WITH YOU. MAKE YOU ONE OF US.
"A KNIGHT OF REN."
WE HAVE A FRIEND. HE TOLD US ABOUT YOU, KARRST. SAID YOU CAN TOUCH THE SHADOW. DO THINGS...
...LIKE THIS.
THAT TRUE?

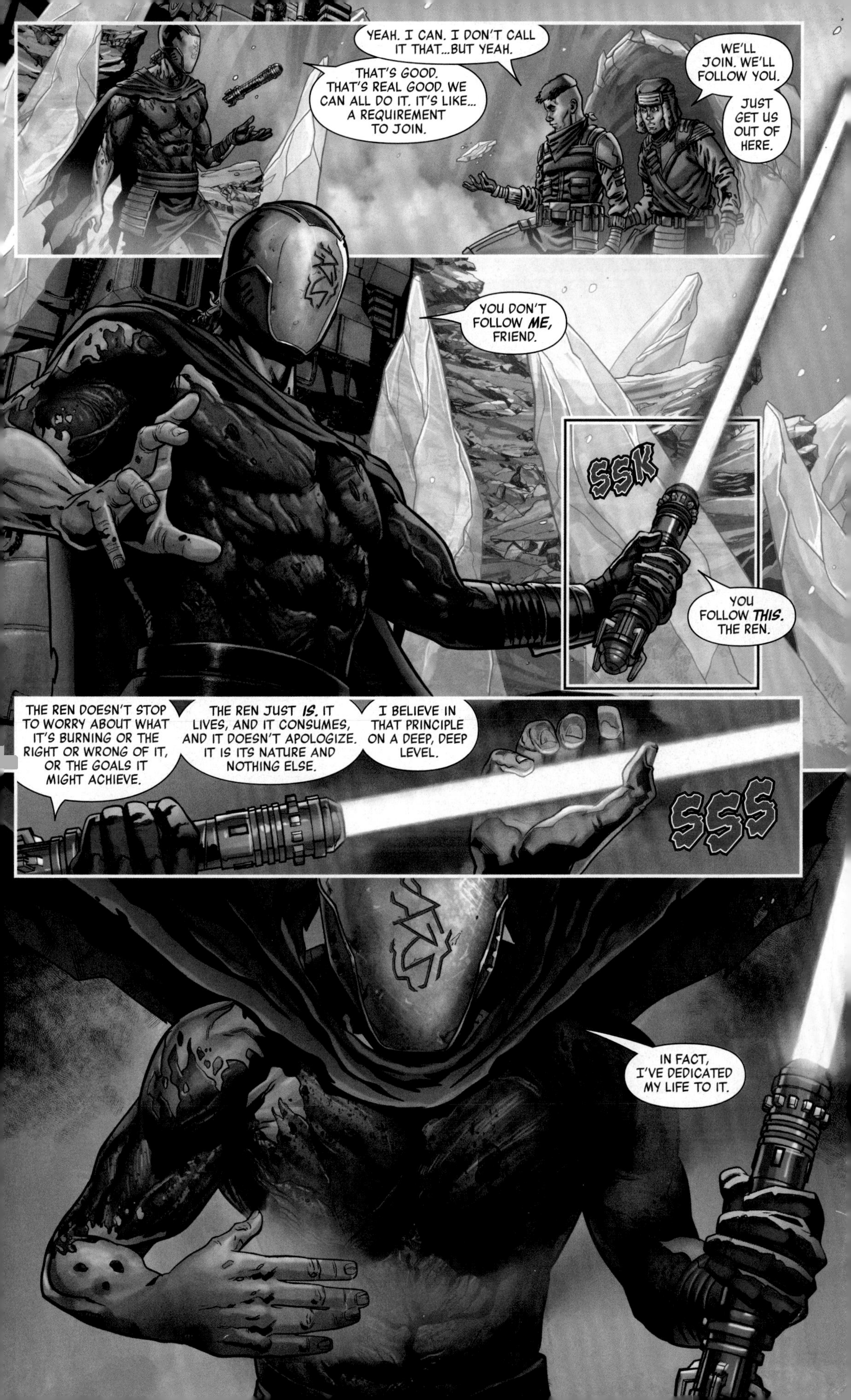
YEAH. I CAN. I DON'T CALL IT THAT...BUT YEAH.
THAT'S GOOD. THAT'S REAL GOOD. WE CAN ALL DO IT. IT'S LIKE... A REQUIREMENT TO JOIN.
WE'LL JOIN. WE'LL FOLLOW YOU.
JUST GET US OUT OF HERE.
YOU DON'T FOLLOW ME, FRIEND.
SSK
YOU FOLLOW THIS. THE REN.
THE REN DOESN'T STOP TO WORRY ABOUT WHAT IT'S BURNING OR THE RIGHT OR WRONG OF IT, OR THE GOALS IT MIGHT ACHIEVE.
THE REN JUST IS. IT LIVES, AND IT CONSUMES, AND IT DOESN'T APOLOGIZE. IT IS ITS NATURE AND NOTHING ELSE.
I BELIEVE IN THAT PRINCIPLE ON A DEEP, DEEP LEVEL.
SSS
IN FACT, I'VE DEDICATED MY LIFE TO IT.

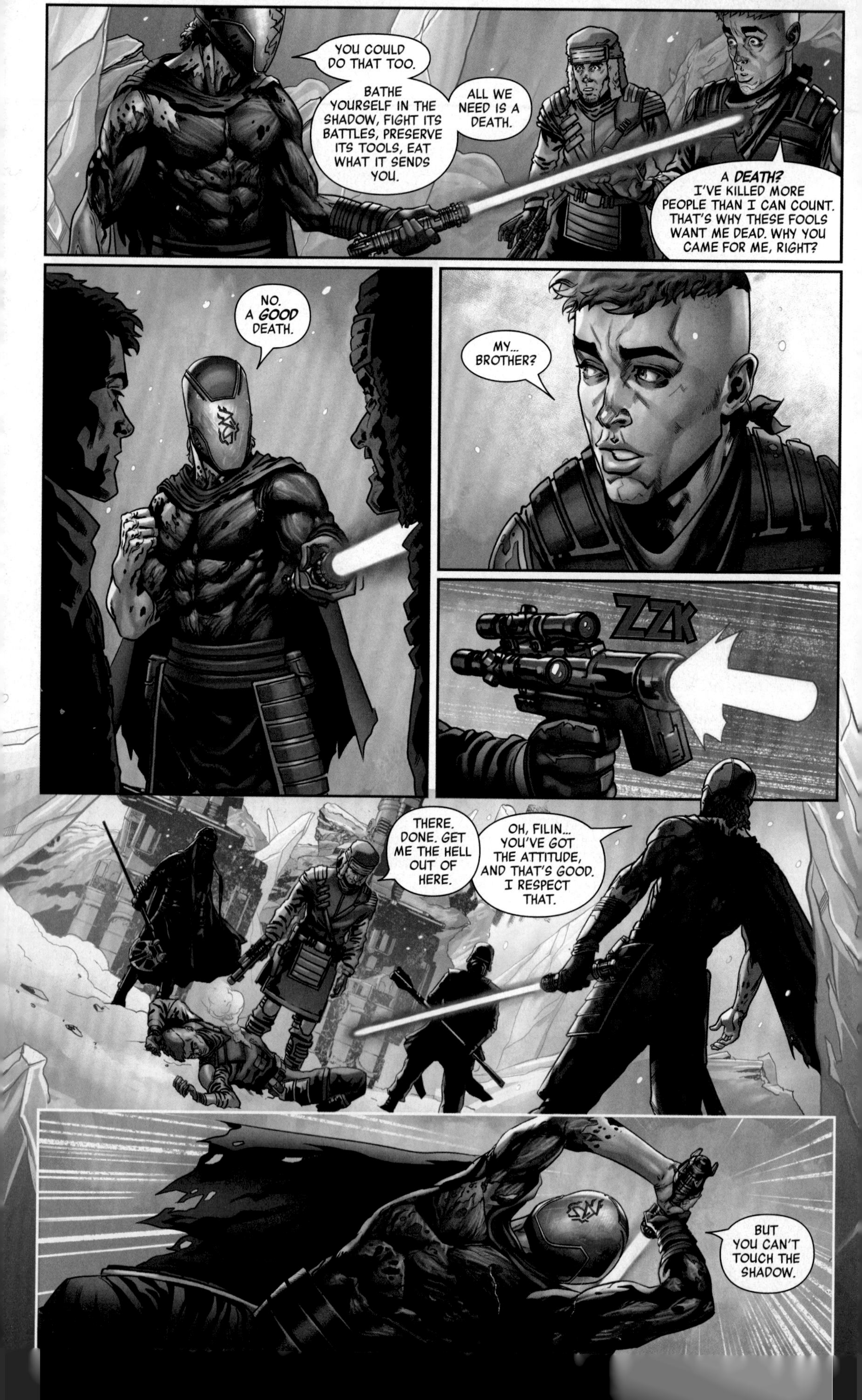
YOU COULD DO THAT TOO.
BATHE YOURSELF IN THE SHADOW, FIGHT ITS BATTLES, PRESERVE ITS TOOLS, EAT WHAT IT SENDS YOU.
ALL WE NEED IS A DEATH.
A *DEATH?* I'VE KILLED MORE PEOPLE THAN I CAN COUNT. THAT'S WHY THESE FOOLS WANT ME DEAD. WHY YOU CAME FOR ME, RIGHT?
NO. A *GOOD* DEATH.
MY... BROTHER?
ZZK
THERE. DONE. GET ME THE HELL OUT OF HERE.
OH, FILIN... YOU'VE GOT THE ATTITUDE, AND THAT'S GOOD. I RESPECT THAT.
BUT YOU CAN'T TOUCH THE SHADOW.

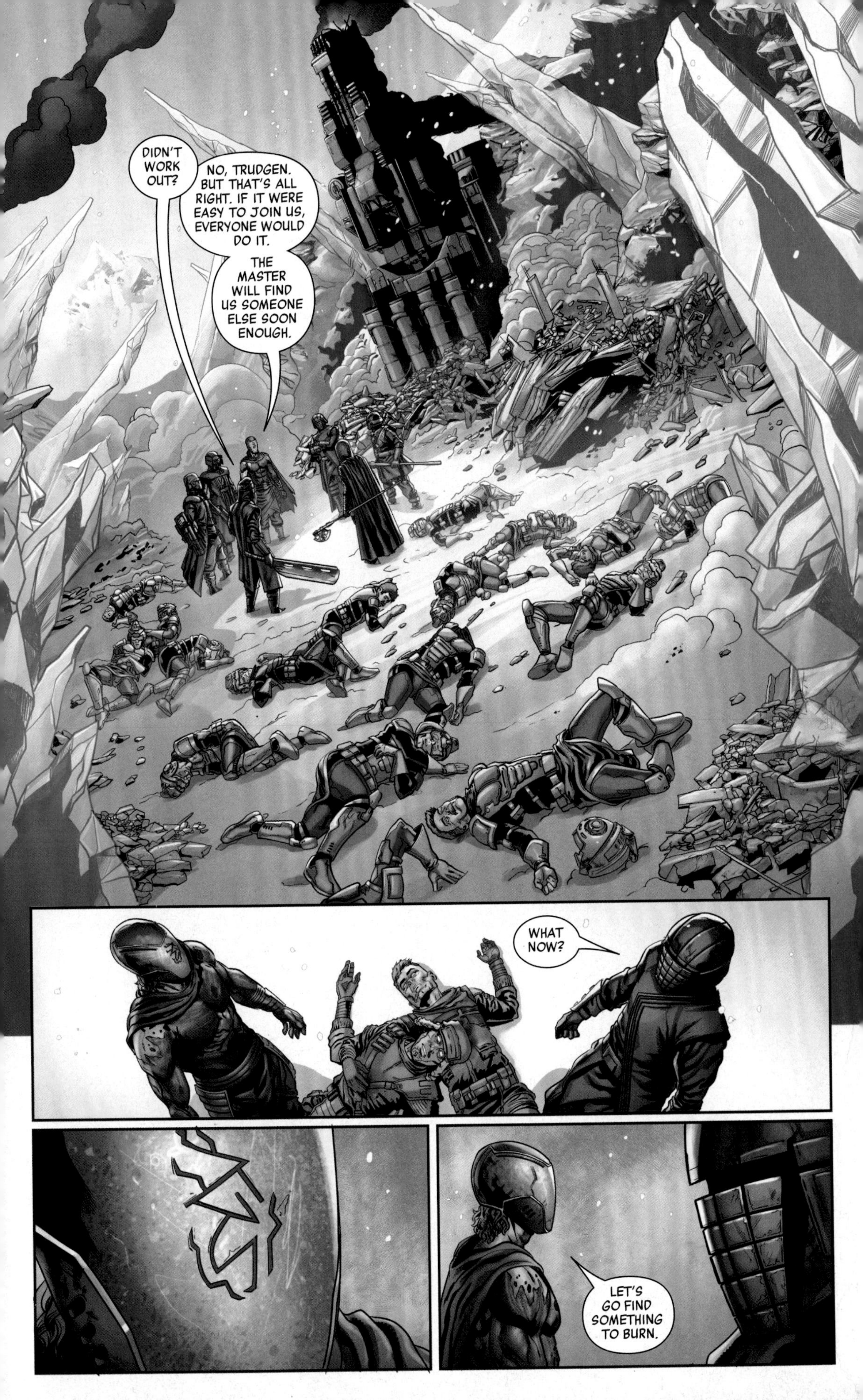
DIDN'T WORK OUT?
NO, TRUDGEN. BUT THAT'S ALL RIGHT. IF IT WERE EASY TO JOIN US, EVERYONE WOULD DO IT.
THE MASTER WILL FIND US SOMEONE ELSE SOON ENOUGH.
WHAT NOW?
LET'S GO FIND SOMETHING TO BURN.

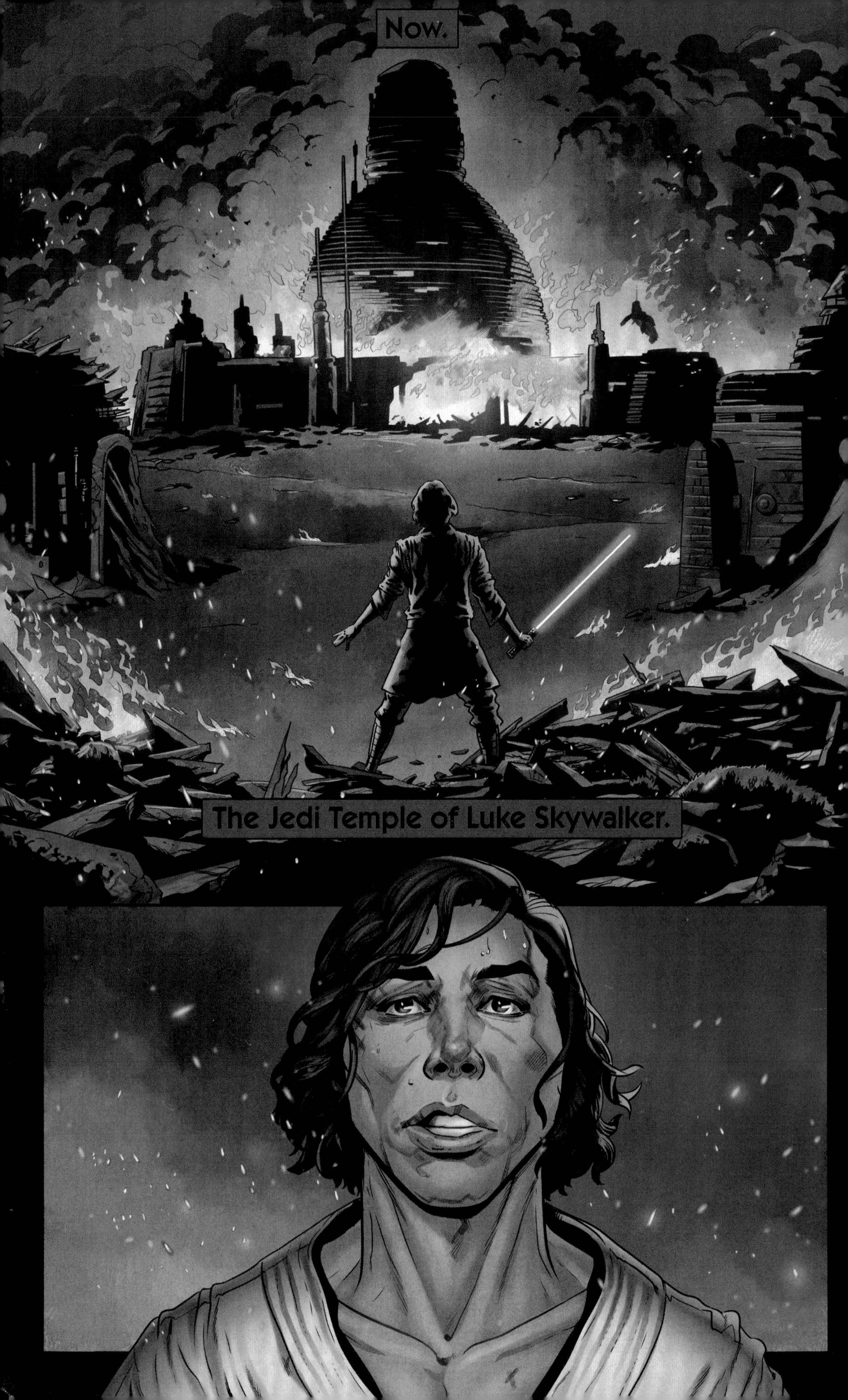
Now.
The Jedi Temple of Luke Skywalker.

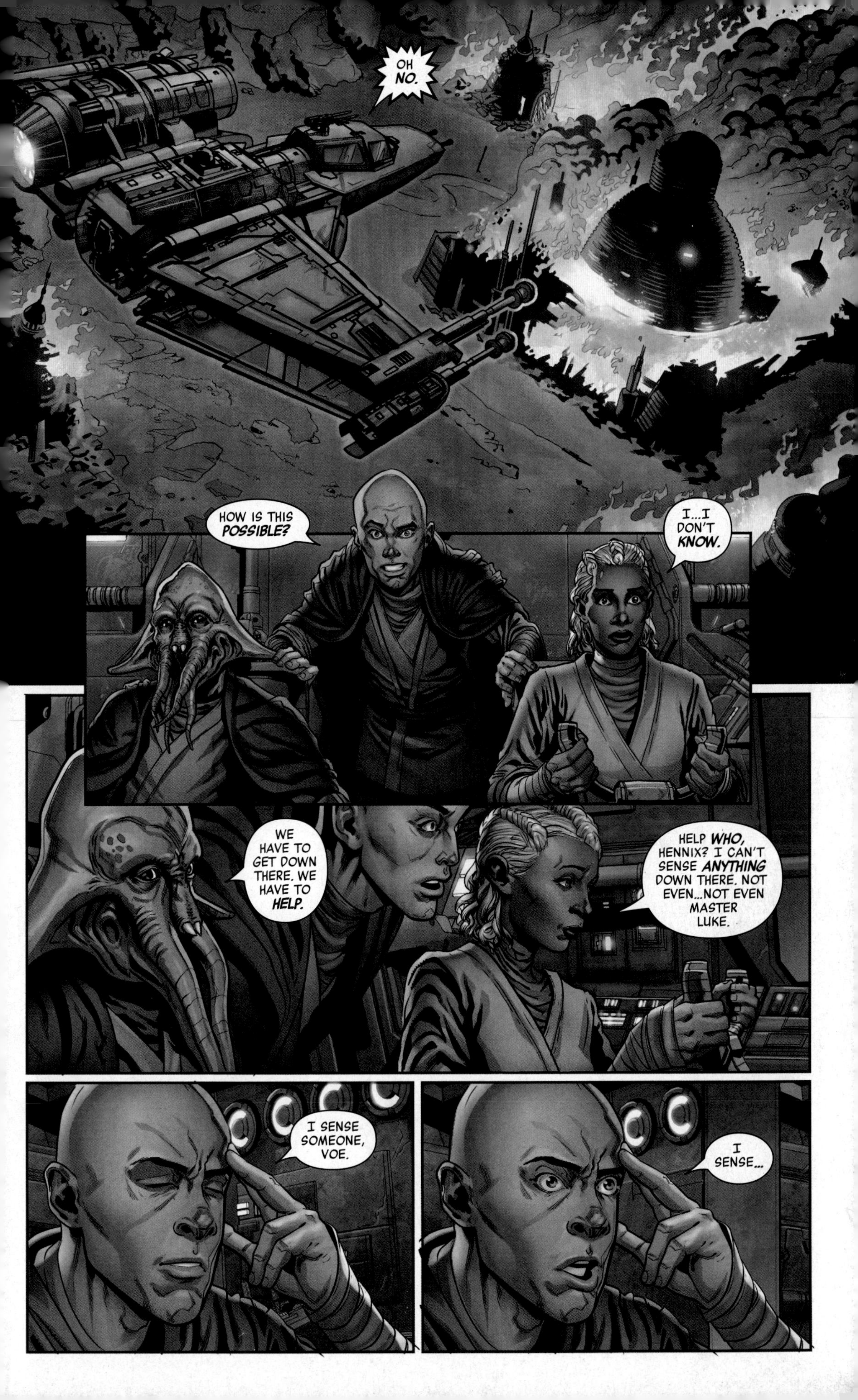
OH NO.
HOW IS THIS POSSIBLE?
I...I DON'T KNOW.
WE HAVE TO GET DOWN THERE. WE HAVE TO HELP.
HELP WHO, HENNIX? I CAN'T SENSE ANYTHING DOWN THERE. NOT EVEN...NOT EVEN MASTER LUKE.
I SENSE SOMEONE, VOE.
I SENSE...

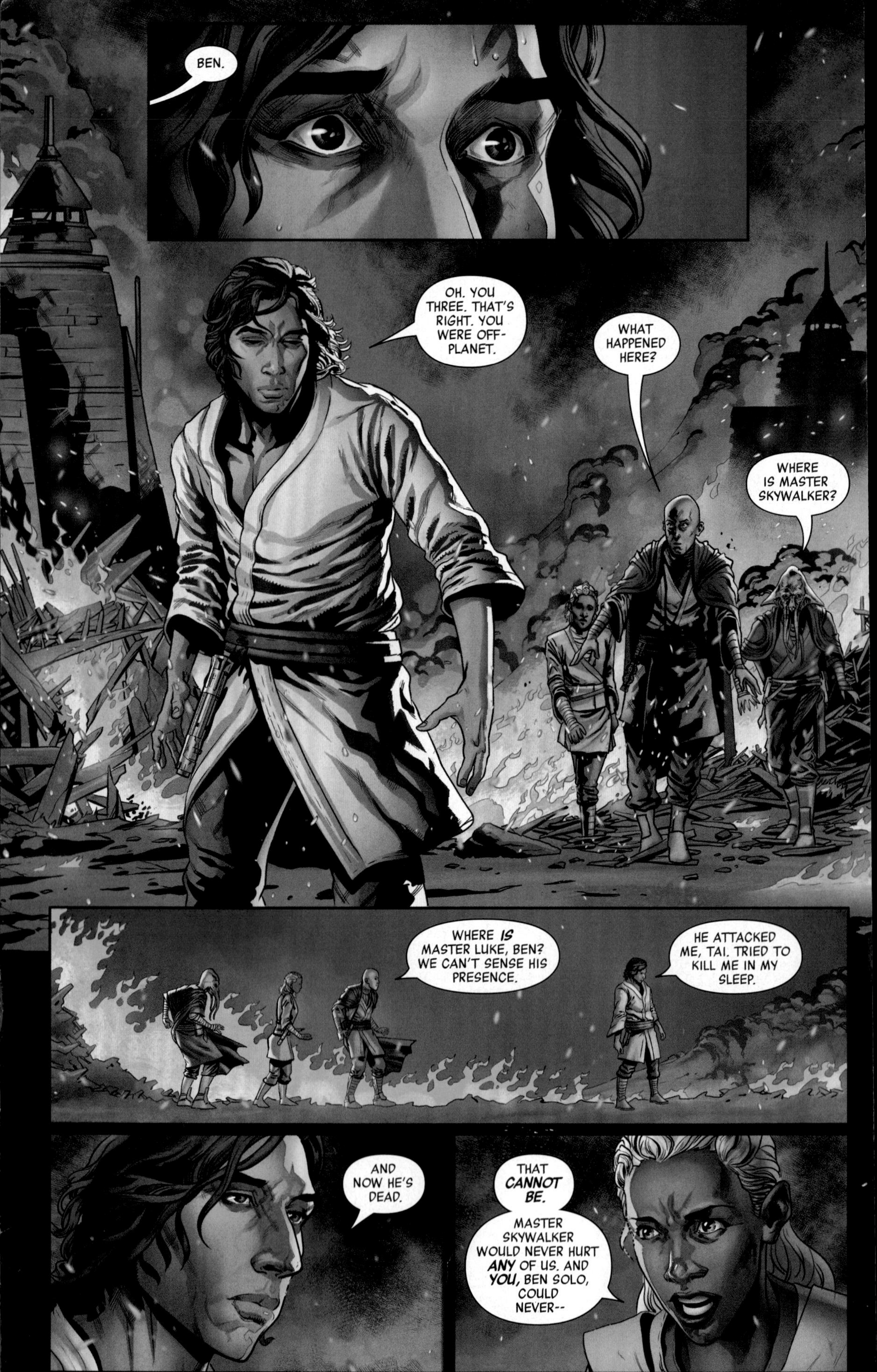
BEN.
OH. YOU THREE. THAT'S RIGHT. YOU WERE OFF-PLANET.
WHAT HAPPENED HERE?
WHERE IS MASTER SKYWALKER?
WHERE *IS* MASTER LUKE, BEN? WE CAN'T SENSE HIS PRESENCE.
HE ATTACKED ME, TAI. TRIED TO KILL ME IN MY SLEEP.
AND NOW HE'S DEAD.
THAT *CANNOT BE.*
MASTER SKYWALKER WOULD NEVER HURT *ANY* OF US. AND *YOU,* BEN SOLO, COULD NEVER--

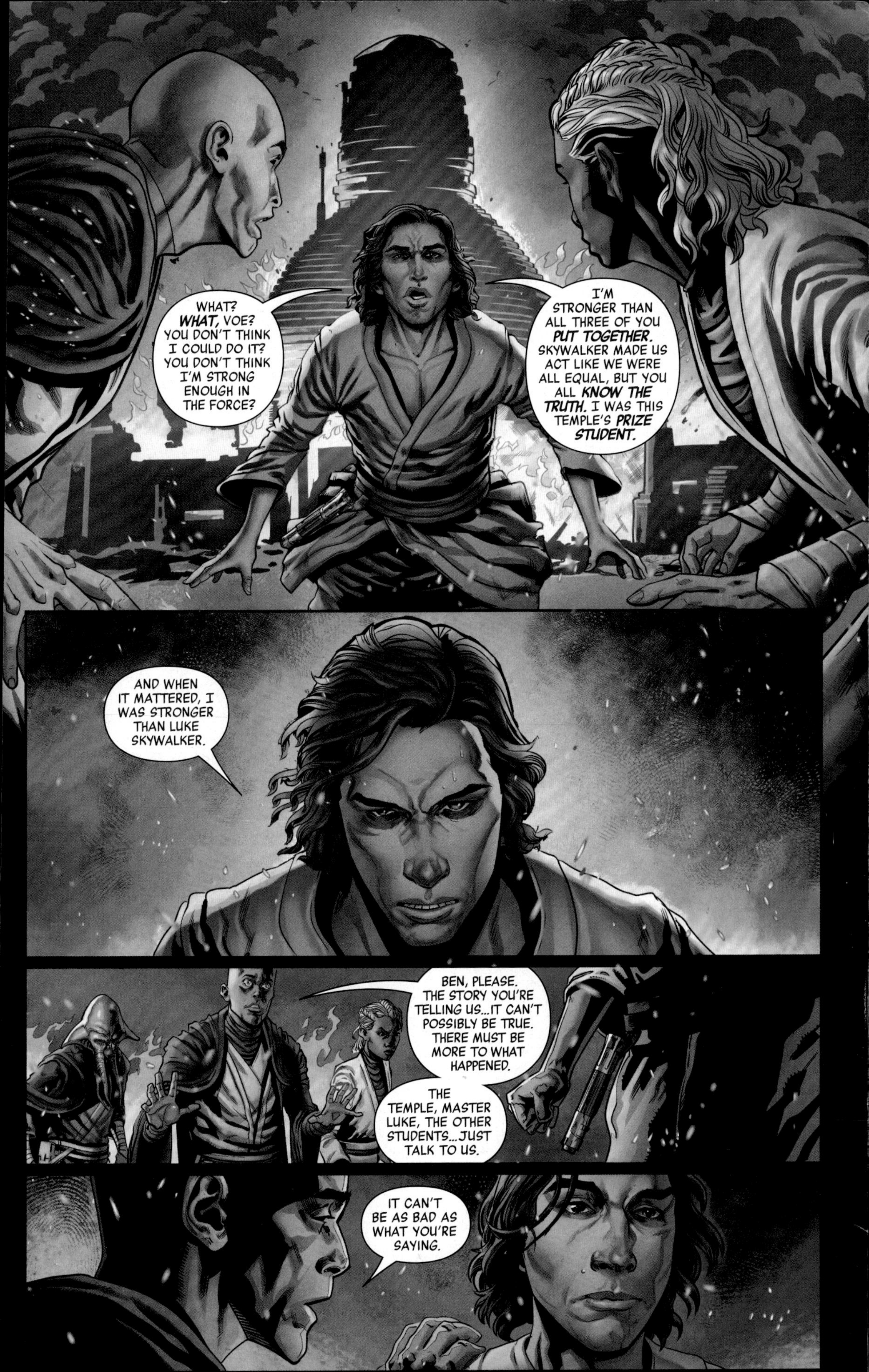
WHAT? **WHAT,** VOE? YOU DON'T THINK I COULD DO IT? YOU DON'T THINK I'M STRONG ENOUGH IN THE FORCE?
I'M STRONGER THAN ALL THREE OF YOU **PUT TOGETHER.** SKYWALKER MADE US ACT LIKE WE WERE ALL EQUAL, BUT YOU ALL **KNOW THE TRUTH.** I WAS THIS TEMPLE'S **PRIZE STUDENT.**
AND WHEN IT MATTERED, I WAS STRONGER THAN LUKE SKYWALKER.
BEN, PLEASE. THE STORY YOU'RE TELLING US...IT CAN'T POSSIBLY BE TRUE. THERE MUST BE MORE TO WHAT HAPPENED.
THE TEMPLE, MASTER LUKE, THE OTHER STUDENTS...JUST TALK TO US.
IT CAN'T BE AS BAD AS WHAT YOU'RE SAYING.

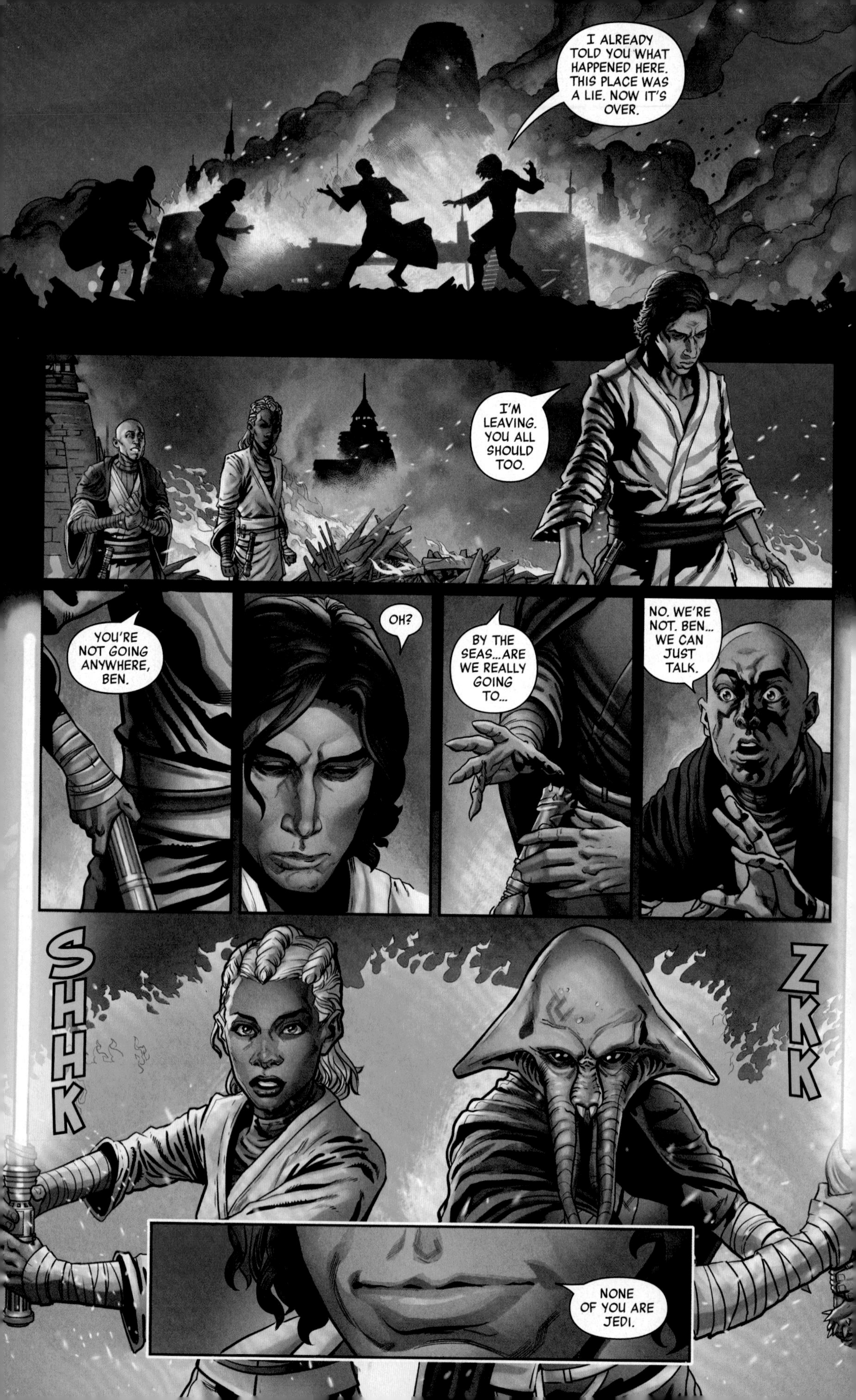
I ALREADY TOLD YOU WHAT HAPPENED HERE. THIS PLACE WAS A LIE. NOW IT'S OVER.
I'M LEAVING. YOU ALL SHOULD TOO.
YOU'RE NOT GOING ANYWHERE, BEN.
OH?
BY THE SEAS...ARE WE REALLY GOING TO...
NO. WE'RE NOT. BEN... WE CAN JUST TALK.
SHHHK
ZKK
NONE OF YOU ARE JEDI.

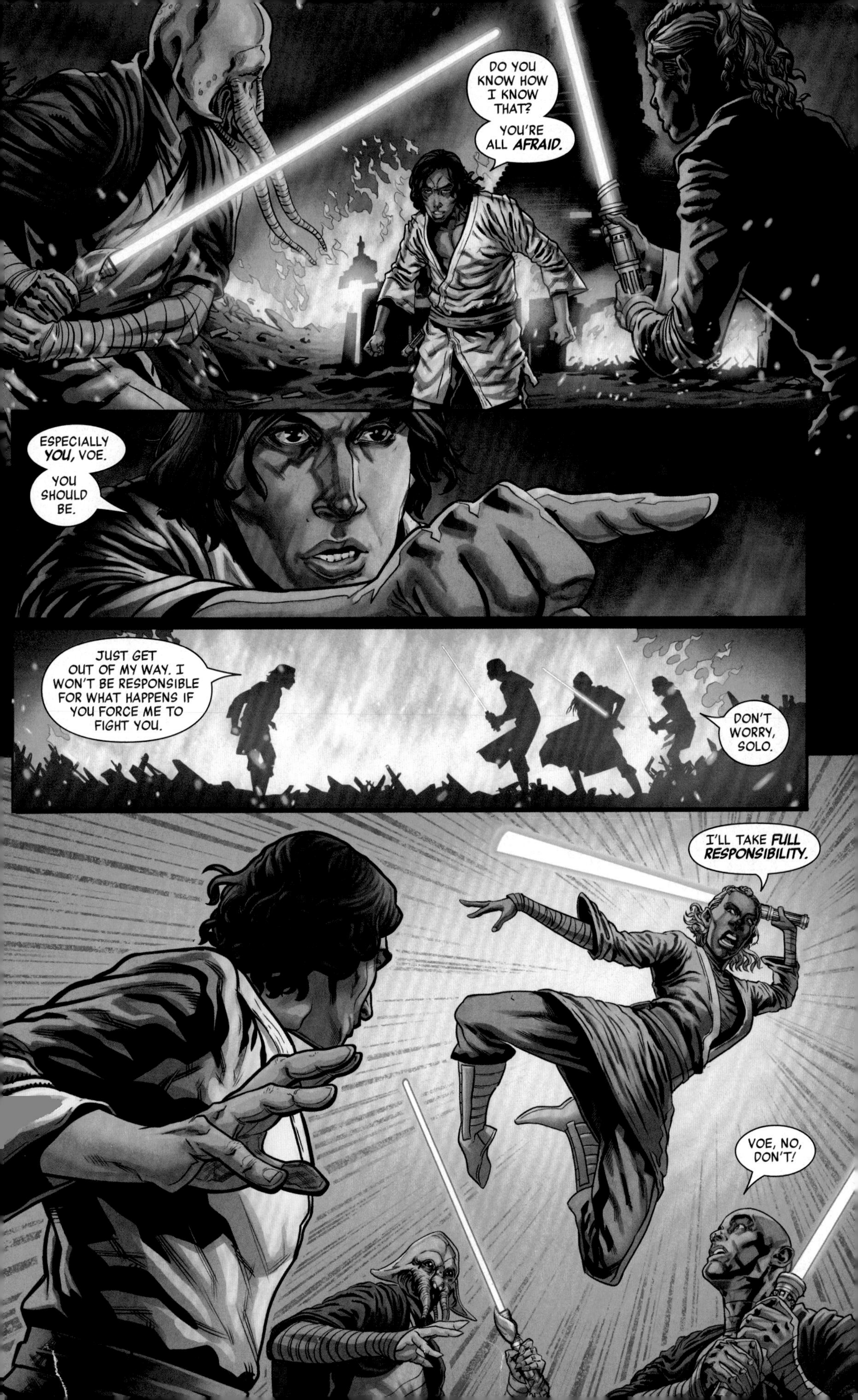
DO YOU KNOW HOW I KNOW THAT?
YOU'RE ALL *AFRAID.*
ESPECIALLY *YOU,* VOE.
YOU SHOULD BE.
JUST GET OUT OF MY WAY. I WON'T BE RESPONSIBLE FOR WHAT HAPPENS IF YOU FORCE ME TO FIGHT YOU.
DON'T WORRY, SOLO.
I'LL TAKE *FULL RESPONSIBILITY.*
VOE, NO, DON'T!

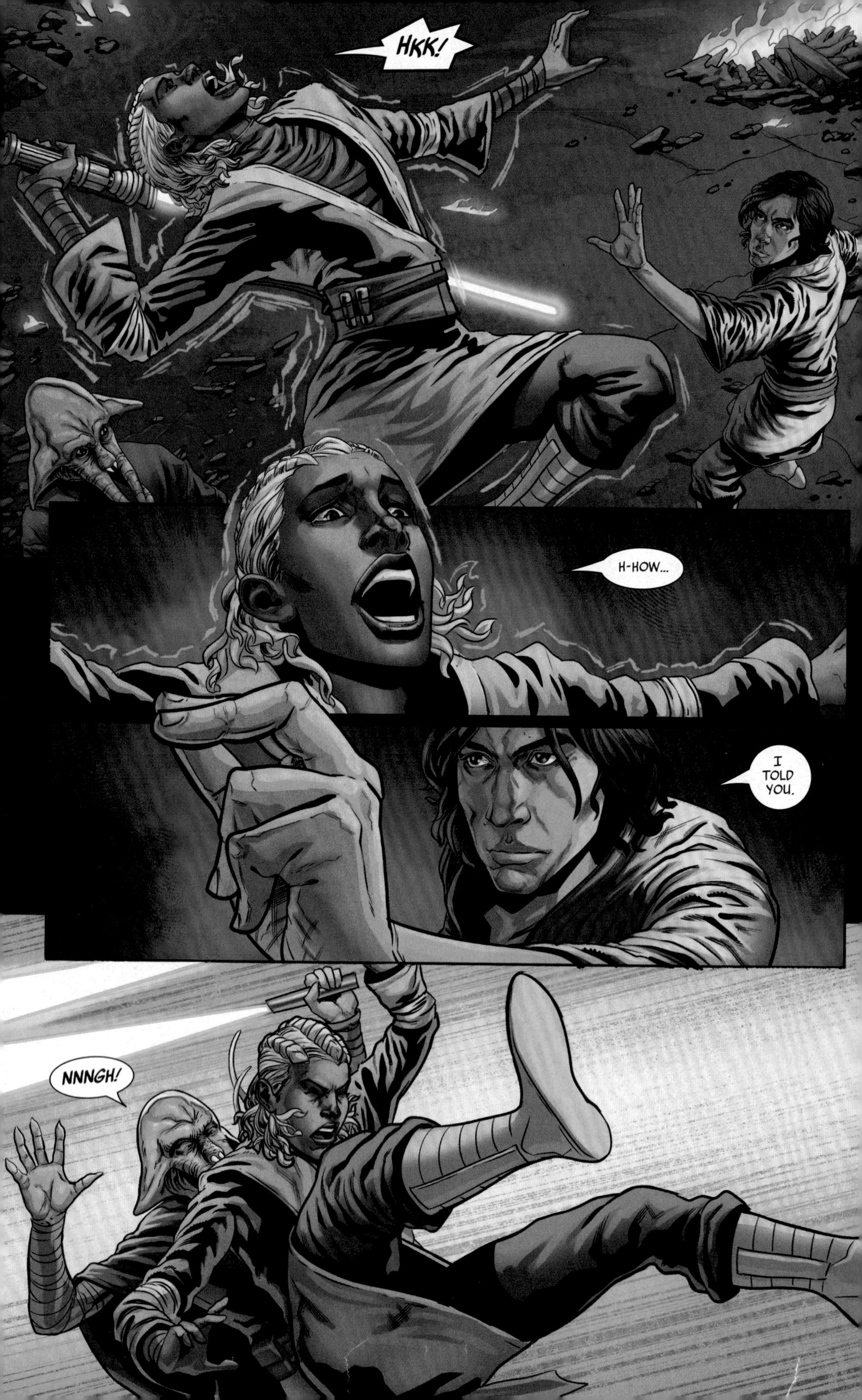
HKK!
H-HOW...
I TOLD YOU.
NNNGH!

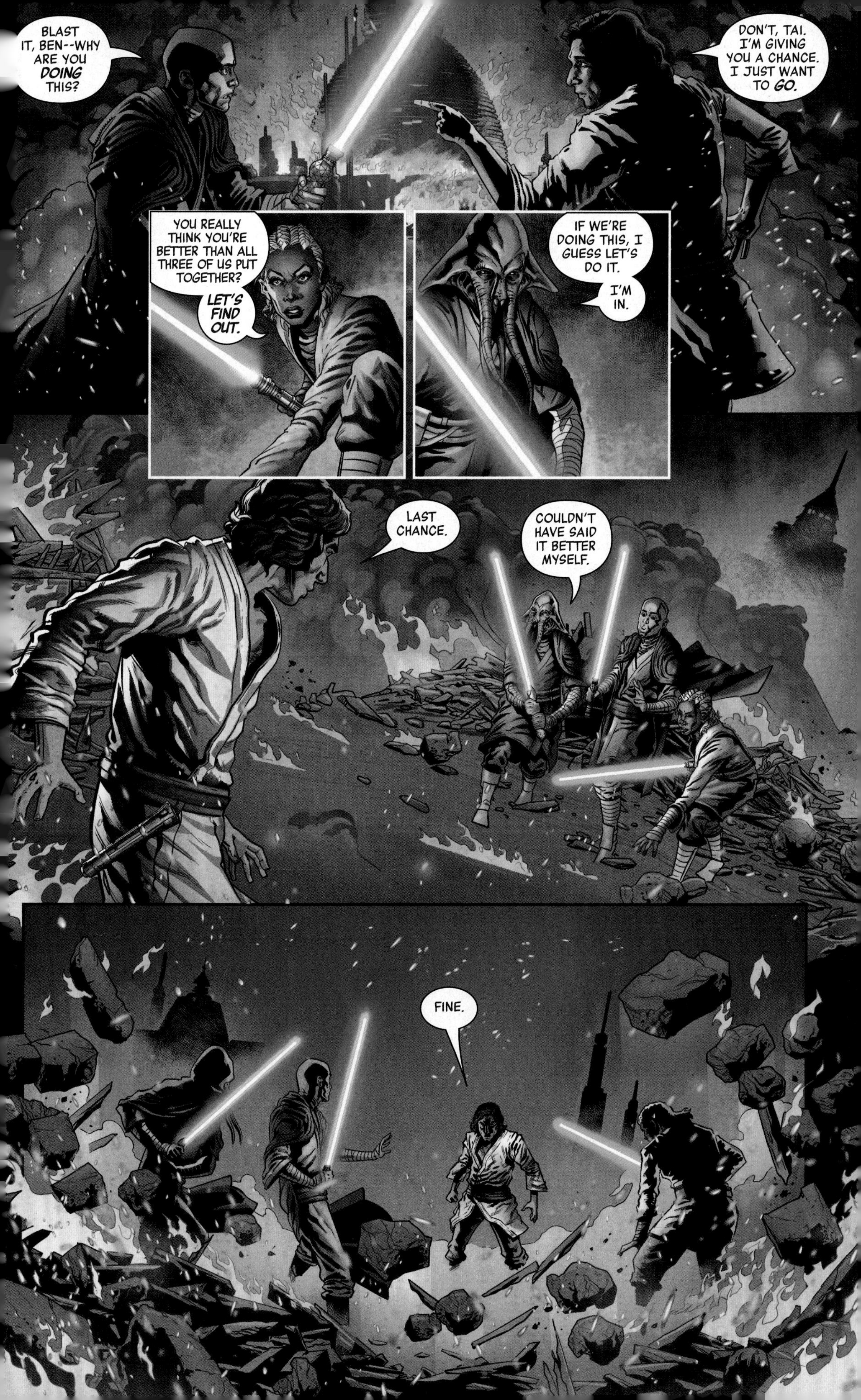
BLAST IT, BEN--WHY ARE YOU *DOING* THIS?
DON'T, TAI. I'M GIVING YOU A CHANCE. I JUST WANT TO *GO.*
YOU REALLY THINK YOU'RE BETTER THAN ALL THREE OF US PUT TOGETHER?
LET'S FIND OUT.
IF WE'RE DOING THIS, I GUESS LET'S DO IT.
I'M IN.
LAST CHANCE.
COULDN'T HAVE SAID IT BETTER MYSELF.
FINE.

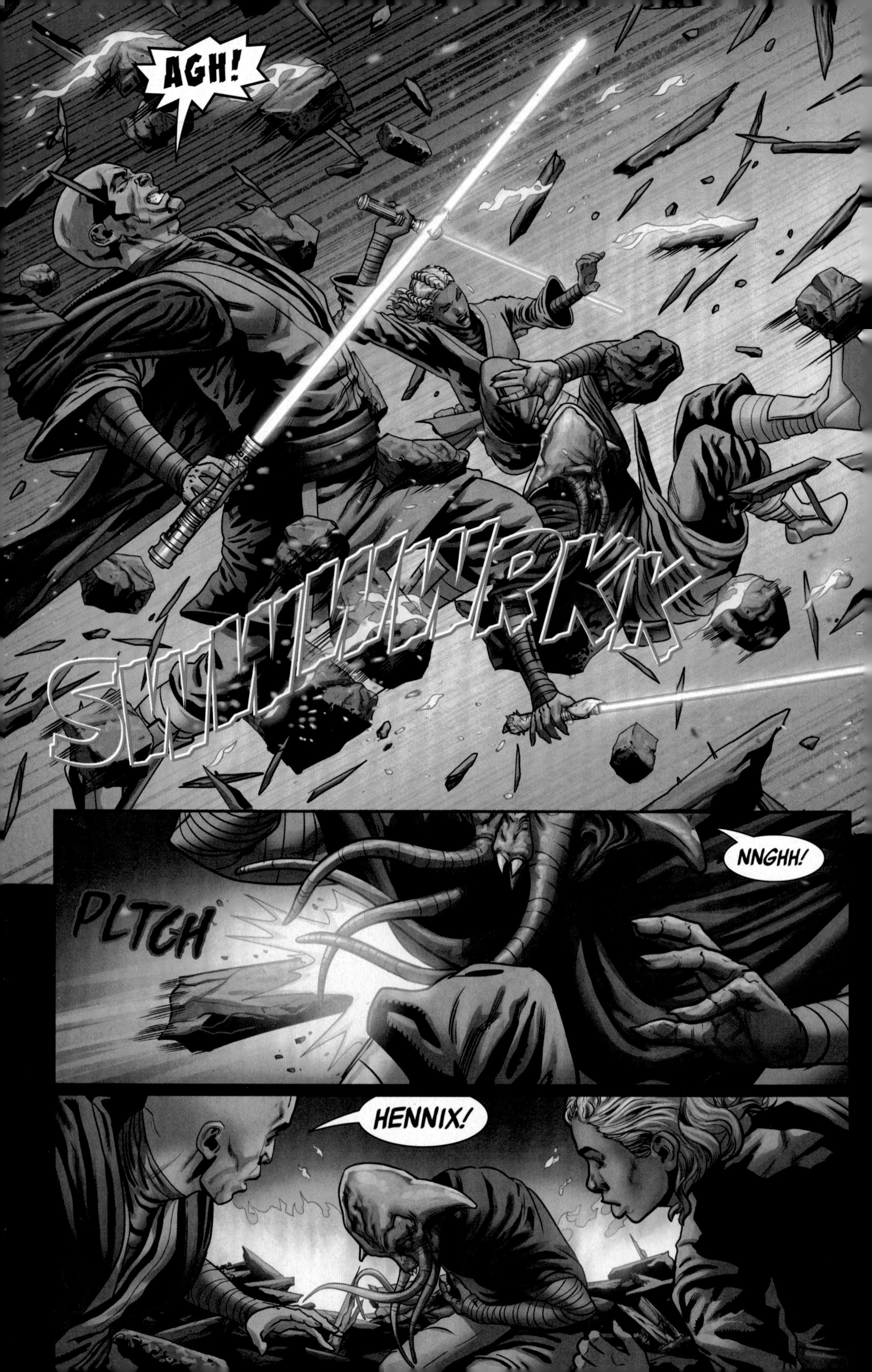
AGH!
SWWWWRKK
NNGHH!
PLTCH
HENNIX!

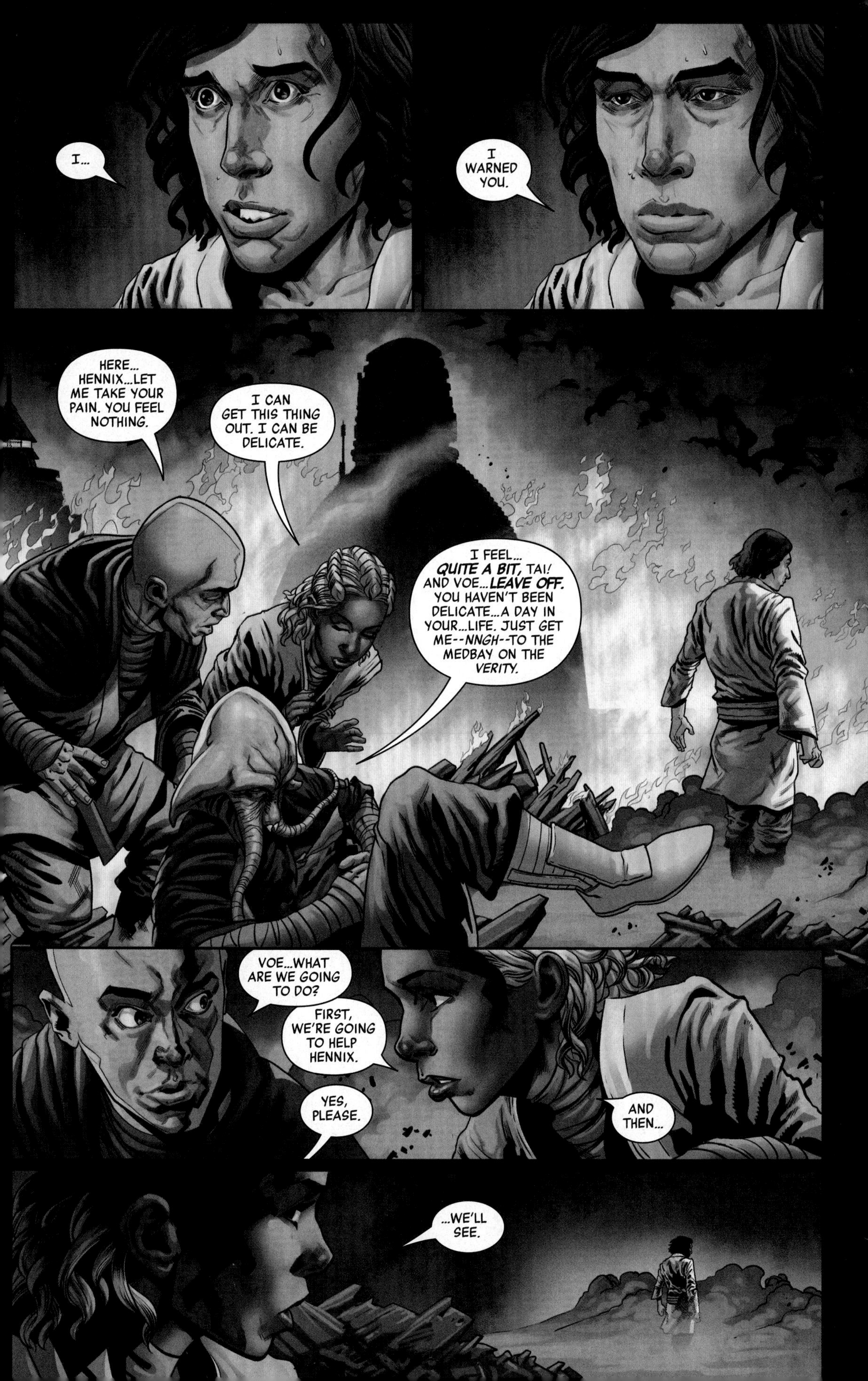
I...
I WARNED YOU.
HERE... HENNIX...LET ME TAKE YOUR PAIN. YOU FEEL NOTHING.
I CAN GET THIS THING OUT. I CAN BE DELICATE.
I FEEL... QUITE A BIT, TAI! AND VOE...LEAVE OFF. YOU HAVEN'T BEEN DELICATE...A DAY IN YOUR...LIFE. JUST GET ME--NNGH--TO THE MEDBAY ON THE VERITY.
VOE...WHAT ARE WE GOING TO DO?
FIRST, WE'RE GOING TO HELP HENNIX.
YES, PLEASE.
AND THEN...
...WE'LL SEE.

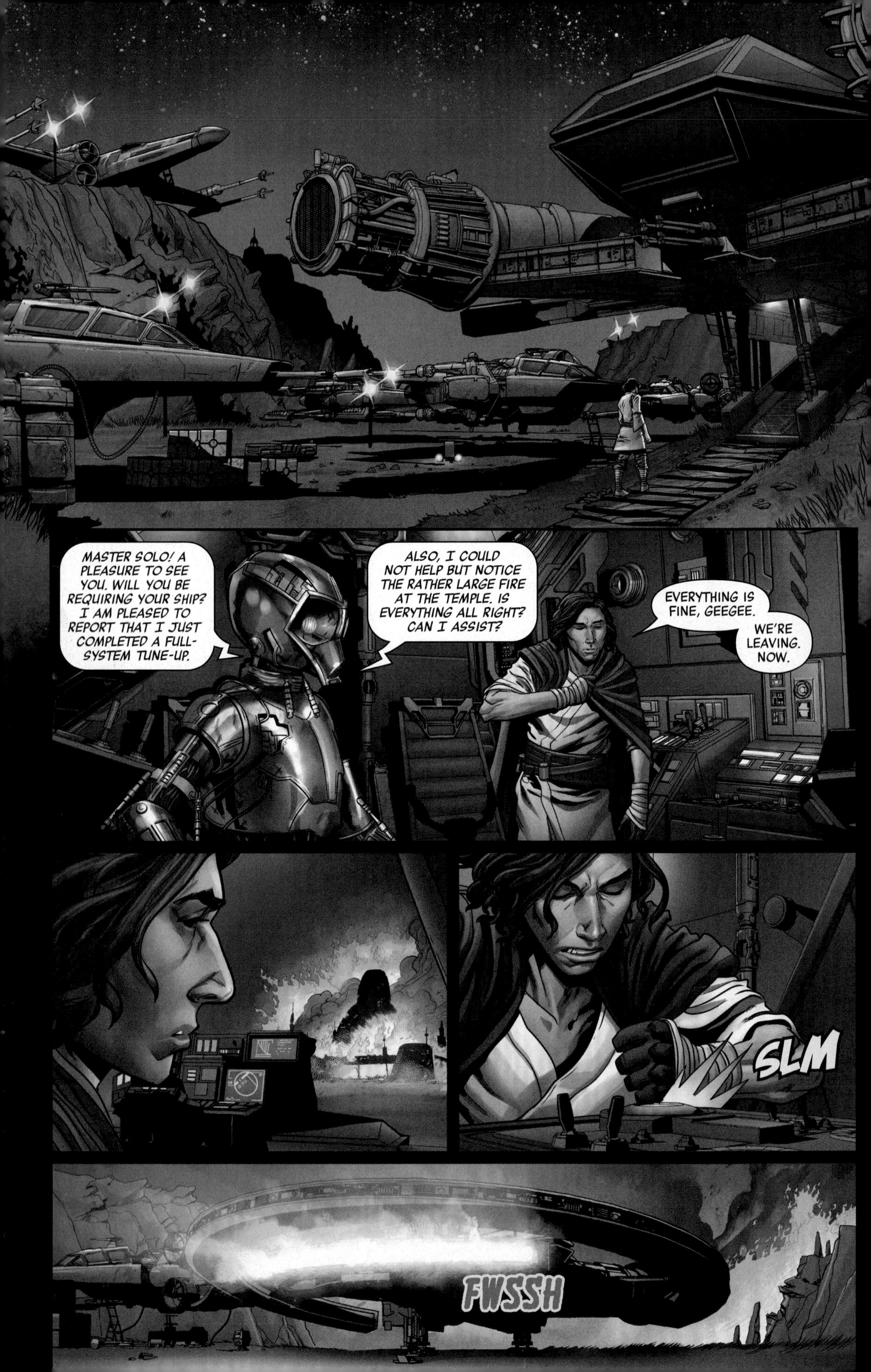
MASTER SOLO! A PLEASURE TO SEE YOU. WILL YOU BE REQUIRING YOUR SHIP? I AM PLEASED TO REPORT THAT I JUST COMPLETED A FULL-SYSTEM TUNE-UP.
ALSO, I COULD NOT HELP BUT NOTICE THE RATHER LARGE FIRE AT THE TEMPLE. IS EVERYTHING ALL RIGHT? CAN I ASSIST?
EVERYTHING IS FINE, GEEGEE.
WE'RE LEAVING. NOW.
SLM
FWSSH

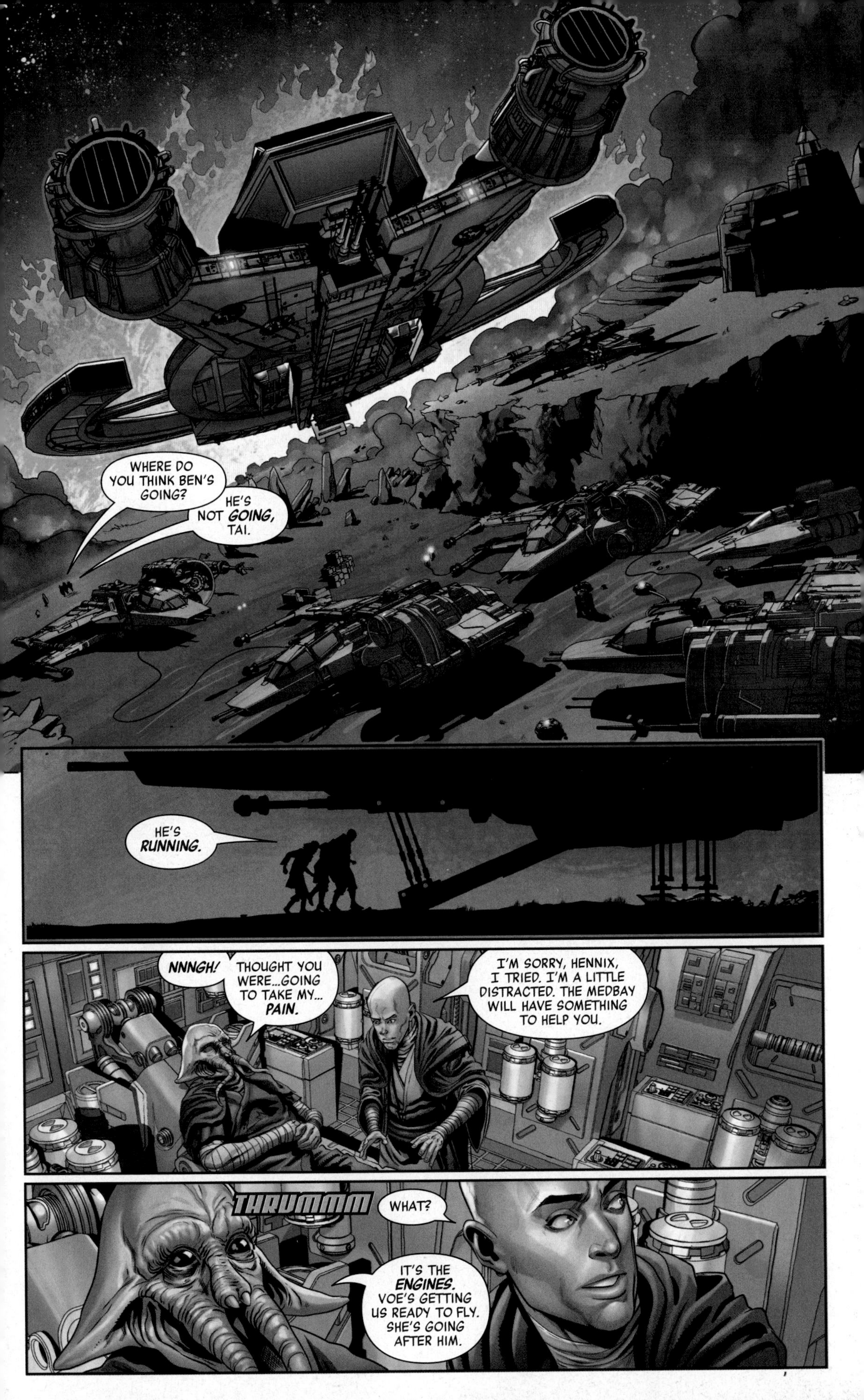
WHERE DO YOU THINK BEN'S GOING?
HE'S NOT GOING, TAI.
HE'S RUNNING.
NNNGH!
THOUGHT YOU WERE...GOING TO TAKE MY... PAIN.
I'M SORRY, HENNIX, I TRIED. I'M A LITTLE DISTRACTED. THE MEDBAY WILL HAVE SOMETHING TO HELP YOU.
THRUMMM
WHAT?
IT'S THE ENGINES. VOE'S GETTING US READY TO FLY. SHE'S GOING AFTER HIM.

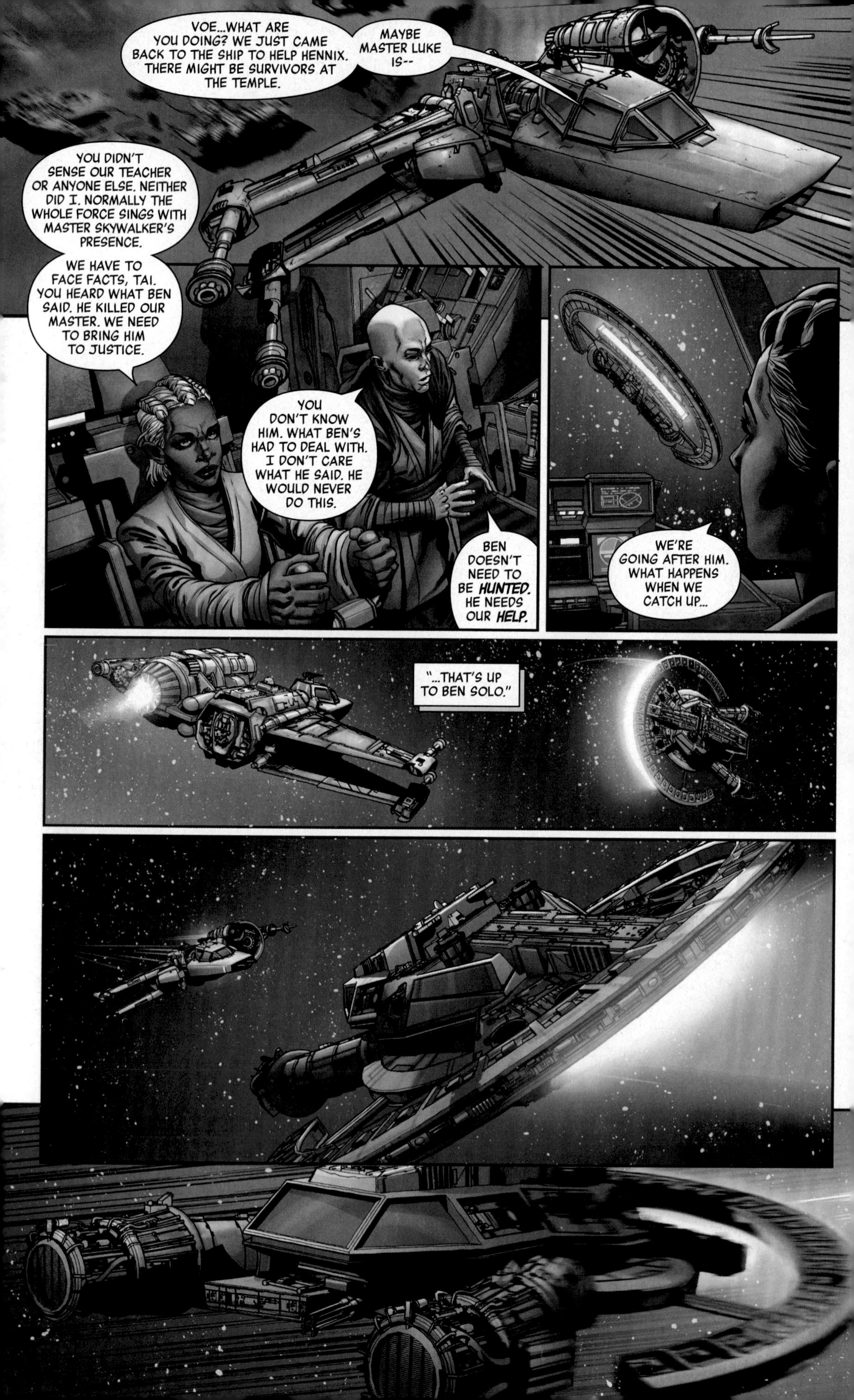
VOE...WHAT ARE YOU DOING? WE JUST CAME BACK TO THE SHIP TO HELP HENNIX. THERE MIGHT BE SURVIVORS AT THE TEMPLE.
MAYBE MASTER LUKE IS--
YOU DIDN'T SENSE OUR TEACHER OR ANYONE ELSE. NEITHER DID I. NORMALLY THE WHOLE FORCE SINGS WITH MASTER SKYWALKER'S PRESENCE.
WE HAVE TO FACE FACTS, TAI. YOU HEARD WHAT BEN SAID. HE KILLED OUR MASTER. WE NEED TO BRING HIM TO JUSTICE.
YOU DON'T KNOW HIM. WHAT BEN'S HAD TO DEAL WITH. I DON'T CARE WHAT HE SAID. HE WOULD NEVER DO THIS.
BEN DOESN'T NEED TO BE *HUNTED.* HE NEEDS OUR *HELP.*
WE'RE GOING AFTER HIM. WHAT HAPPENS WHEN WE CATCH UP...
"...THAT'S UP TO BEN SOLO."

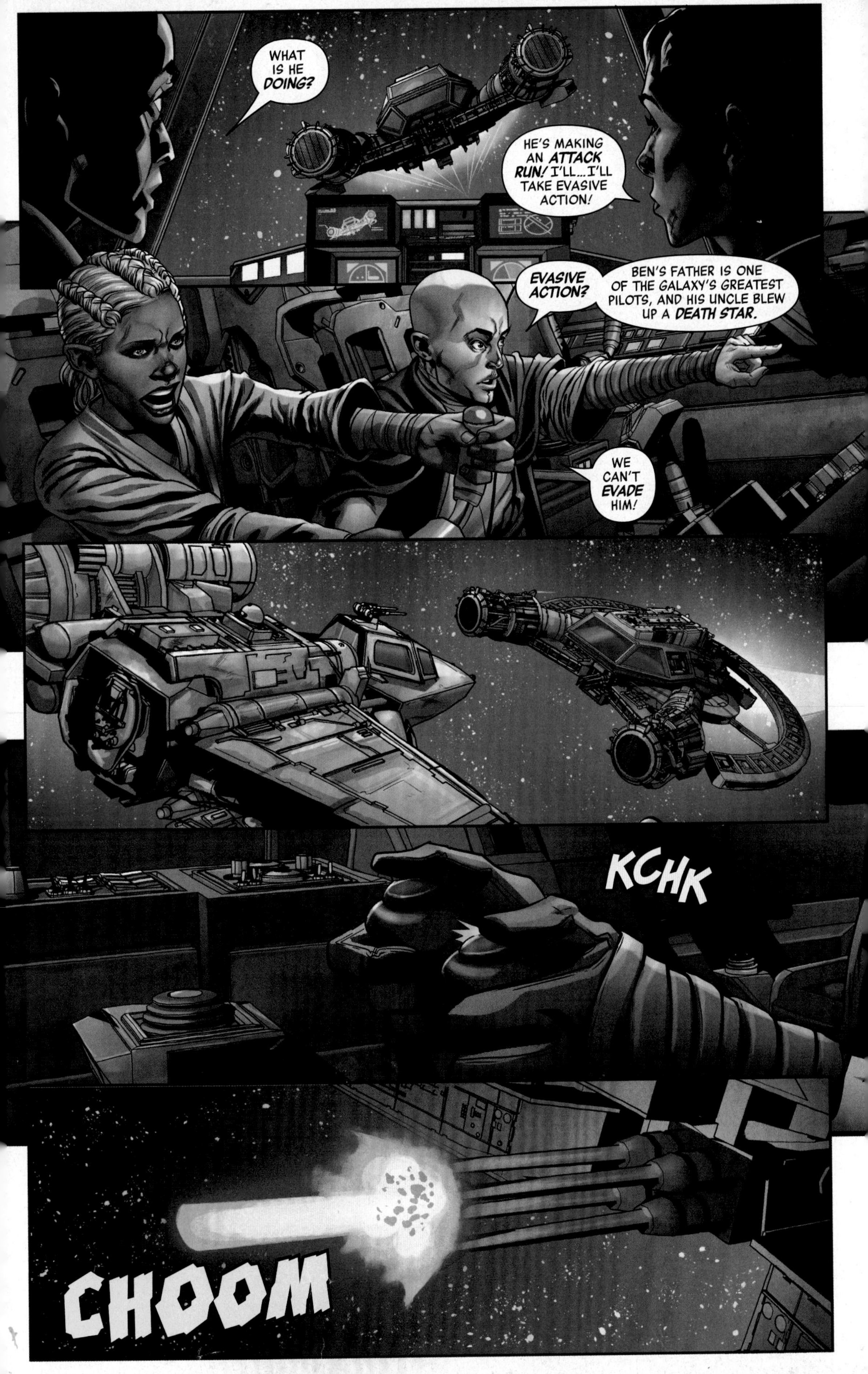
WHAT IS HE DOING?
HE'S MAKING AN ATTACK RUN! I'LL... I'LL TAKE EVASIVE ACTION!
EVASIVE ACTION?
BEN'S FATHER IS ONE OF THE GALAXY'S GREATEST PILOTS, AND HIS UNCLE BLEW UP A DEATH STAR.
WE CAN'T EVADE HIM!
KCHK
CHOOM

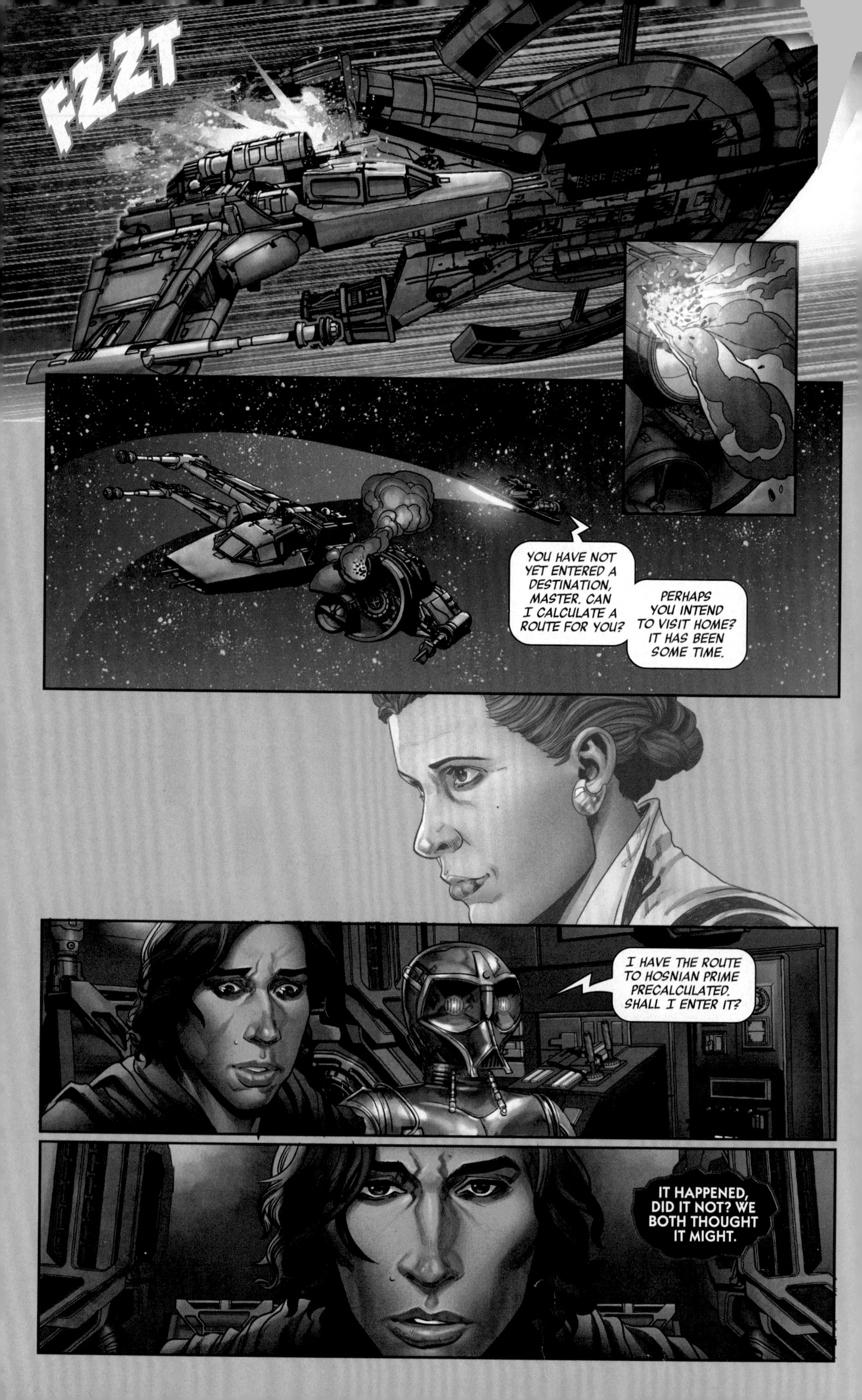
FZZT
YOU HAVE NOT YET ENTERED A DESTINATION, MASTER. CAN I CALCULATE A ROUTE FOR YOU?
PERHAPS YOU INTEND TO VISIT HOME? IT HAS BEEN SOME TIME.
I HAVE THE ROUTE TO HOSNIAN PRIME PRECALCULATED. SHALL I ENTER IT?
IT HAPPENED, DID IT NOT? WE BOTH THOUGHT IT MIGHT.

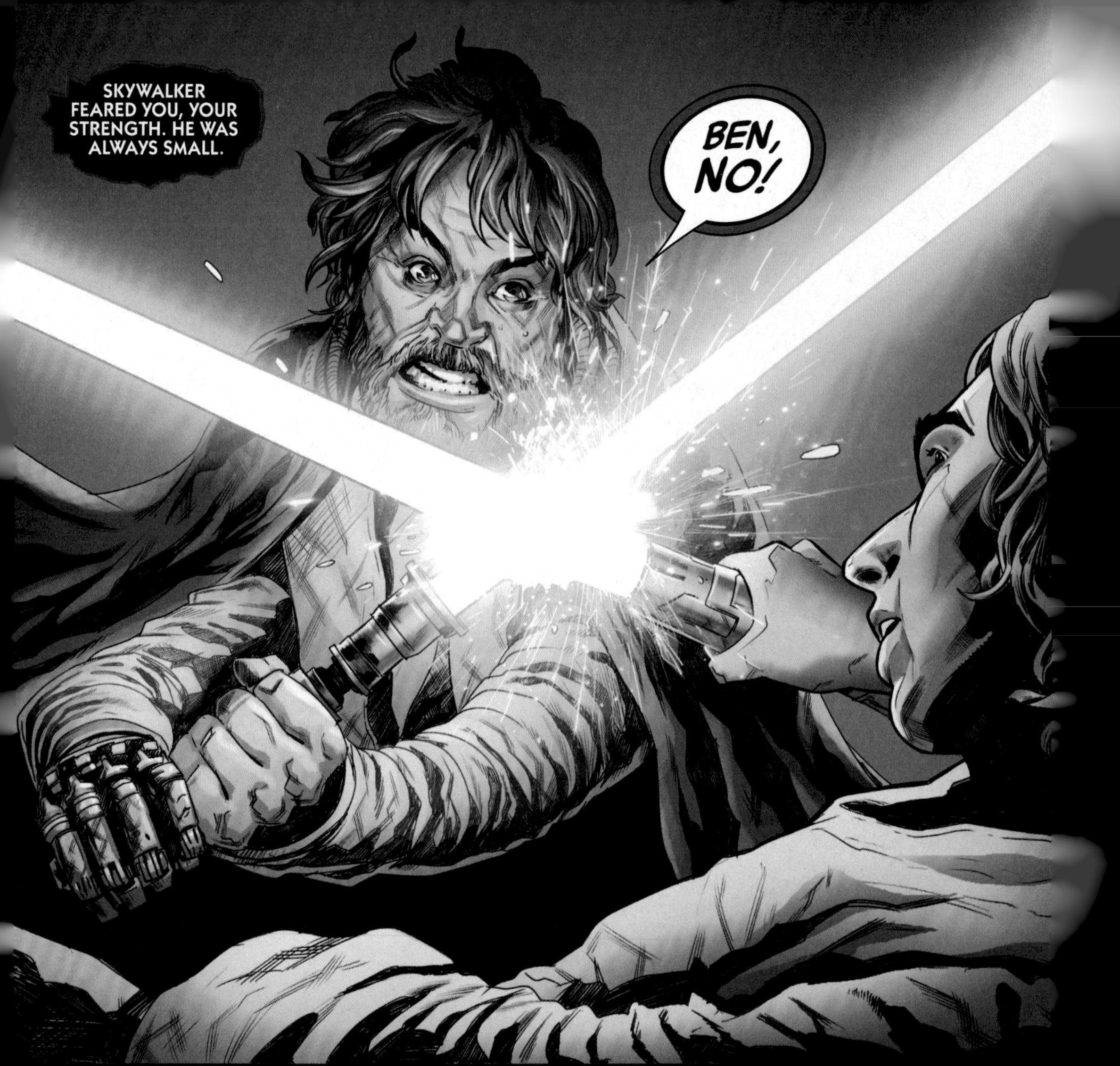
SKYWALKER FEARED YOU, YOUR STRENGTH. HE WAS ALWAYS SMALL.
BEN, NO!

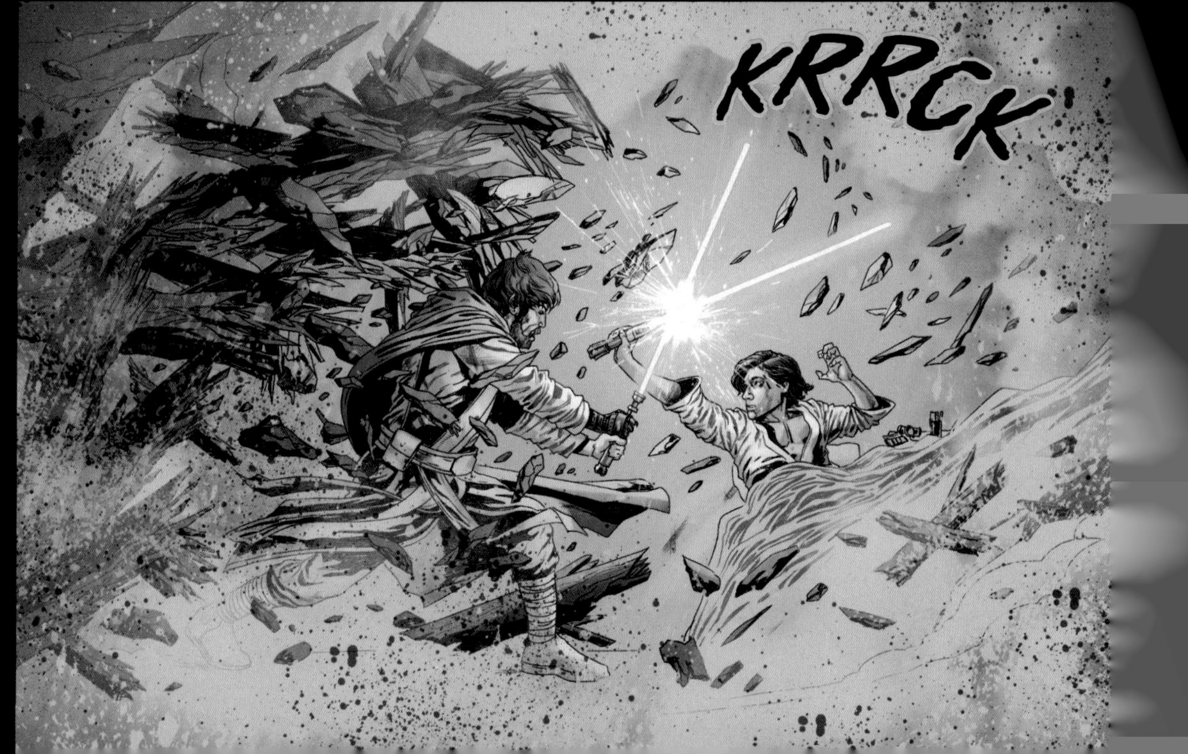
KRRCK

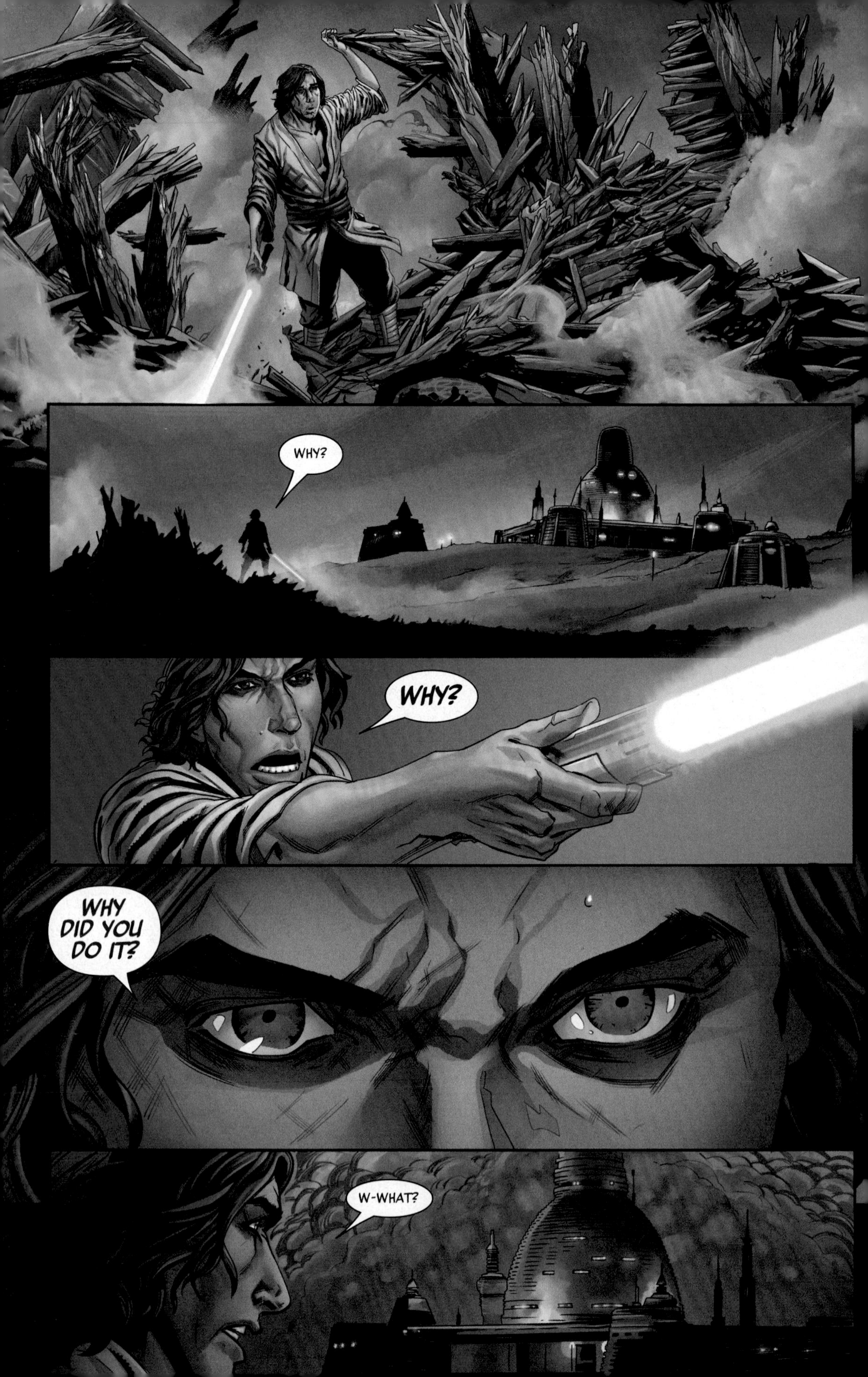
WHY?
WHY?
WHY DID YOU DO IT?
W-WHAT?

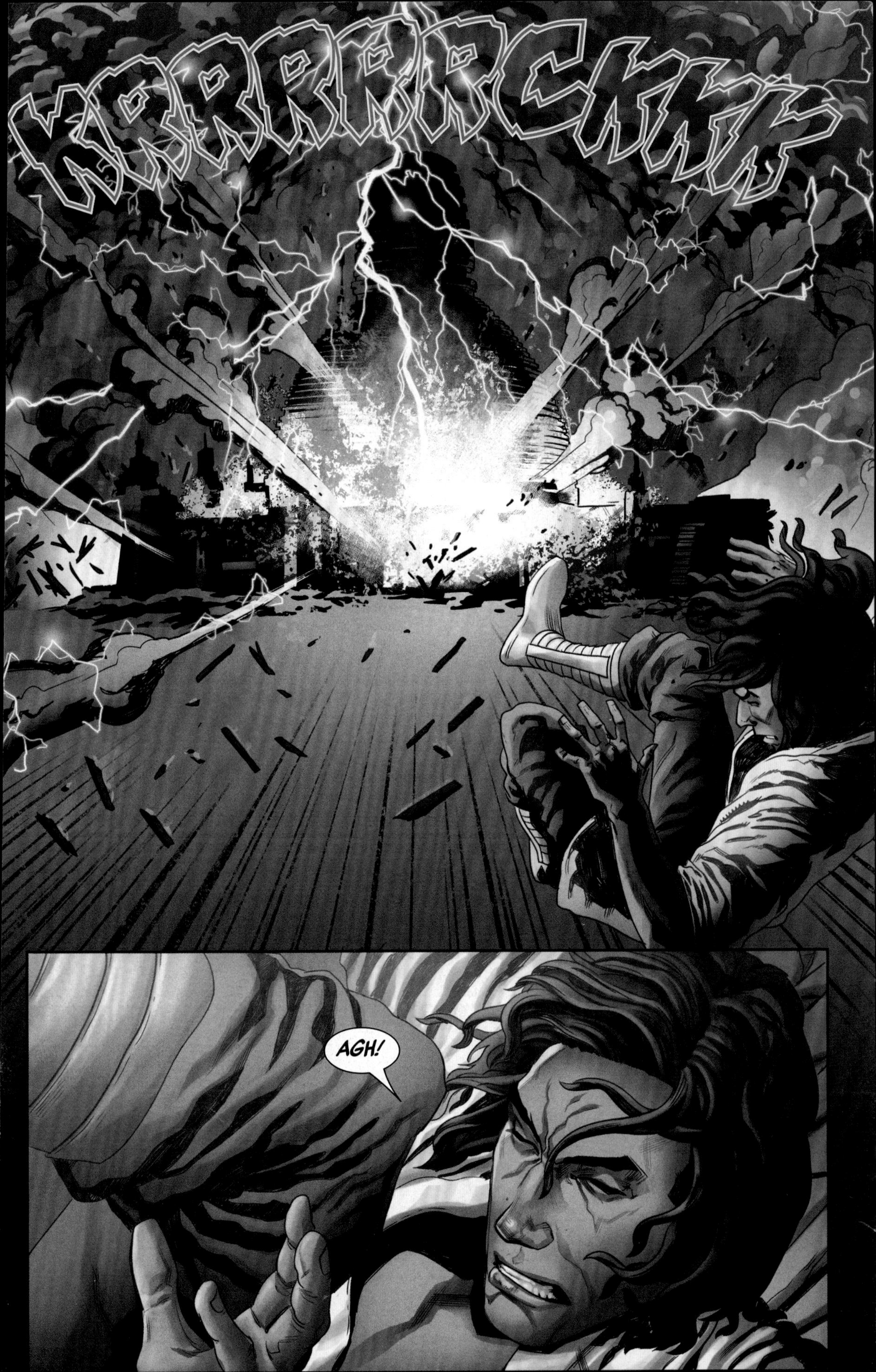
KRRRRRCKKK
AGH!

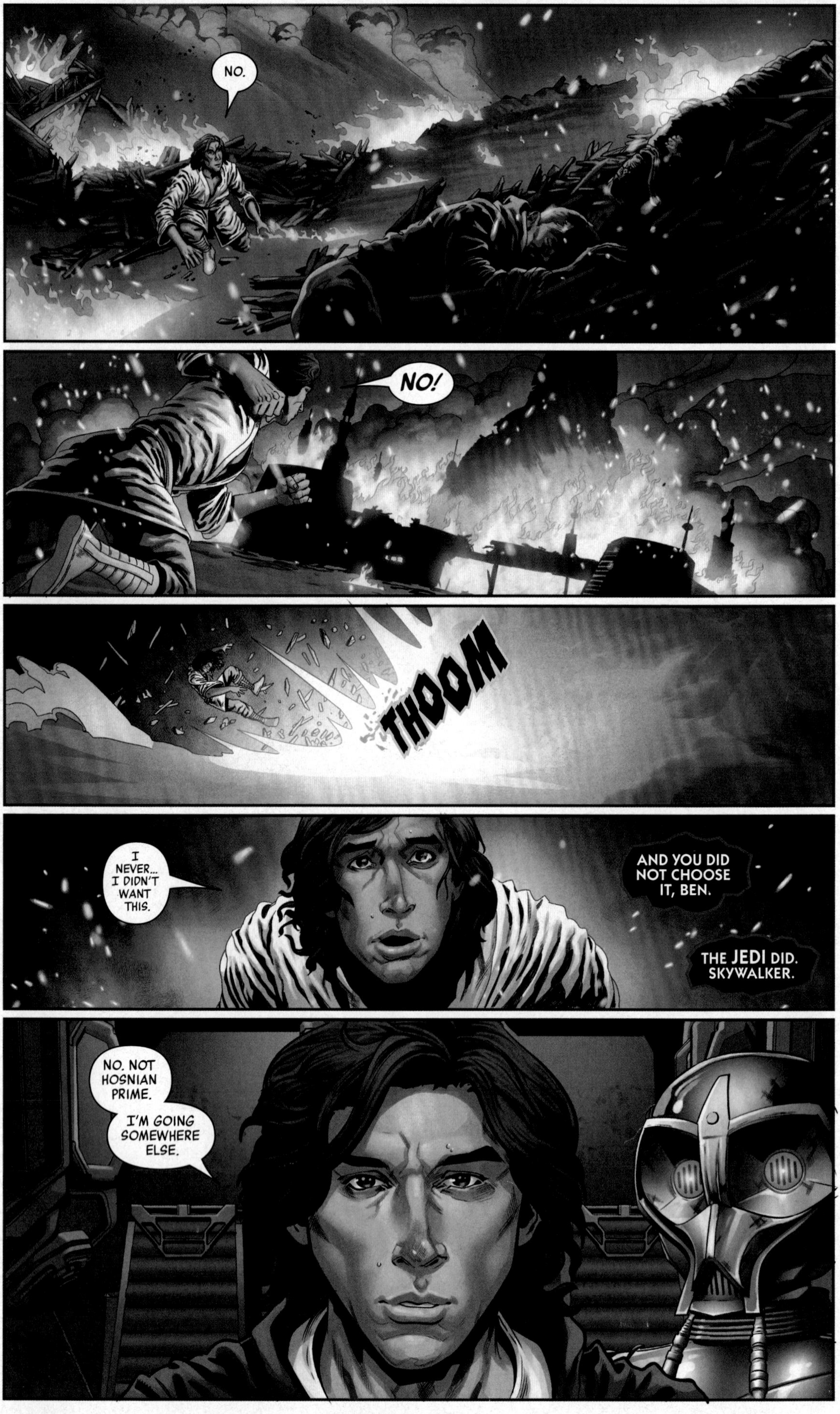
NO.
NO!
THOOM
I NEVER... I DIDN'T WANT THIS.
AND YOU DID NOT CHOOSE IT, BEN.
THE JEDI DID. SKYWALKER.
NO. NOT HOSNIAN PRIME.
I'M GOING SOMEWHERE ELSE.

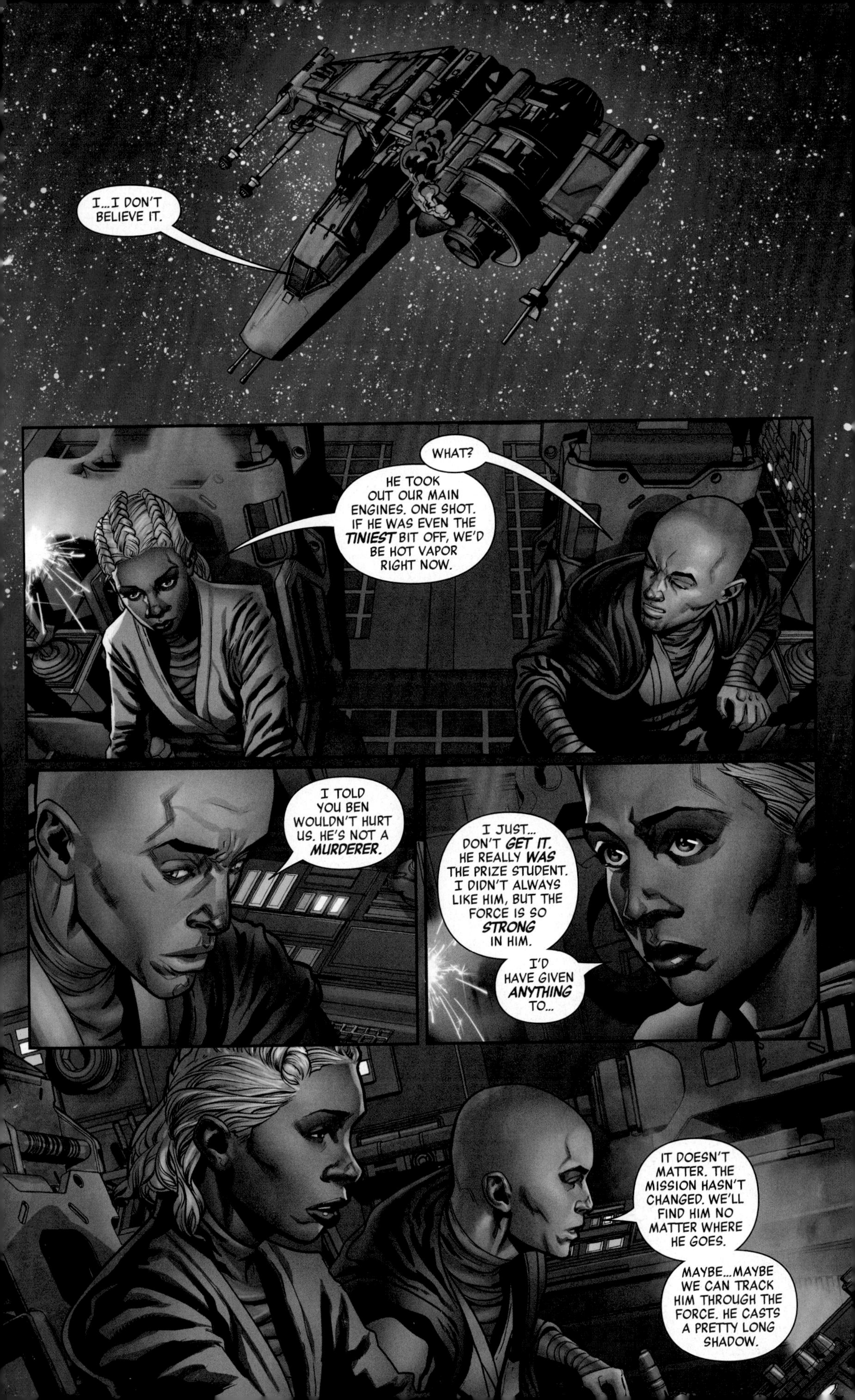
I...I DON'T BELIEVE IT.
WHAT?
HE TOOK OUT OUR MAIN ENGINES. ONE SHOT. IF HE WAS EVEN THE TINIEST BIT OFF, WE'D BE HOT VAPOR RIGHT NOW.
I TOLD YOU BEN WOULDN'T HURT US. HE'S NOT A MURDERER.
I JUST... DON'T GET IT. HE REALLY WAS THE PRIZE STUDENT. I DIDN'T ALWAYS LIKE HIM, BUT THE FORCE IS SO STRONG IN HIM.
I'D HAVE GIVEN ANYTHING TO...
IT DOESN'T MATTER. THE MISSION HASN'T CHANGED. WE'LL FIND HIM NO MATTER WHERE HE GOES.
MAYBE...MAYBE WE CAN TRACK HIM THROUGH THE FORCE. HE CASTS A PRETTY LONG SHADOW.

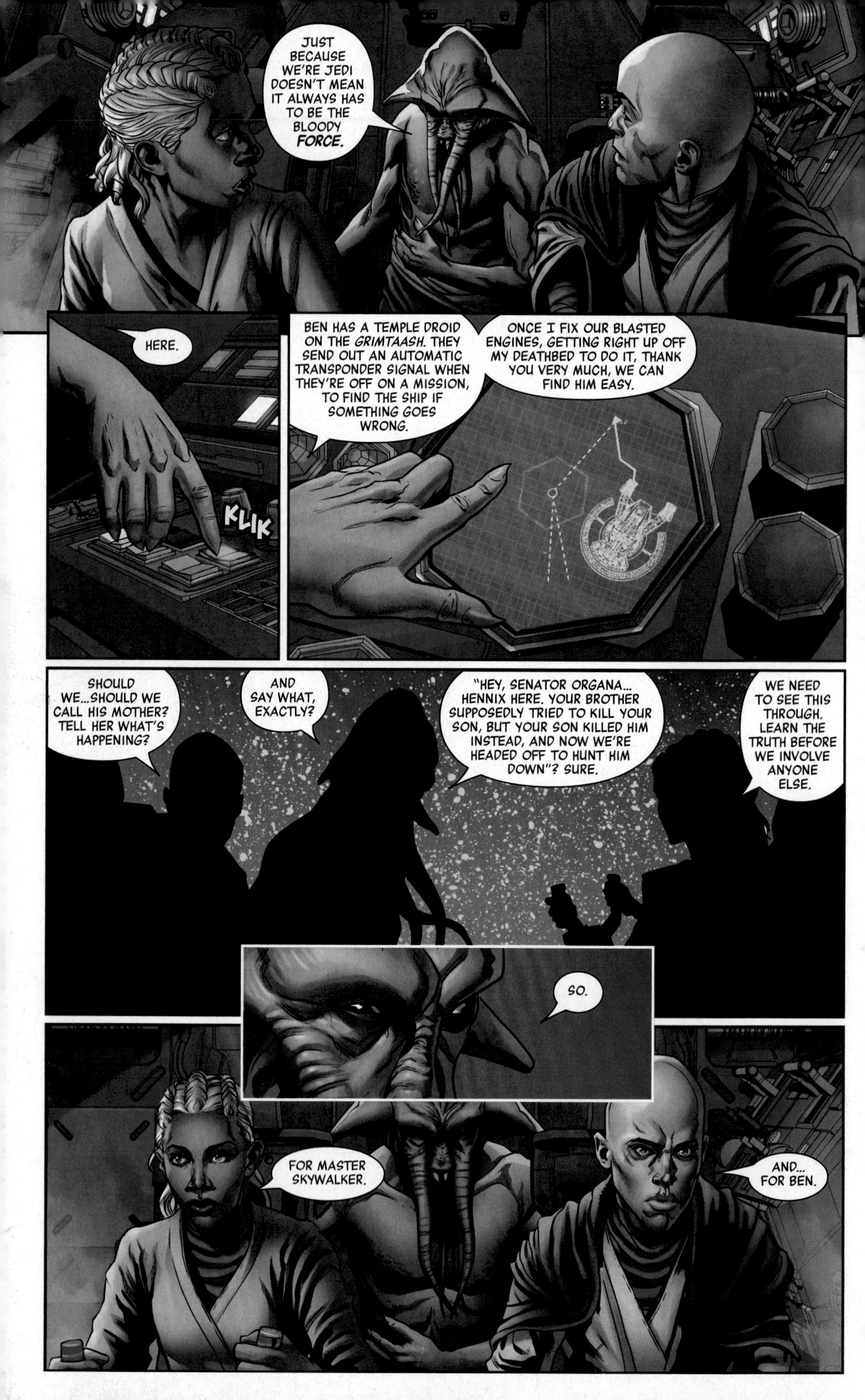
JUST BECAUSE WE'RE JEDI DOESN'T MEAN IT ALWAYS HAS TO BE THE BLOODY *FORCE.*
HERE.
KLIK
BEN HAS A TEMPLE DROID ON THE *GRIMTAASH.* THEY SEND OUT AN AUTOMATIC TRANSPONDER SIGNAL WHEN THEY'RE OFF ON A MISSION, TO FIND THE SHIP IF SOMETHING GOES WRONG.
ONCE I FIX OUR BLASTED ENGINES, GETTING RIGHT UP OFF MY DEATHBED TO DO IT, THANK YOU VERY MUCH, WE CAN FIND HIM EASY.
SHOULD WE...SHOULD WE CALL HIS MOTHER? TELL HER WHAT'S HAPPENING?
AND SAY WHAT, EXACTLY?
"HEY, SENATOR ORGANA... HENNIX HERE. YOUR BROTHER SUPPOSEDLY TRIED TO KILL YOUR SON, BUT YOUR SON KILLED HIM INSTEAD, AND NOW WE'RE HEADED OFF TO HUNT HIM DOWN"? SURE.
WE NEED TO SEE THIS THROUGH. LEARN THE TRUTH BEFORE WE INVOLVE ANYONE ELSE.
SO.
FOR MASTER SKYWALKER.
AND... FOR BEN.

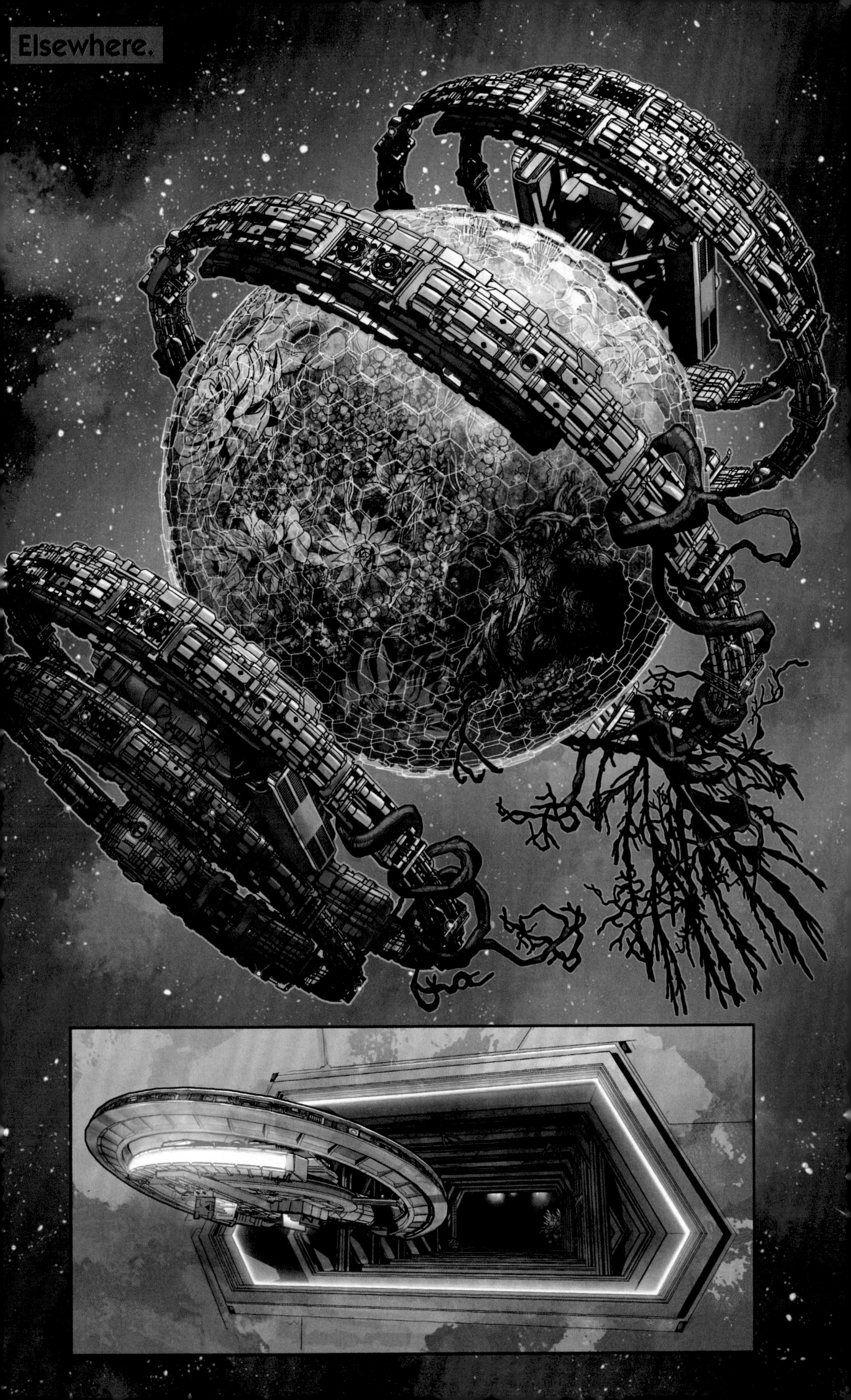
Elsewhere.

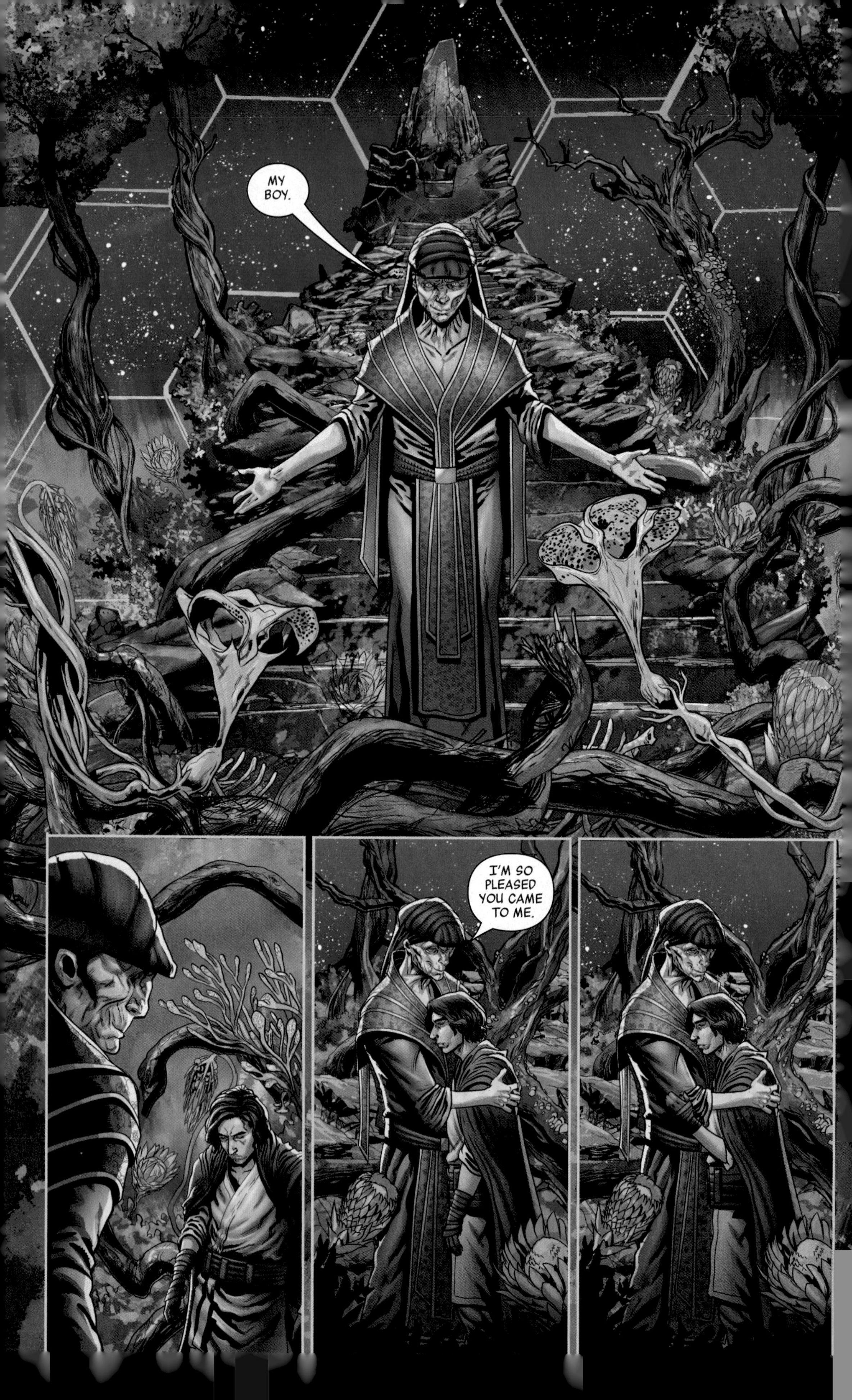
MY BOY.
I'M SO PLEASED YOU CAME TO ME.

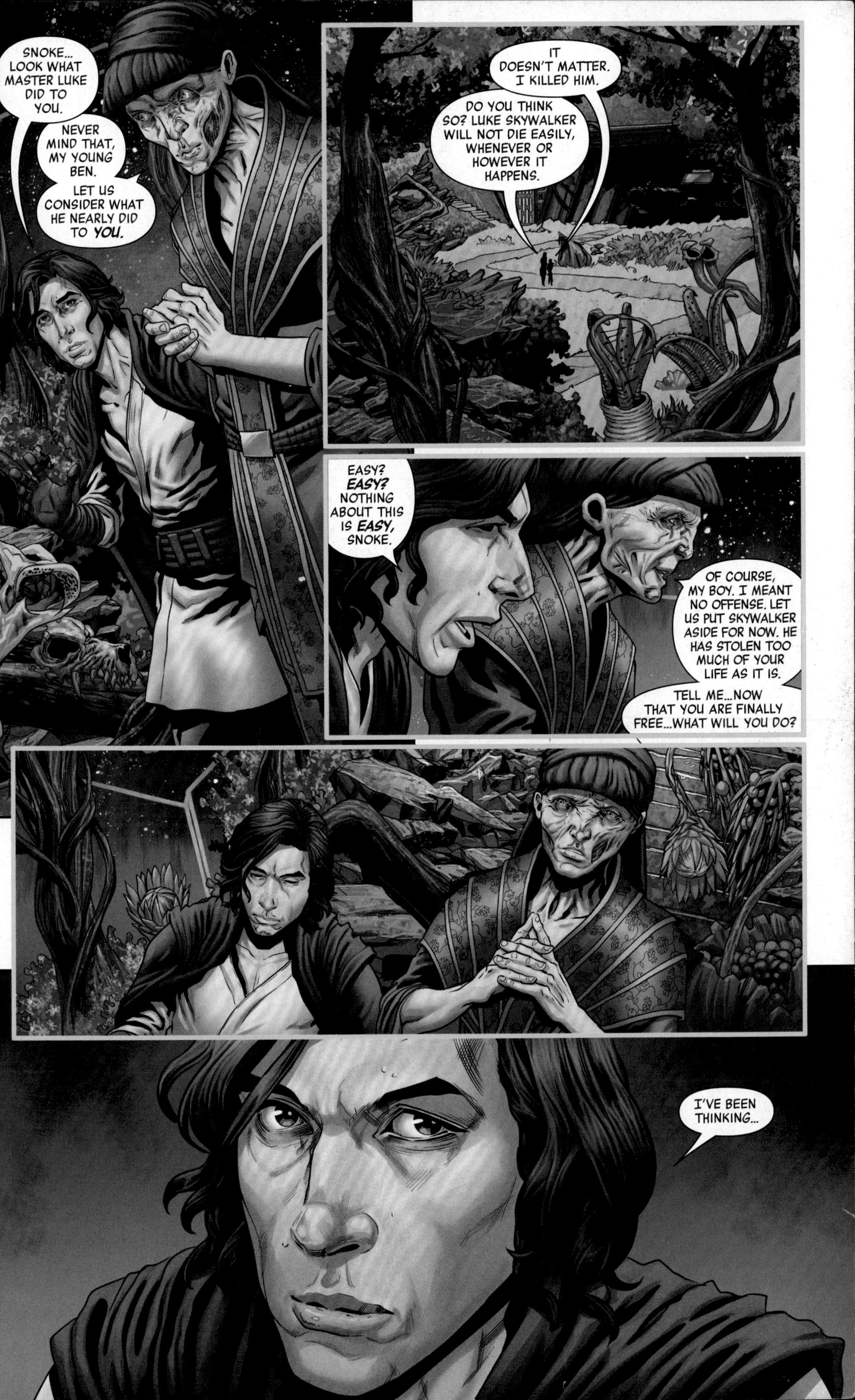

SNOKE... LOOK WHAT MASTER LUKE DID TO YOU.
NEVER MIND THAT, MY YOUNG BEN.
LET US CONSIDER WHAT HE NEARLY DID TO YOU.
IT DOESN'T MATTER. I KILLED HIM.
DO YOU THINK SO? LUKE SKYWALKER WILL NOT DIE EASILY, WHENEVER OR HOWEVER IT HAPPENS.
EASY? EASY? NOTHING ABOUT THIS IS EASY, SNOKE.
OF COURSE, MY BOY. I MEANT NO OFFENSE. LET US PUT SKYWALKER ASIDE FOR NOW. HE HAS STOLEN TOO MUCH OF YOUR LIFE AS IT IS.
TELL ME...NOW THAT YOU ARE FINALLY FREE...WHAT WILL YOU DO?
I'VE BEEN THINKING...

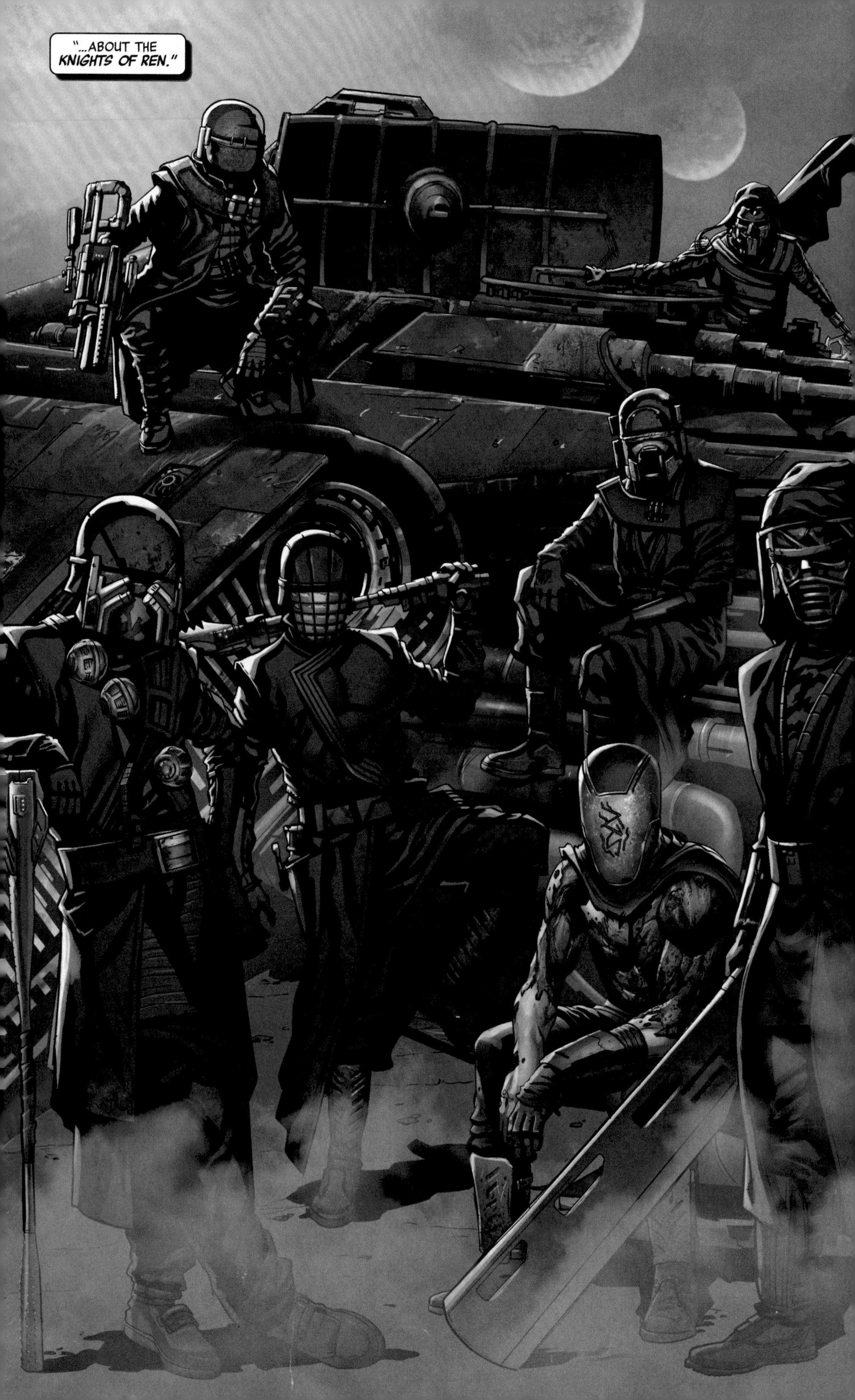
"...ABOUT THE KNIGHTS OF REN."

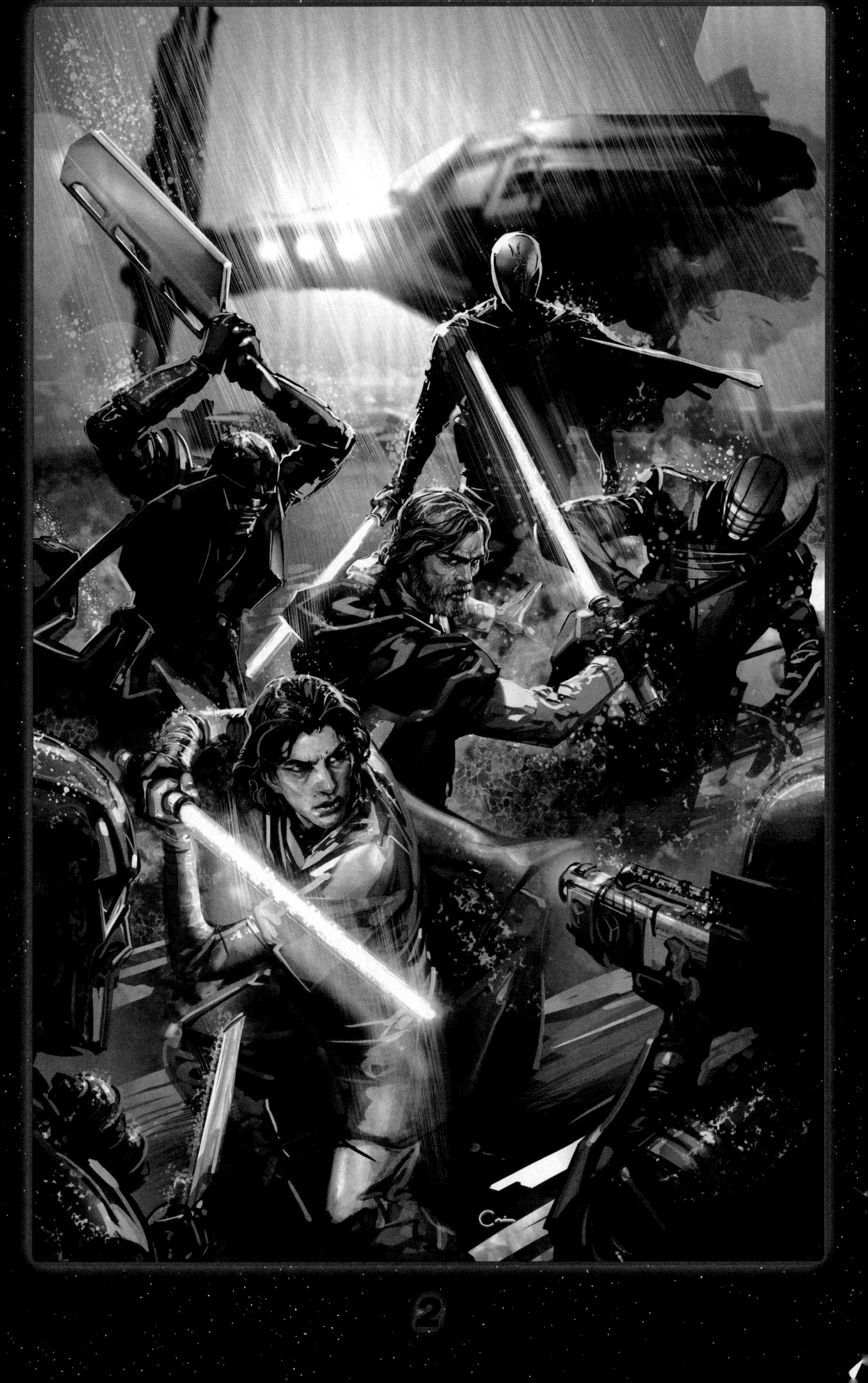

2

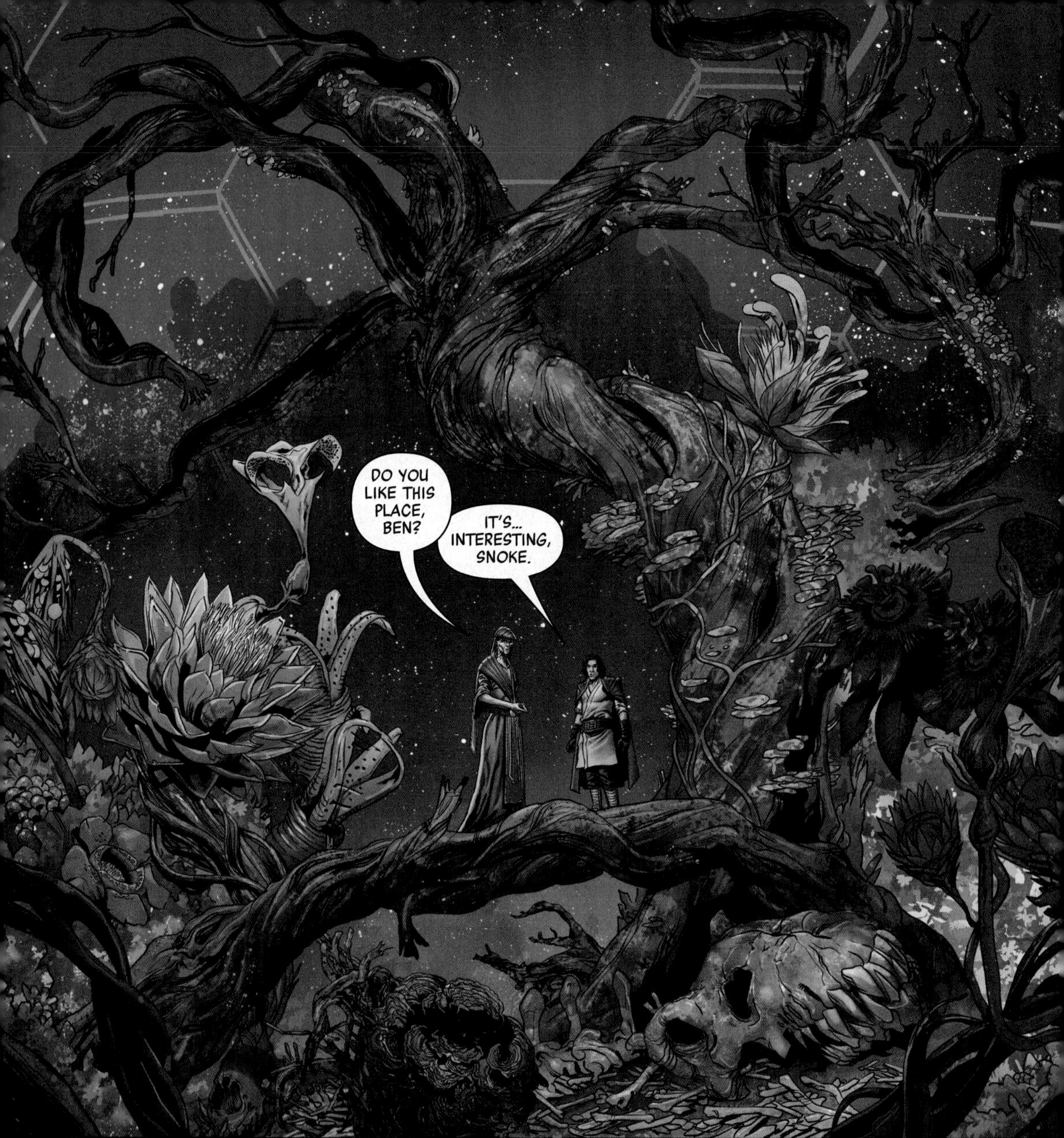
DO YOU LIKE THIS PLACE, BEN?
IT'S... INTERESTING, SNOKE.

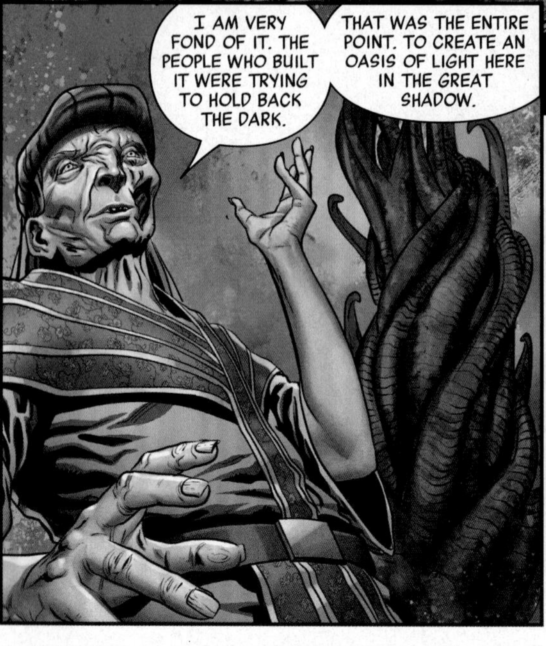
I AM VERY FOND OF IT. THE PEOPLE WHO BUILT IT WERE TRYING TO HOLD BACK THE DARK.
THAT WAS THE ENTIRE POINT. TO CREATE AN OASIS OF LIGHT HERE IN THE GREAT SHADOW.

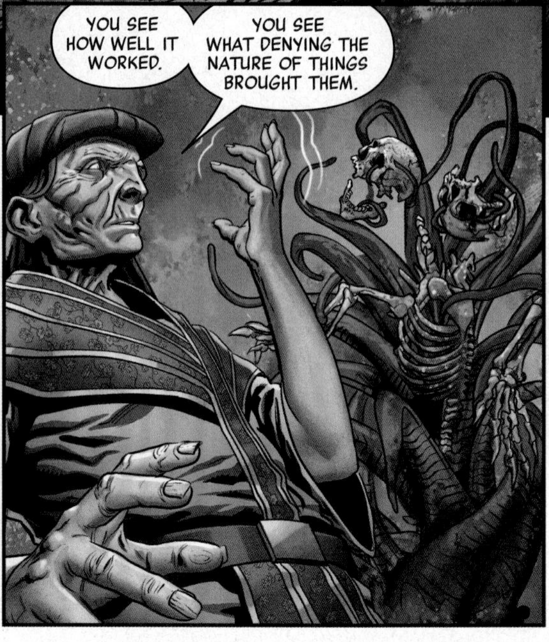
YOU SEE HOW WELL IT WORKED.
YOU SEE WHAT DENYING THE NATURE OF THINGS BROUGHT THEM.

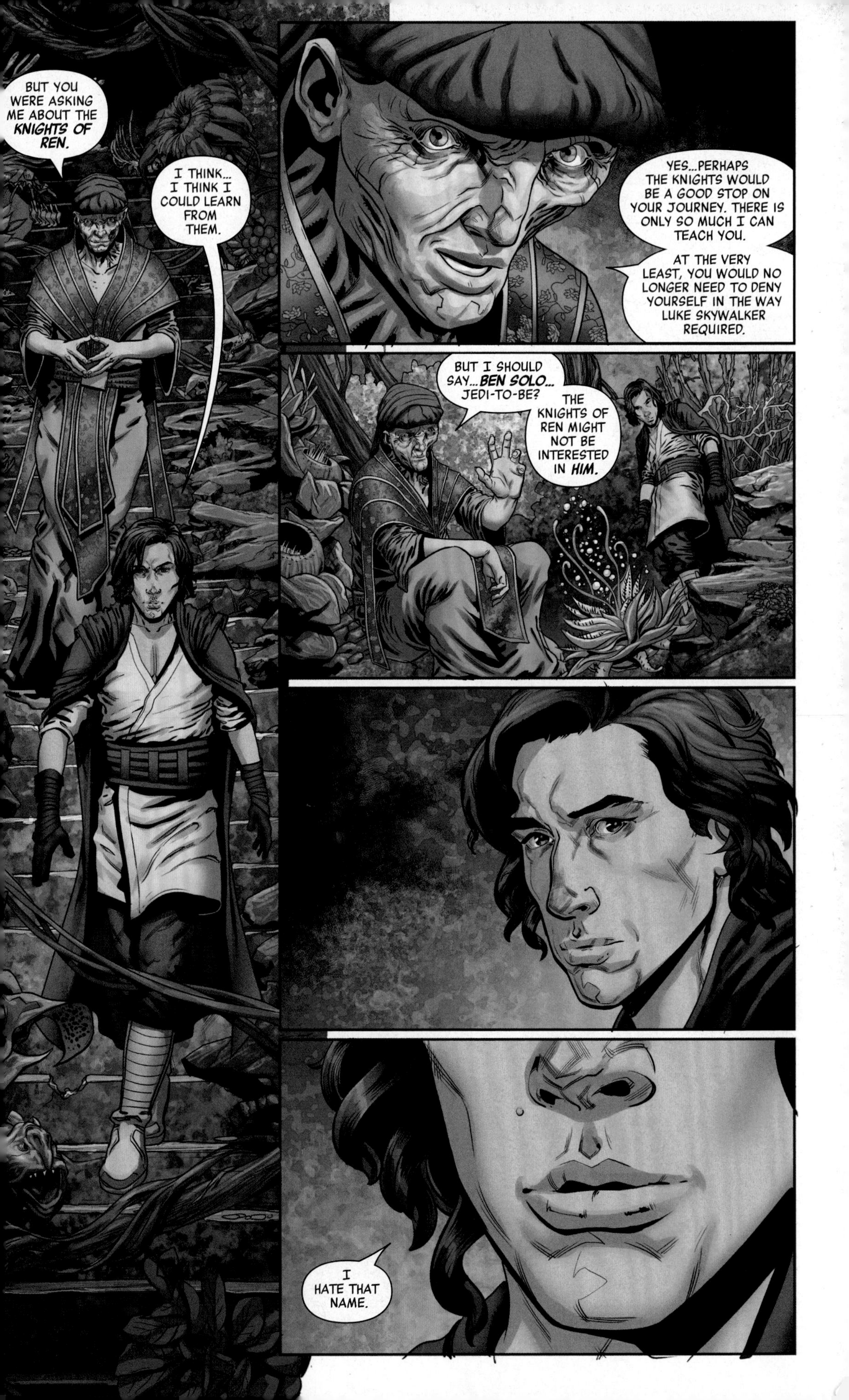
BUT YOU WERE ASKING ME ABOUT THE *KNIGHTS OF REN.*
I THINK... I THINK I COULD LEARN FROM THEM.
YES...PERHAPS THE KNIGHTS WOULD BE A GOOD STOP ON YOUR JOURNEY. THERE IS ONLY SO MUCH I CAN TEACH YOU.
AT THE VERY LEAST, YOU WOULD NO LONGER NEED TO DENY YOURSELF IN THE WAY LUKE SKYWALKER REQUIRED.
BUT I SHOULD SAY...*BEN SOLO...* JEDI-TO-BE?
THE KNIGHTS OF REN MIGHT NOT BE INTERESTED IN *HIM.*
I HATE THAT NAME.

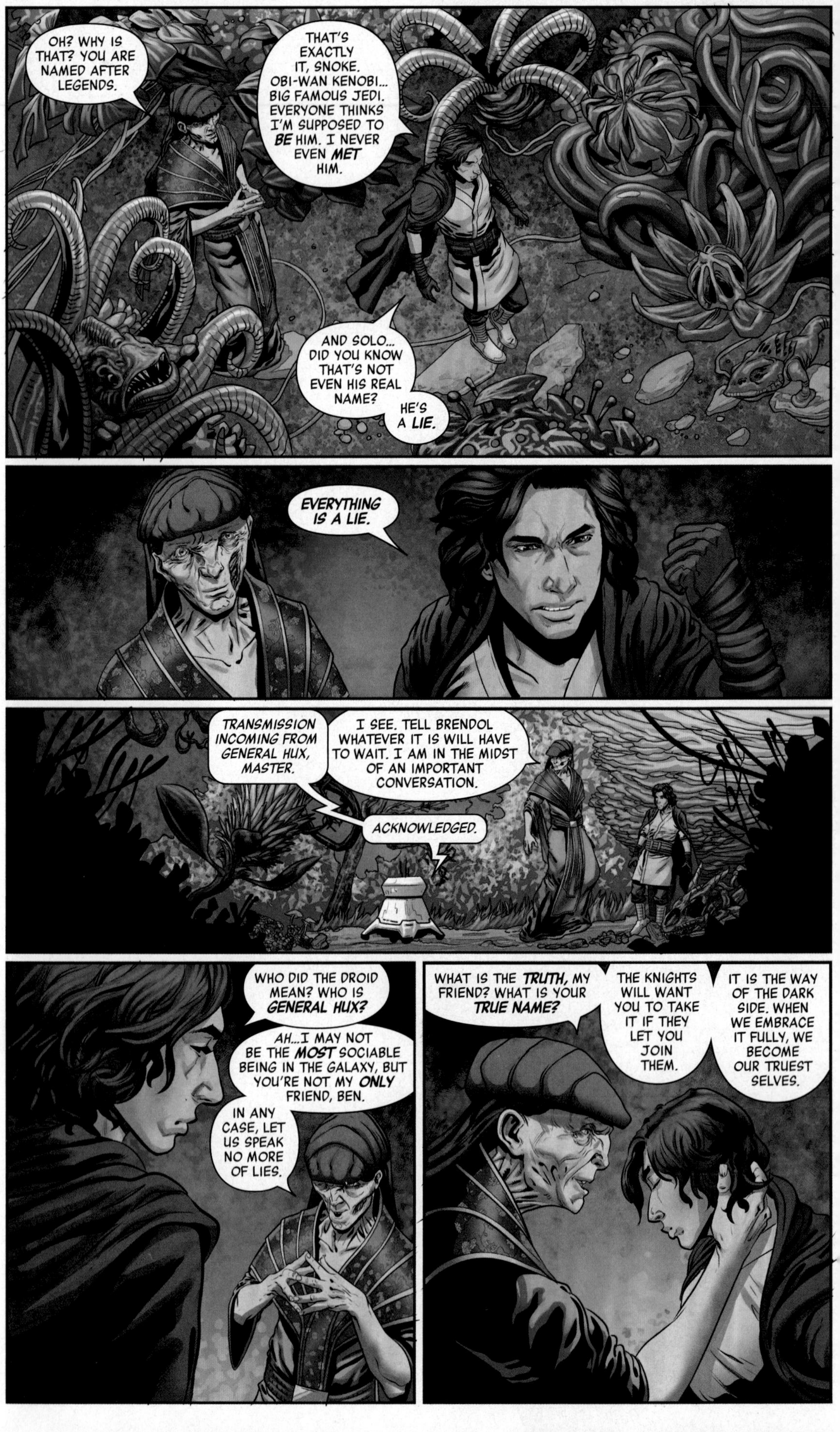
OH? WHY IS THAT? YOU ARE NAMED AFTER LEGENDS.
THAT'S EXACTLY IT, SNOKE. OBI-WAN KENOBI... BIG FAMOUS JEDI. EVERYONE THINKS I'M SUPPOSED TO BE HIM. I NEVER EVEN MET HIM.
AND SOLO... DID YOU KNOW THAT'S NOT EVEN HIS REAL NAME?
HE'S A LIE.
EVERYTHING IS A LIE.
TRANSMISSION INCOMING FROM GENERAL HUX, MASTER.
I SEE. TELL BRENDOL WHATEVER IT IS WILL HAVE TO WAIT. I AM IN THE MIDST OF AN IMPORTANT CONVERSATION.
ACKNOWLEDGED.
WHO DID THE DROID MEAN? WHO IS GENERAL HUX?
AH...I MAY NOT BE THE MOST SOCIABLE BEING IN THE GALAXY, BUT YOU'RE NOT MY ONLY FRIEND, BEN.
IN ANY CASE, LET US SPEAK NO MORE OF LIES.
WHAT IS THE TRUTH, MY FRIEND? WHAT IS YOUR TRUE NAME?
THE KNIGHTS WILL WANT YOU TO TAKE IT IF THEY LET YOU JOIN THEM.
IT IS THE WAY OF THE DARK SIDE. WHEN WE EMBRACE IT FULLY, WE BECOME OUR TRUEST SELVES.

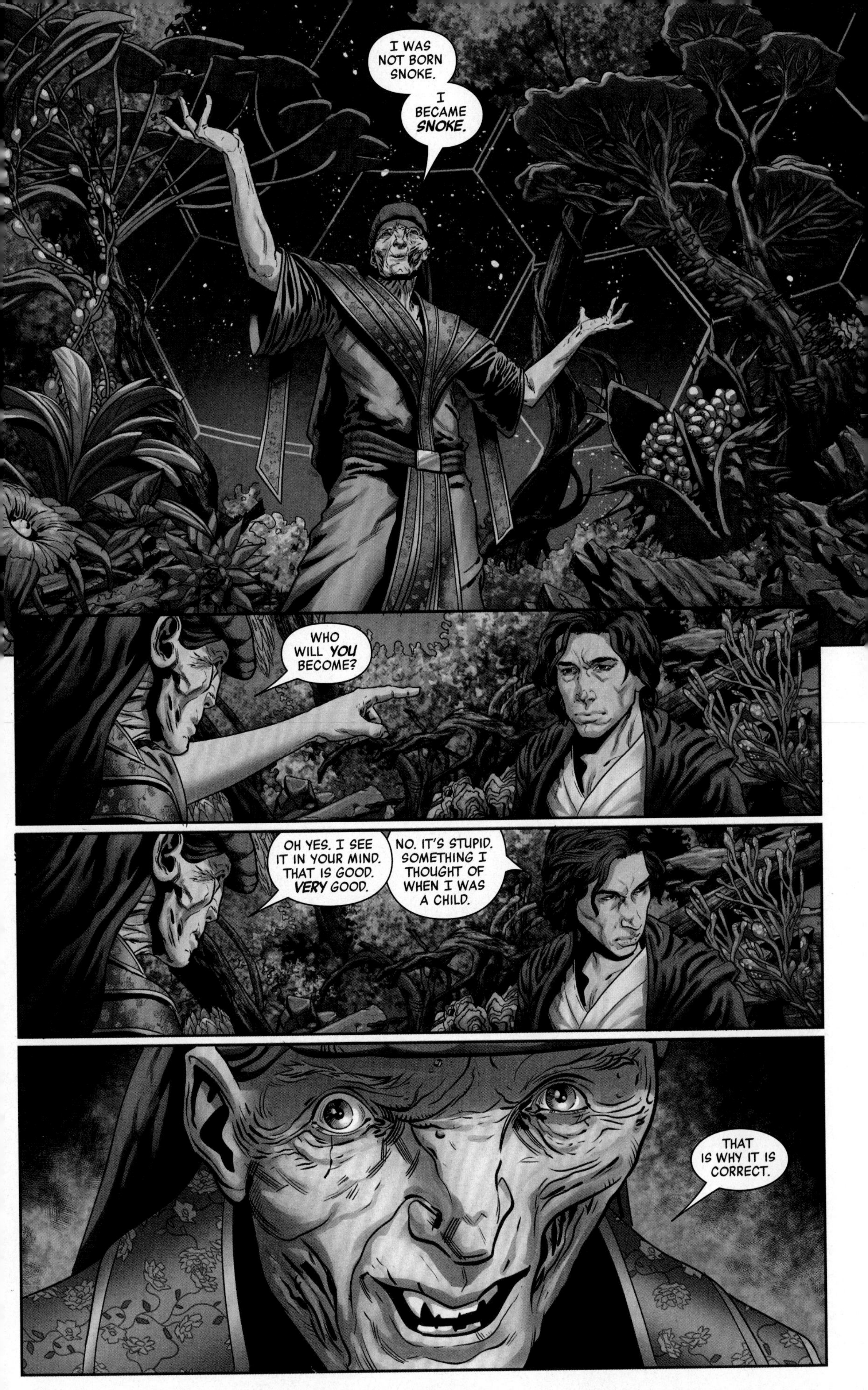
I WAS NOT BORN SNOKE.
I BECAME SNOKE.
WHO WILL YOU BECOME?
OH YES. I SEE IT IN YOUR MIND. THAT IS GOOD. VERY GOOD.
NO. IT'S STUPID. SOMETHING I THOUGHT OF WHEN I WAS A CHILD.
THAT IS WHY IT IS CORRECT.

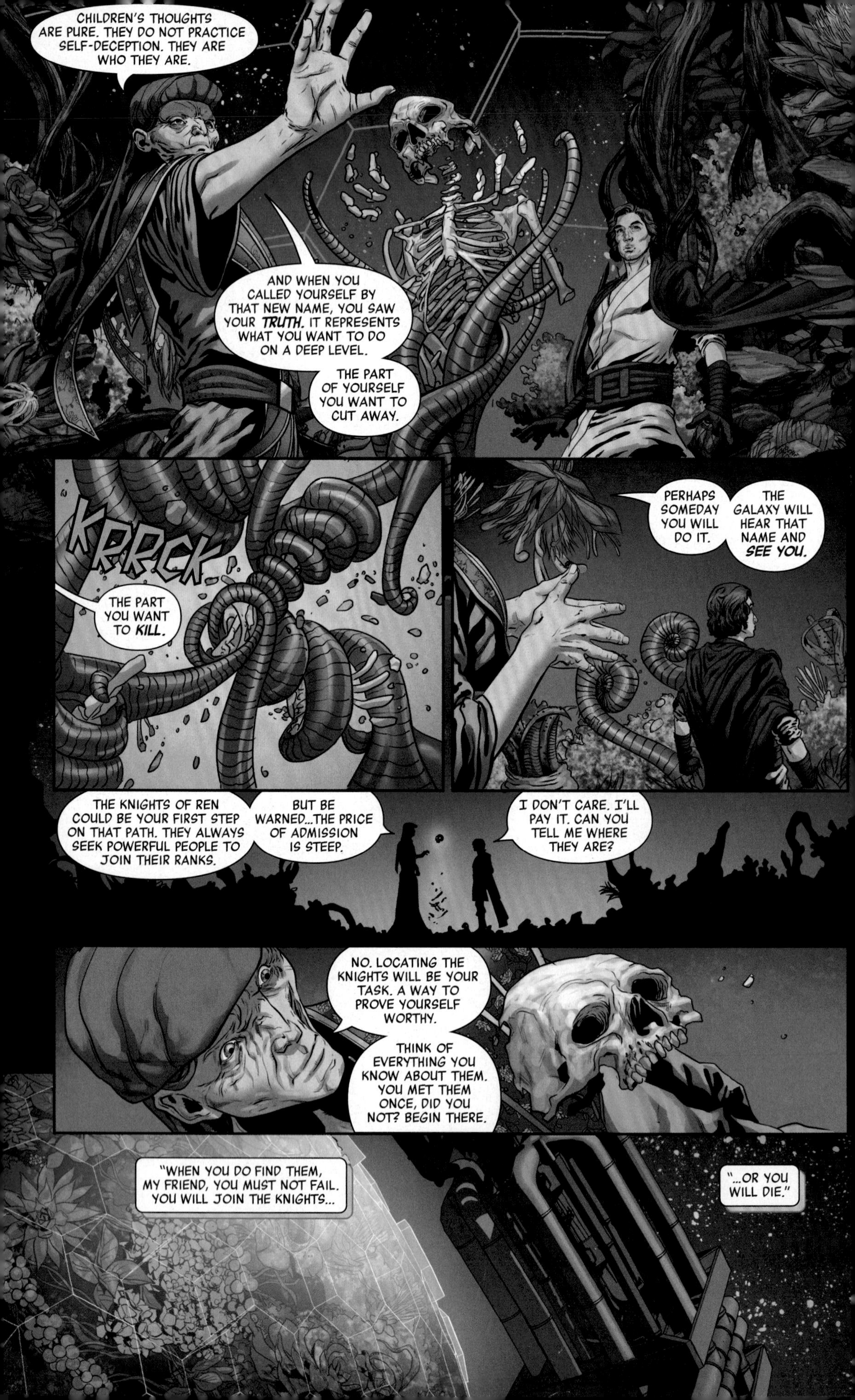
CHILDREN'S THOUGHTS ARE PURE. THEY DO NOT PRACTICE SELF-DECEPTION. THEY ARE WHO THEY ARE.
AND WHEN YOU CALLED YOURSELF BY THAT NEW NAME, YOU SAW YOUR ***TRUTH.*** IT REPRESENTS WHAT YOU WANT TO DO ON A DEEP LEVEL.
THE PART OF YOURSELF YOU WANT TO CUT AWAY.
KRRCK
THE PART YOU WANT TO ***KILL.***
PERHAPS SOMEDAY YOU WILL DO IT.
THE GALAXY WILL HEAR THAT NAME AND ***SEE YOU.***
THE KNIGHTS OF REN COULD BE YOUR FIRST STEP ON THAT PATH. THEY ALWAYS SEEK POWERFUL PEOPLE TO JOIN THEIR RANKS.
BUT BE WARNED...THE PRICE OF ADMISSION IS STEEP.
I DON'T CARE. I'LL PAY IT. CAN YOU TELL ME WHERE THEY ARE?
NO. LOCATING THE KNIGHTS WILL BE YOUR TASK. A WAY TO PROVE YOURSELF WORTHY.
THINK OF EVERYTHING YOU KNOW ABOUT THEM. YOU MET THEM ONCE, DID YOU NOT? BEGIN THERE.
"WHEN YOU DO FIND THEM, MY FRIEND, YOU MUST NOT FAIL. YOU WILL JOIN THE KNIGHTS...
"...OR YOU WILL DIE."

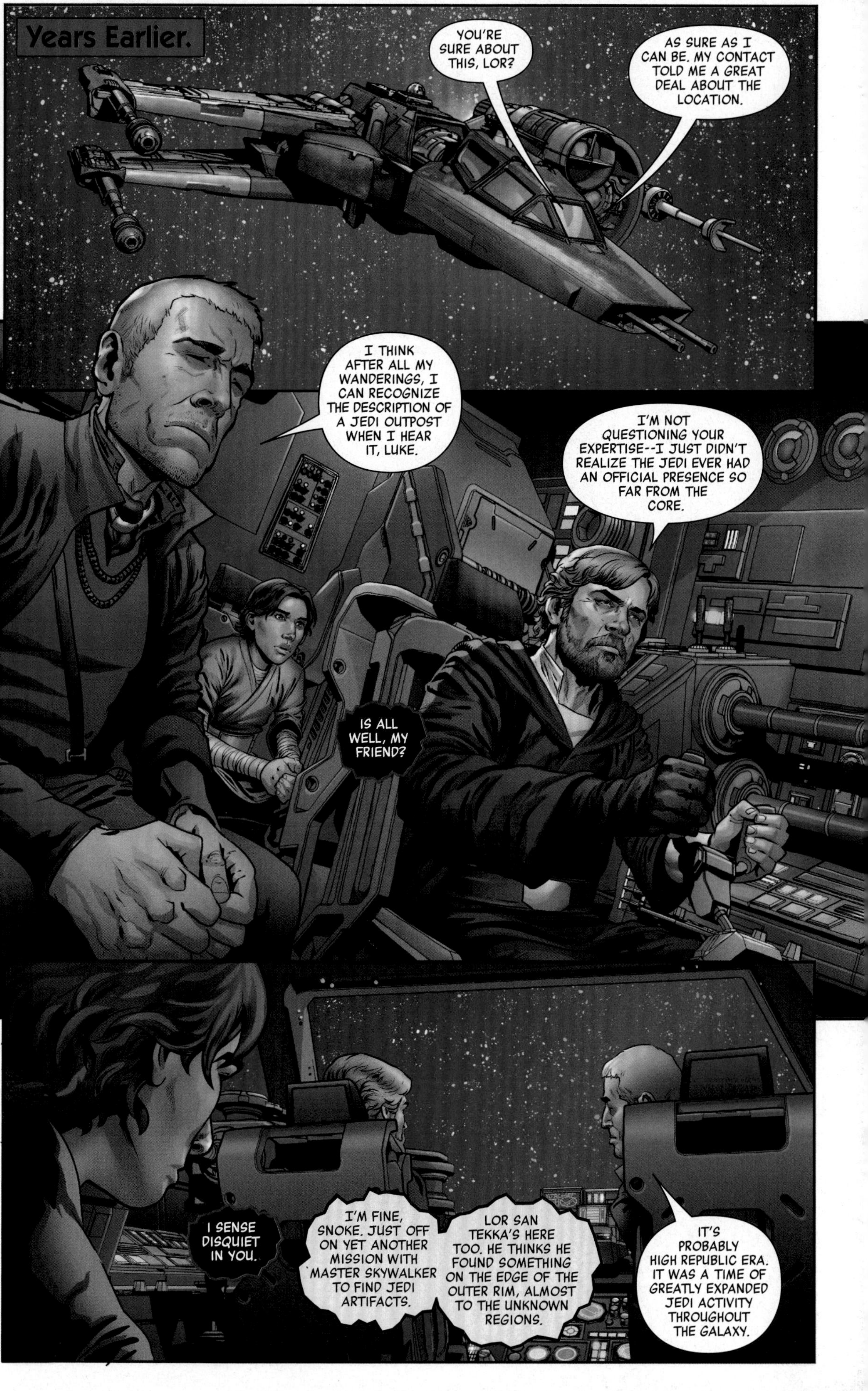

Years Earlier.
YOU'RE SURE ABOUT THIS, LOR?
AS SURE AS I CAN BE. MY CONTACT TOLD ME A GREAT DEAL ABOUT THE LOCATION.
I THINK AFTER ALL MY WANDERINGS, I CAN RECOGNIZE THE DESCRIPTION OF A JEDI OUTPOST WHEN I HEAR IT, LUKE.
I'M NOT QUESTIONING YOUR EXPERTISE--I JUST DIDN'T REALIZE THE JEDI EVER HAD AN OFFICIAL PRESENCE SO FAR FROM THE CORE.
IS ALL WELL, MY FRIEND?
I SENSE DISQUIET IN YOU.
I'M FINE, SNOKE. JUST OFF ON YET ANOTHER MISSION WITH MASTER SKYWALKER TO FIND JEDI ARTIFACTS.
LOR SAN TEKKA'S HERE TOO. HE THINKS HE FOUND SOMETHING ON THE EDGE OF THE OUTER RIM, ALMOST TO THE UNKNOWN REGIONS.
IT'S PROBABLY HIGH REPUBLIC ERA. IT WAS A TIME OF GREATLY EXPANDED JEDI ACTIVITY THROUGHOUT THE GALAXY.

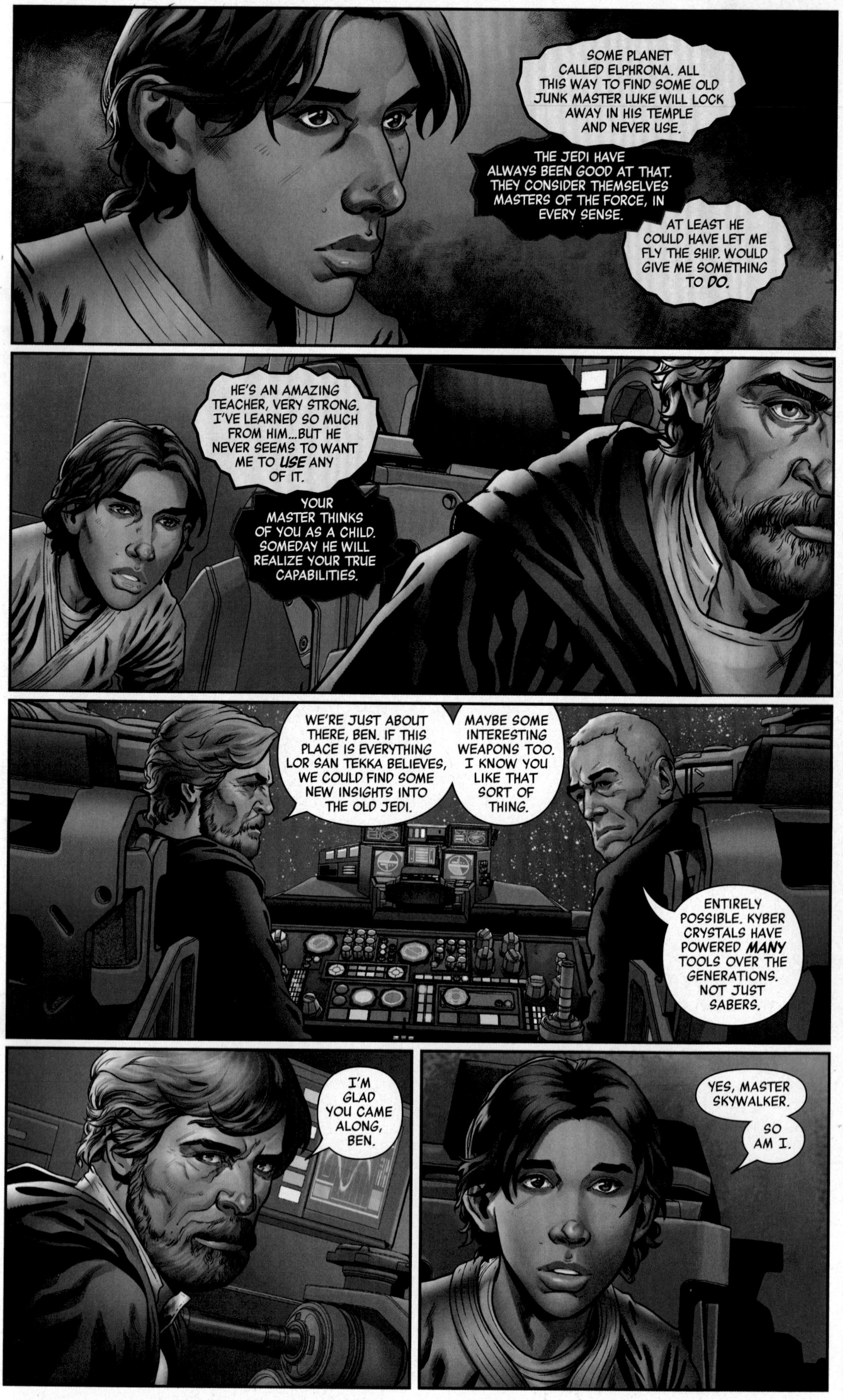
SOME PLANET CALLED ELPHRONA. ALL THIS WAY TO FIND SOME OLD JUNK MASTER LUKE WILL LOCK AWAY IN HIS TEMPLE AND NEVER USE.
THE JEDI HAVE ALWAYS BEEN GOOD AT THAT. THEY CONSIDER THEMSELVES MASTERS OF THE FORCE, IN EVERY SENSE.
AT LEAST HE COULD HAVE LET ME FLY THE SHIP. WOULD GIVE ME SOMETHING TO *DO*.
HE'S AN AMAZING TEACHER, VERY STRONG. I'VE LEARNED SO MUCH FROM HIM...BUT HE NEVER SEEMS TO WANT ME TO *USE* ANY OF IT.
YOUR MASTER THINKS OF YOU AS A CHILD. SOMEDAY HE WILL REALIZE YOUR TRUE CAPABILITIES.
WE'RE JUST ABOUT THERE, BEN. IF THIS PLACE IS EVERYTHING LOR SAN TEKKA BELIEVES, WE COULD FIND SOME NEW INSIGHTS INTO THE OLD JEDI.
MAYBE SOME INTERESTING WEAPONS TOO. I KNOW YOU LIKE THAT SORT OF THING.
ENTIRELY POSSIBLE. KYBER CRYSTALS HAVE POWERED **MANY** TOOLS OVER THE GENERATIONS. NOT JUST SABERS.
I'M GLAD YOU CAME ALONG, BEN.
YES, MASTER SKYWALKER.
SO AM I.

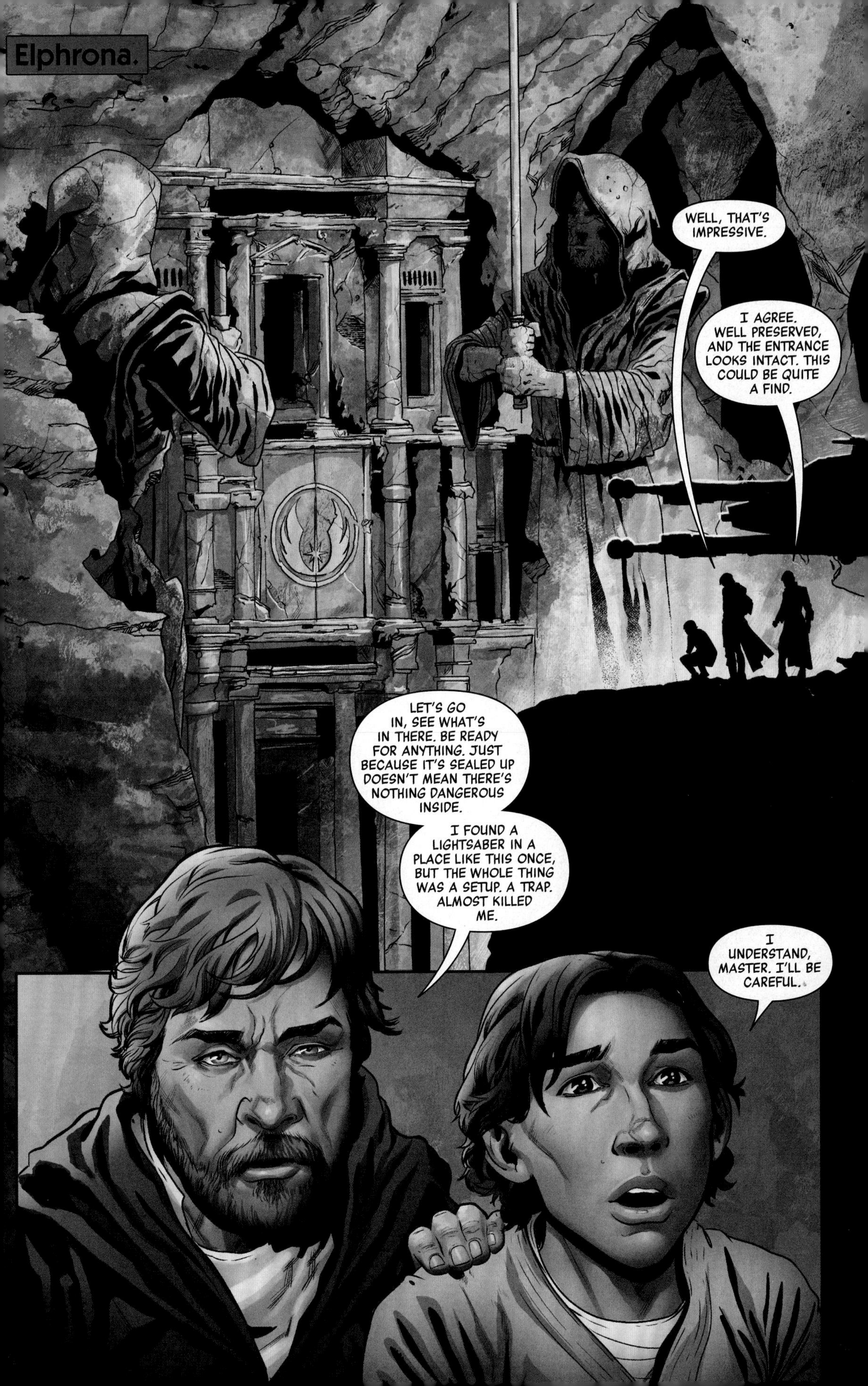
Elphrona.
WELL, THAT'S IMPRESSIVE.
I AGREE. WELL PRESERVED, AND THE ENTRANCE LOOKS INTACT. THIS COULD BE QUITE A FIND.
LET'S GO IN, SEE WHAT'S IN THERE. BE READY FOR ANYTHING. JUST BECAUSE IT'S SEALED UP DOESN'T MEAN THERE'S NOTHING DANGEROUS INSIDE.
I FOUND A LIGHTSABER IN A PLACE LIKE THIS ONCE, BUT THE WHOLE THING WAS A SETUP. A TRAP. ALMOST KILLED ME.
I UNDERSTAND, MASTER. I'LL BE CAREFUL.

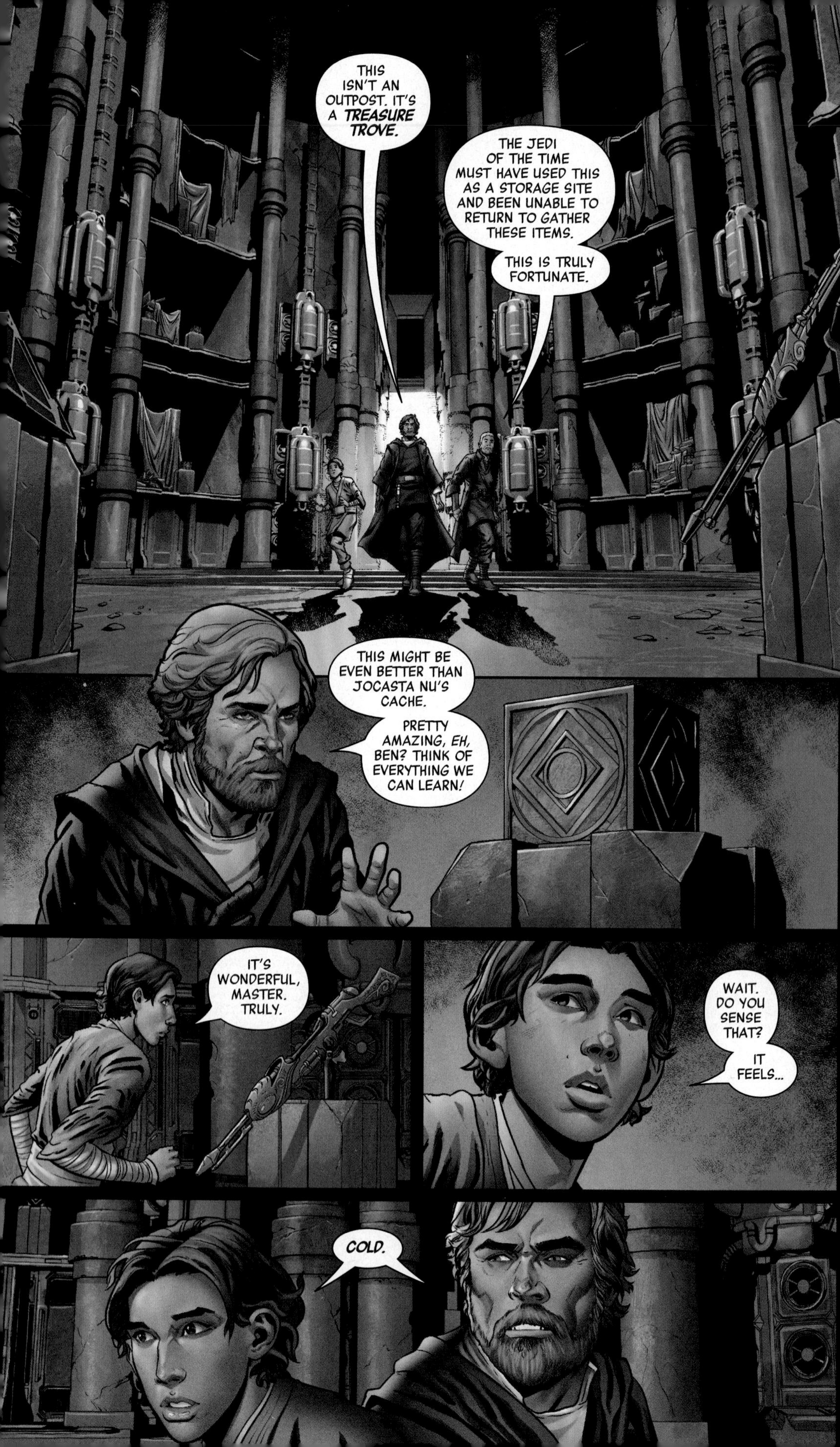
THIS ISN'T AN OUTPOST. IT'S A *TREASURE TROVE.*
THE JEDI OF THE TIME MUST HAVE USED THIS AS A STORAGE SITE AND BEEN UNABLE TO RETURN TO GATHER THESE ITEMS.
THIS IS TRULY FORTUNATE.
THIS MIGHT BE EVEN BETTER THAN JOCASTA NU'S CACHE.
PRETTY AMAZING, *EH,* BEN? THINK OF EVERYTHING WE CAN LEARN!
IT'S WONDERFUL, MASTER. TRULY.
WAIT. DO YOU SENSE THAT?
IT FEELS...
COLD.

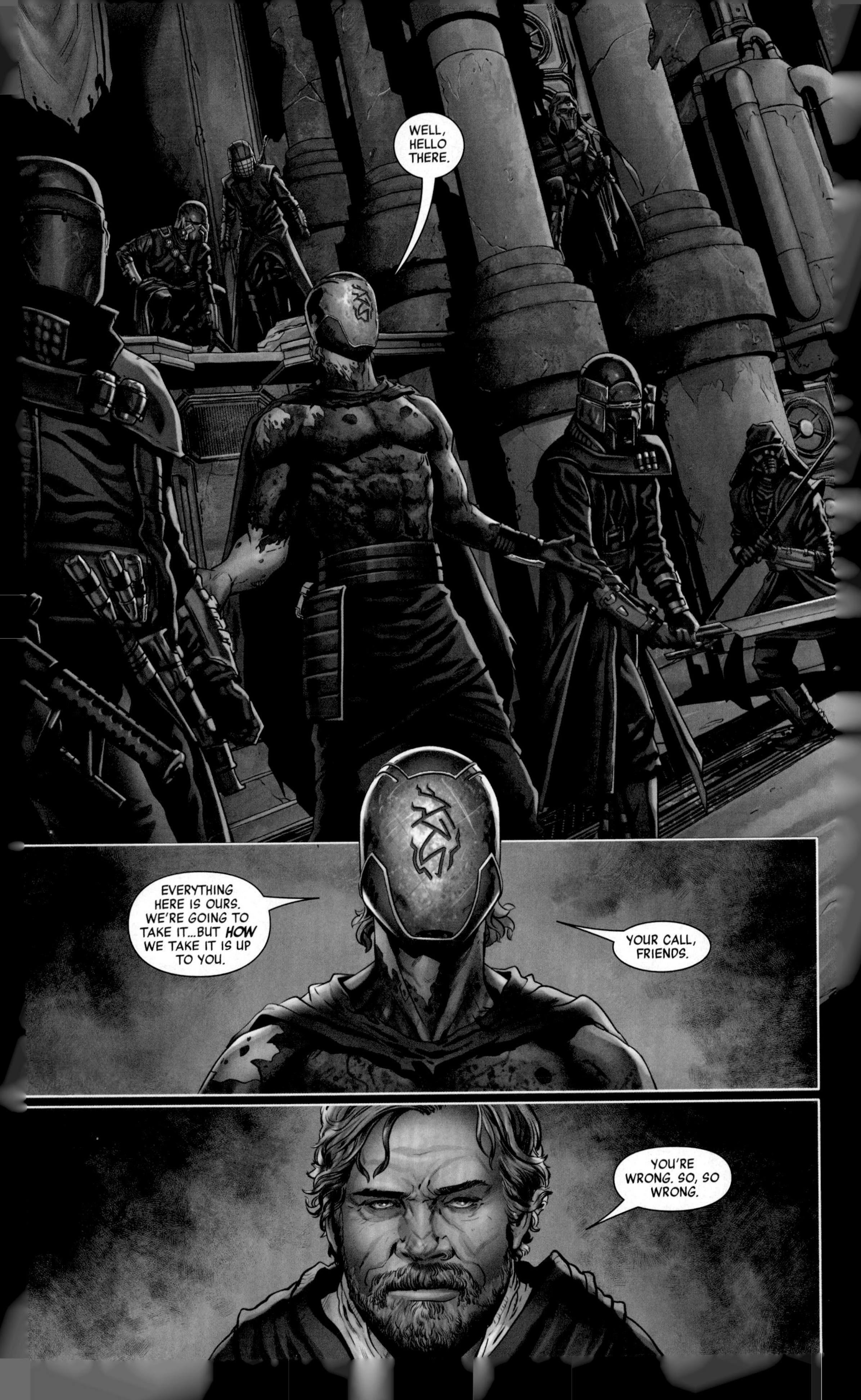
WELL, HELLO THERE.
EVERYTHING HERE IS OURS. WE'RE GOING TO TAKE IT...BUT *HOW* WE TAKE IT IS UP TO YOU.
YOUR CALL, FRIENDS.
YOU'RE WRONG. SO, SO WRONG.

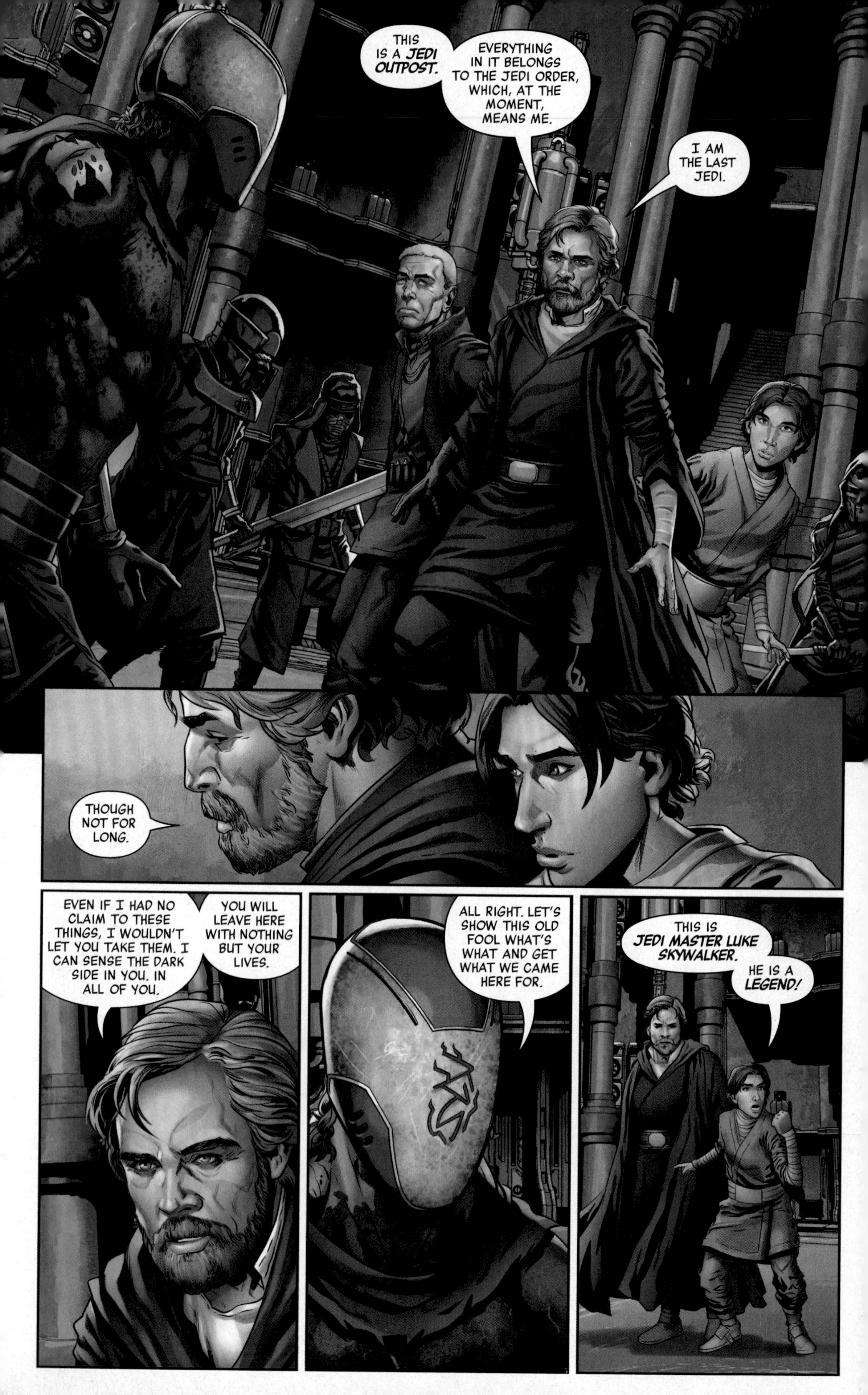
THIS IS A JEDI OUTPOST.
EVERYTHING IN IT BELONGS TO THE JEDI ORDER, WHICH, AT THE MOMENT, MEANS ME.
I AM THE LAST JEDI.
THOUGH NOT FOR LONG.
EVEN IF I HAD NO CLAIM TO THESE THINGS, I WOULDN'T LET YOU TAKE THEM. I CAN SENSE THE DARK SIDE IN YOU. IN ALL OF YOU.
YOU WILL LEAVE HERE WITH NOTHING BUT YOUR LIVES.
ALL RIGHT. LET'S SHOW THIS OLD FOOL WHAT'S WHAT AND GET WHAT WE CAME HERE FOR.
THIS IS JEDI MASTER LUKE SKYWALKER.
HE IS A LEGEND!

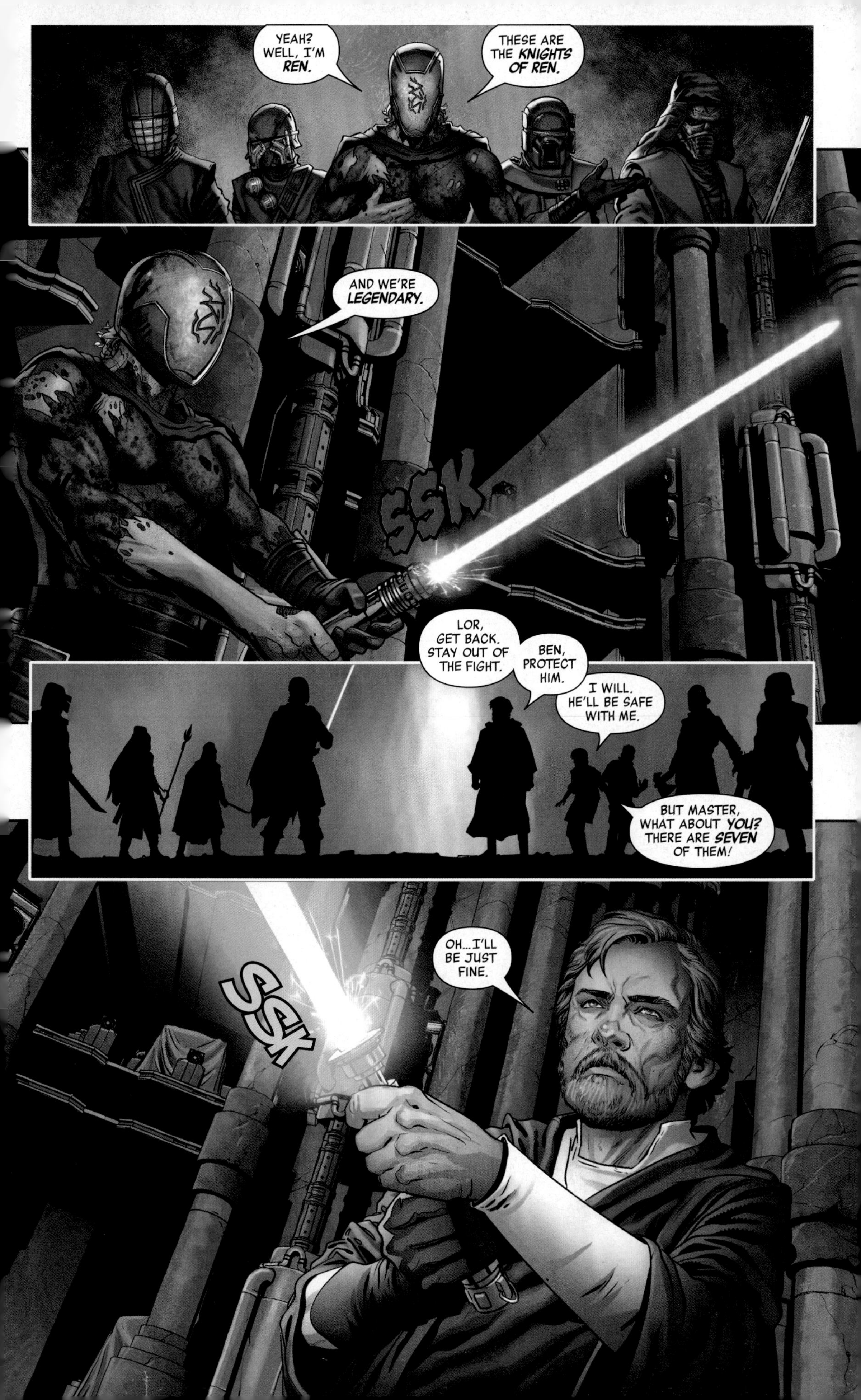
YEAH? WELL, I'M REN.
THESE ARE THE KNIGHTS OF REN.
AND WE'RE LEGENDARY.
SSK
LOR, GET BACK. STAY OUT OF THE FIGHT.
BEN, PROTECT HIM.
I WILL. HE'LL BE SAFE WITH ME.
BUT MASTER, WHAT ABOUT YOU? THERE ARE SEVEN OF THEM!
OH...I'LL BE JUST FINE.
SSK

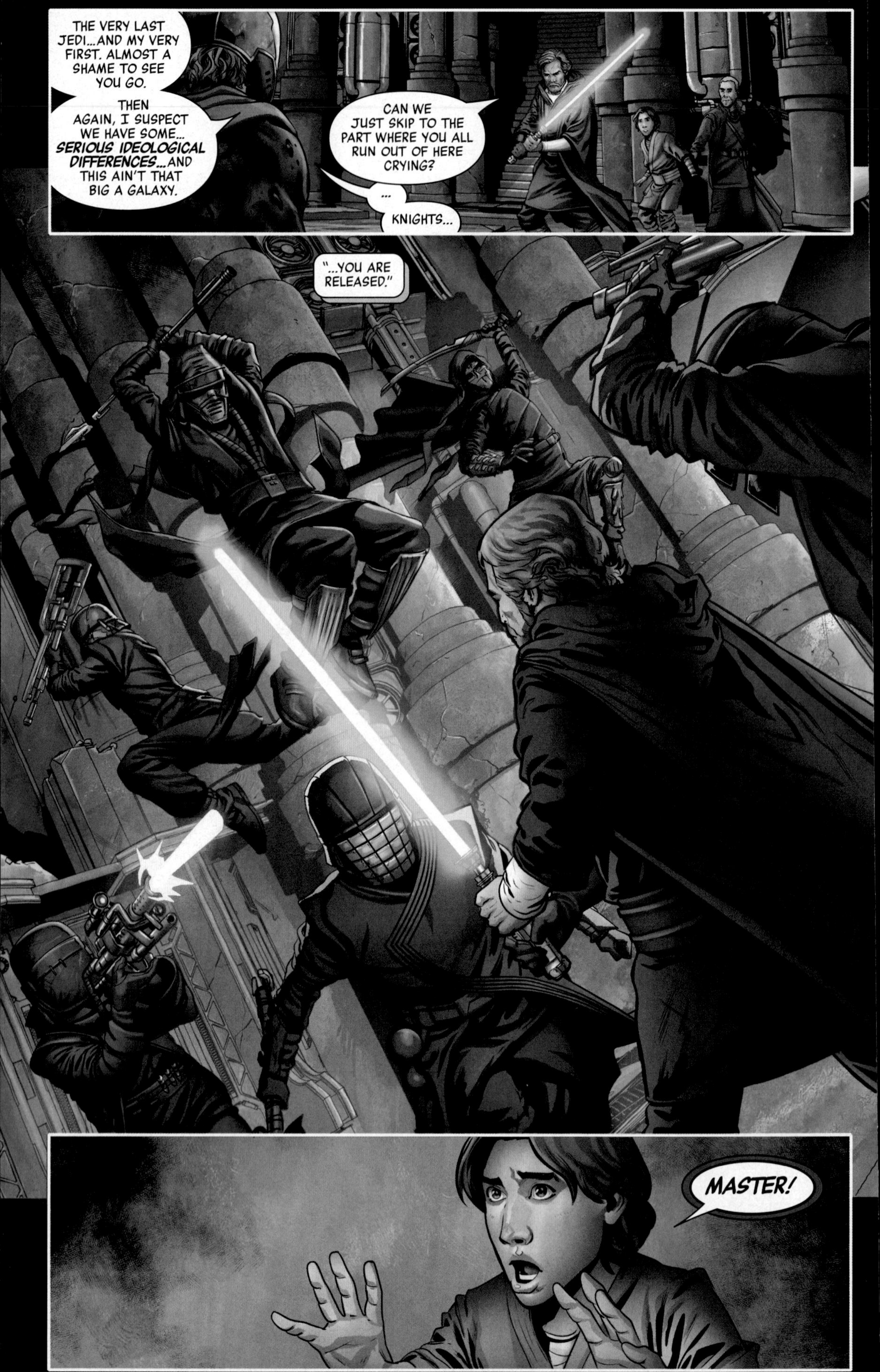
THE VERY LAST JEDI...AND MY VERY FIRST. ALMOST A SHAME TO SEE YOU GO.
THEN AGAIN, I SUSPECT WE HAVE SOME... SERIOUS IDEOLOGICAL DIFFERENCES...AND THIS AIN'T THAT BIG A GALAXY.
CAN WE JUST SKIP TO THE PART WHERE YOU ALL RUN OUT OF HERE CRYING?
...
KNIGHTS...
"...YOU ARE RELEASED."
MASTER!

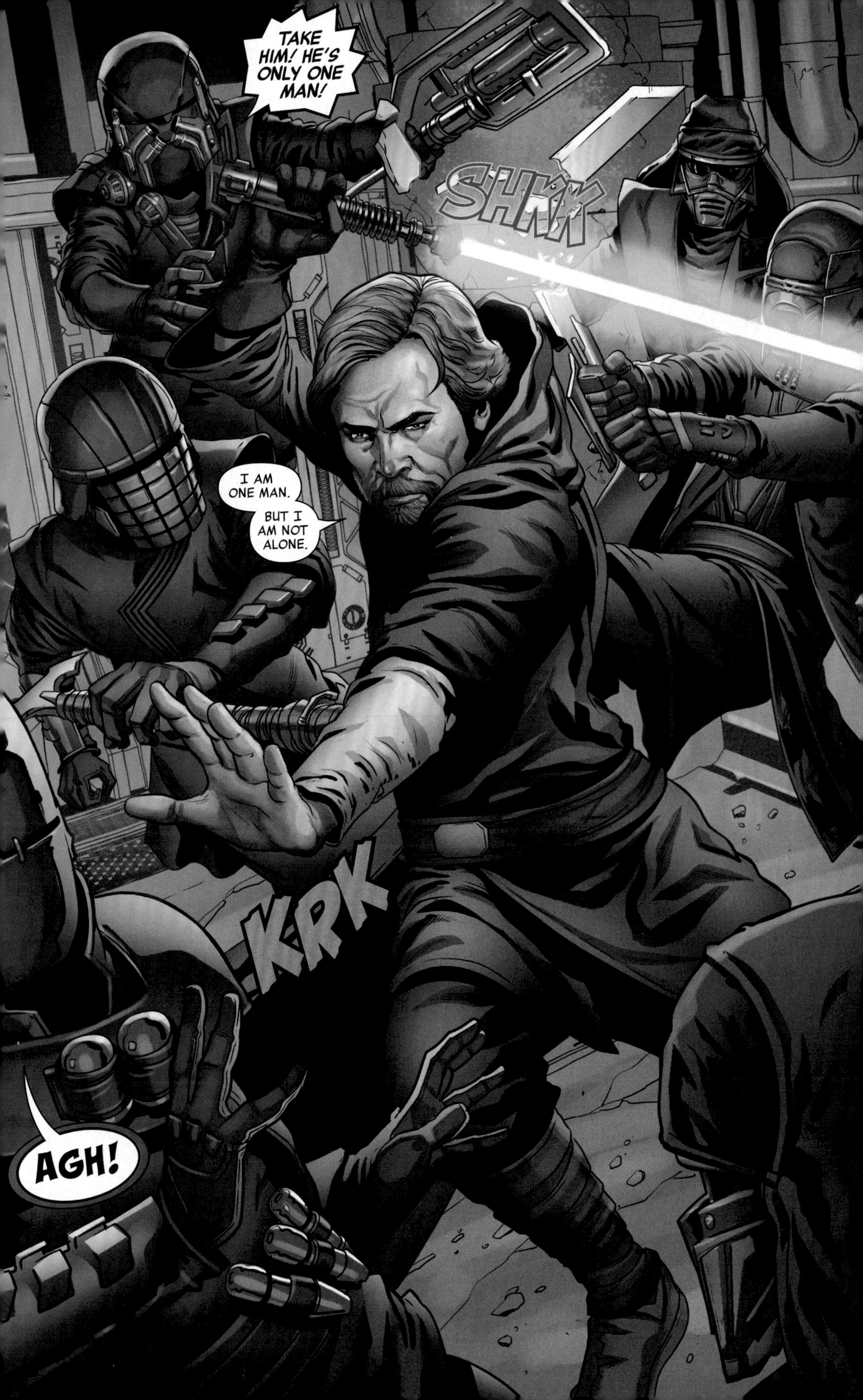
TAKE HIM! HE'S ONLY ONE MAN!
SHNK
I AM ONE MAN.
BUT I AM NOT ALONE.
KRK
AGH!

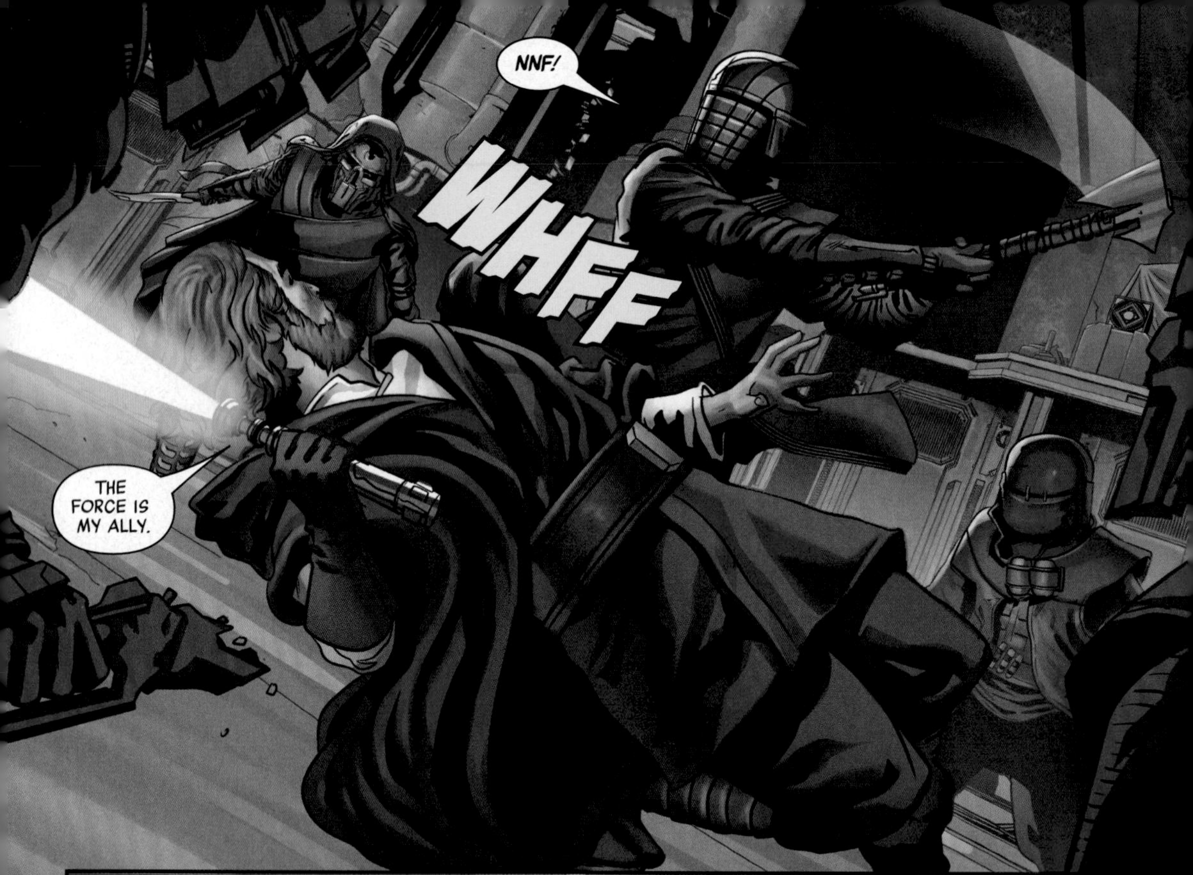
NNF!
WHFF
THE FORCE IS MY ALLY.
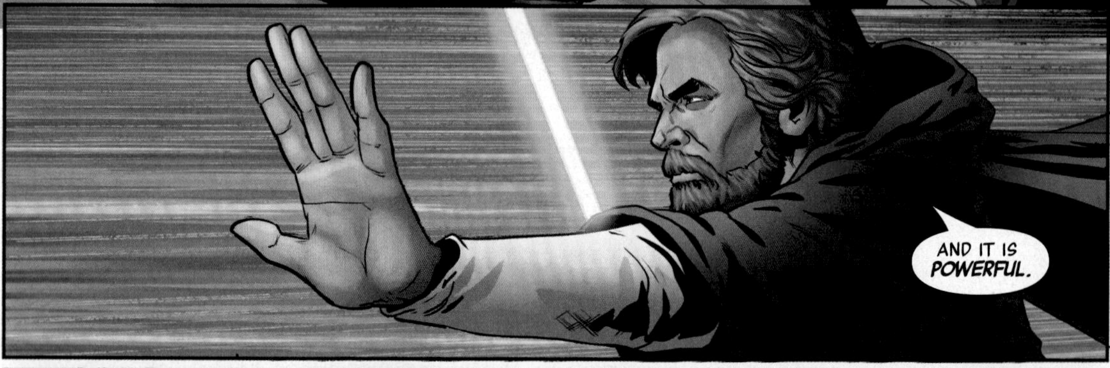
AND IT IS POWERFUL.
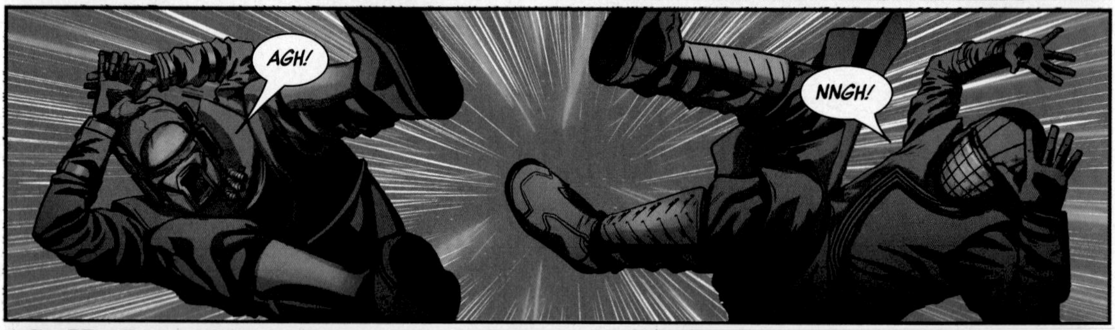
AGH!
NNGH!
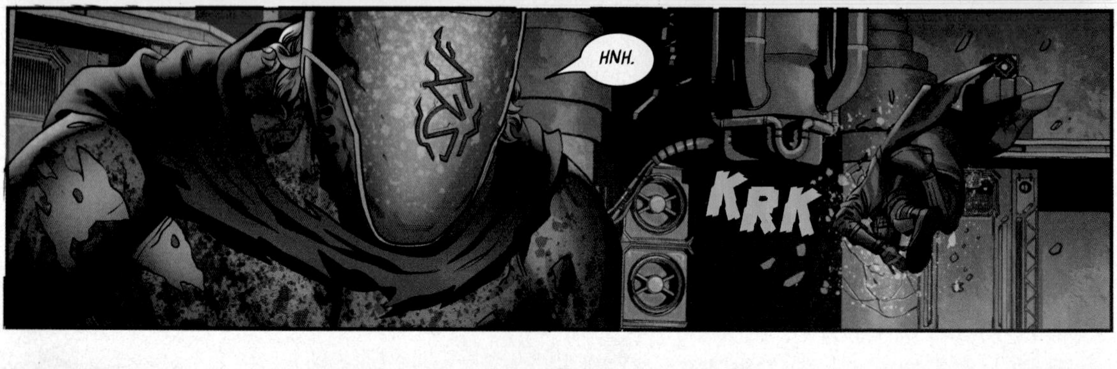
HNH.
KRK

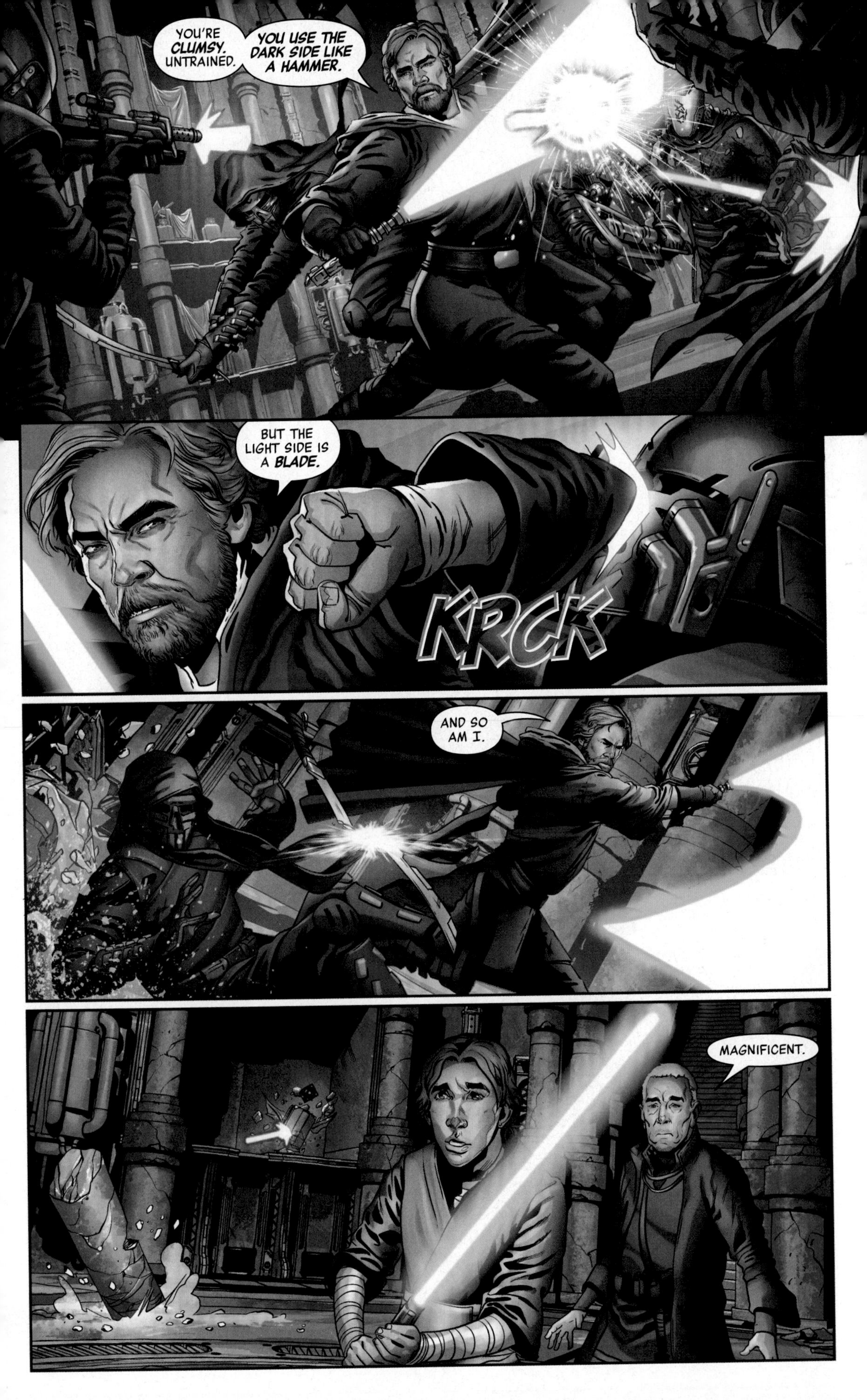
YOU'RE CLUMSY. UNTRAINED.
YOU USE THE DARK SIDE LIKE A HAMMER.
BUT THE LIGHT SIDE IS A BLADE.
KRCK
AND SO AM I.
MAGNIFICENT.

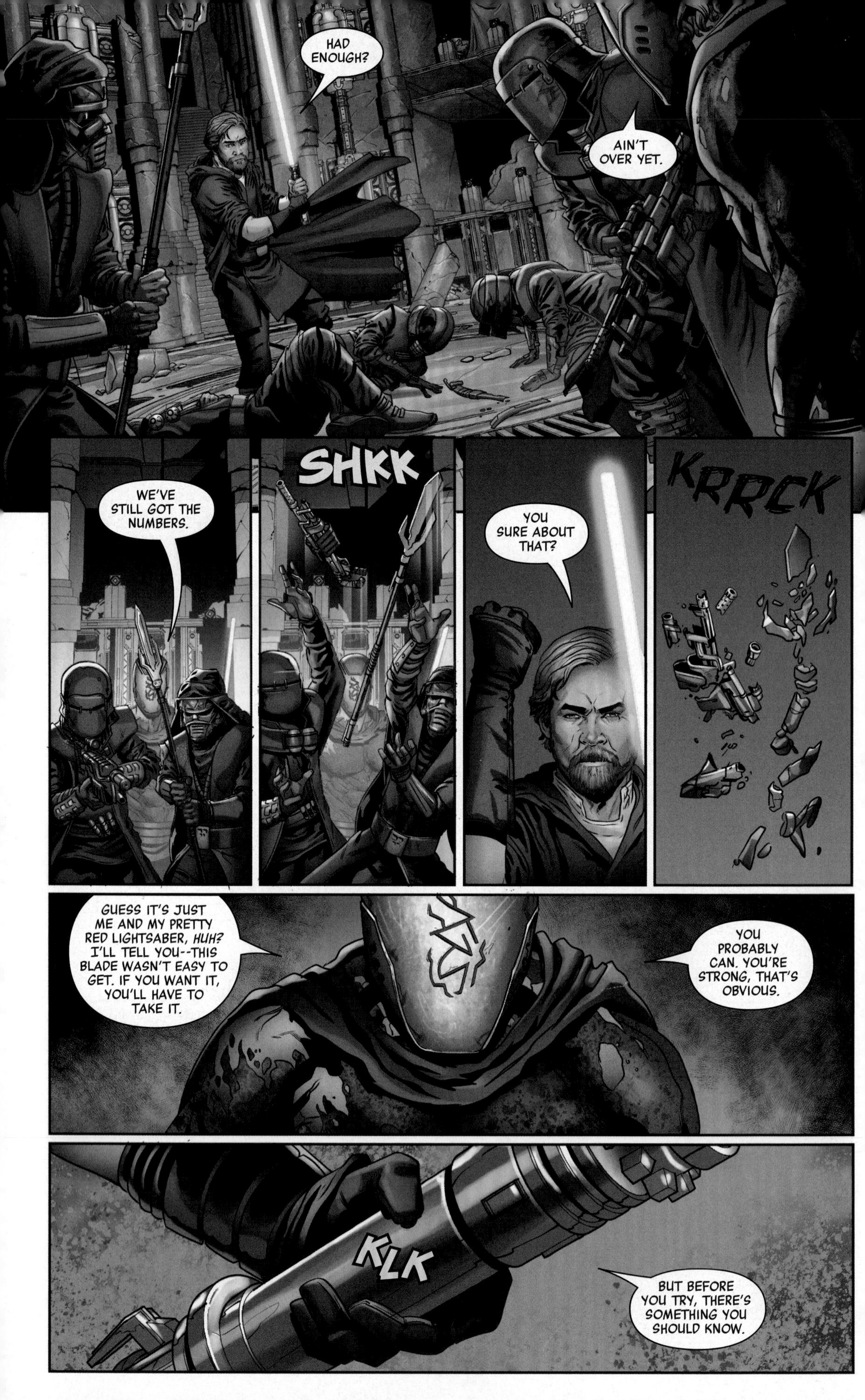

HAD ENOUGH?
AIN'T OVER YET.
WE'VE STILL GOT THE NUMBERS.
SHKK
YOU SURE ABOUT THAT?
KRRCK
GUESS IT'S JUST ME AND MY PRETTY RED LIGHTSABER, *HUH?* I'LL TELL YOU--THIS BLADE WASN'T EASY TO GET. IF YOU WANT IT, YOU'LL HAVE TO TAKE IT.
YOU PROBABLY CAN. YOU'RE STRONG, THAT'S OBVIOUS.
KLK
BUT BEFORE YOU TRY, THERE'S SOMETHING YOU SHOULD KNOW.

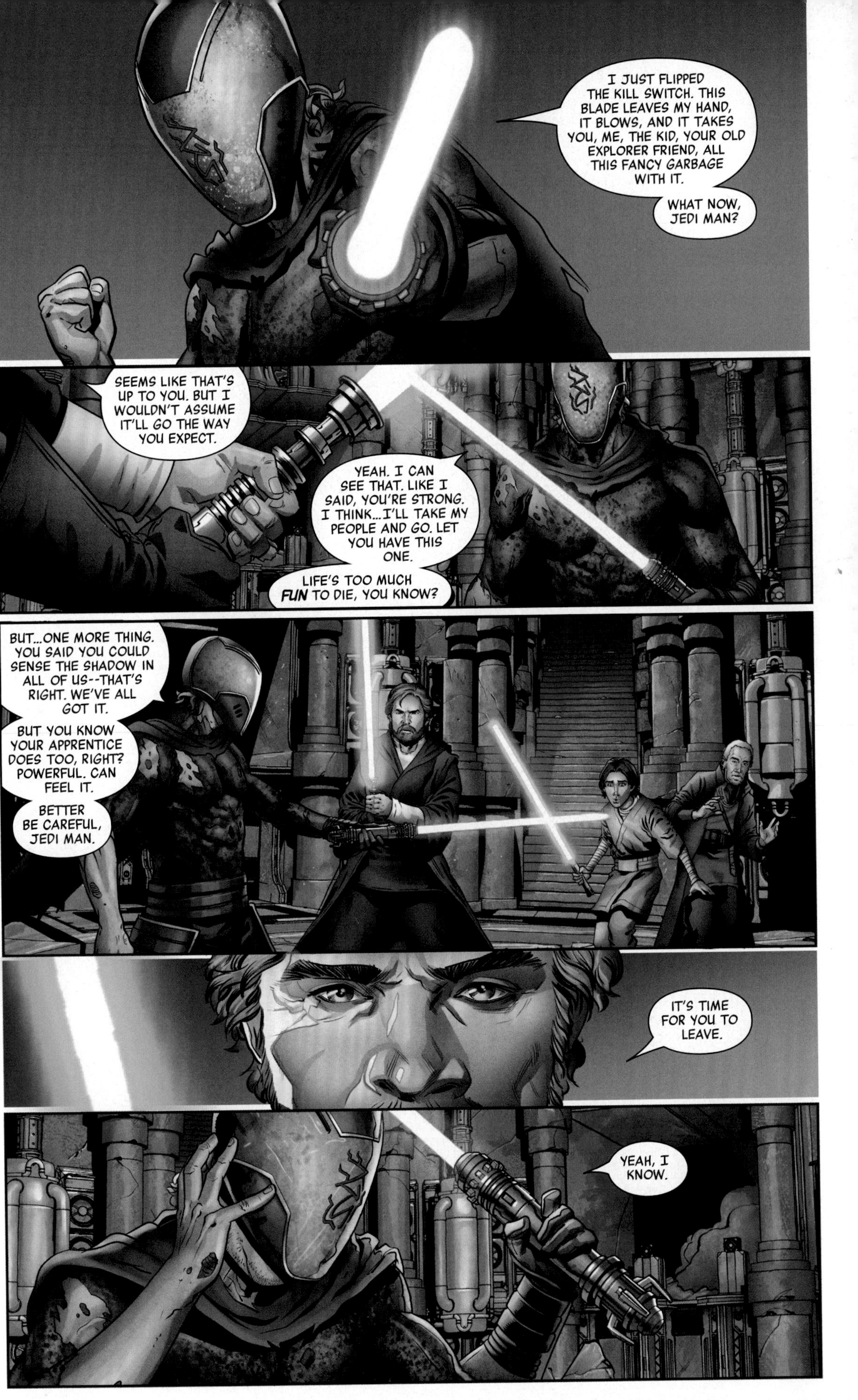
I JUST FLIPPED THE KILL SWITCH. THIS BLADE LEAVES MY HAND, IT BLOWS, AND IT TAKES YOU, ME, THE KID, YOUR OLD EXPLORER FRIEND, ALL THIS FANCY GARBAGE WITH IT.
WHAT NOW, JEDI MAN?
SEEMS LIKE THAT'S UP TO YOU. BUT I WOULDN'T ASSUME IT'LL GO THE WAY YOU EXPECT.
YEAH. I CAN SEE THAT. LIKE I SAID, YOU'RE STRONG. I THINK...I'LL TAKE MY PEOPLE AND GO. LET YOU HAVE THIS ONE.
LIFE'S TOO MUCH ***FUN*** TO DIE, YOU KNOW?
BUT...ONE MORE THING. YOU SAID YOU COULD SENSE THE SHADOW IN ALL OF US--THAT'S RIGHT. WE'VE ALL GOT IT.
BUT YOU KNOW YOUR APPRENTICE DOES TOO, RIGHT? POWERFUL. CAN FEEL IT.
BETTER BE CAREFUL, JEDI MAN.
IT'S TIME FOR YOU TO LEAVE.
YEAH, I KNOW.

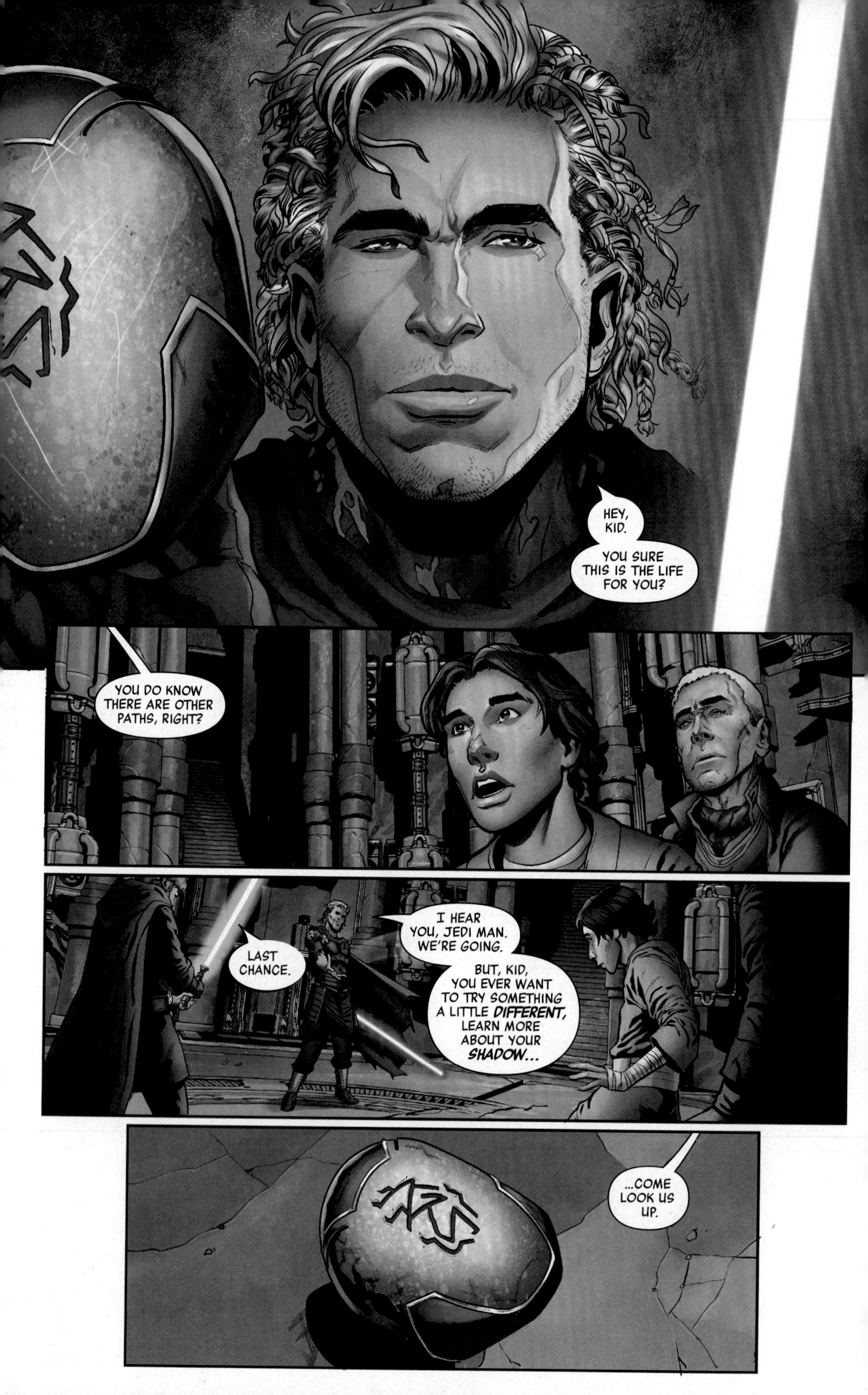
HEY, KID.
YOU SURE THIS IS THE LIFE FOR YOU?
YOU DO KNOW THERE ARE OTHER PATHS, RIGHT?
LAST CHANCE.
I HEAR YOU, JEDI MAN. WE'RE GOING.
BUT, KID, YOU EVER WANT TO TRY SOMETHING A LITTLE DIFFERENT, LEARN MORE ABOUT YOUR SHADOW...
...COME LOOK US UP.

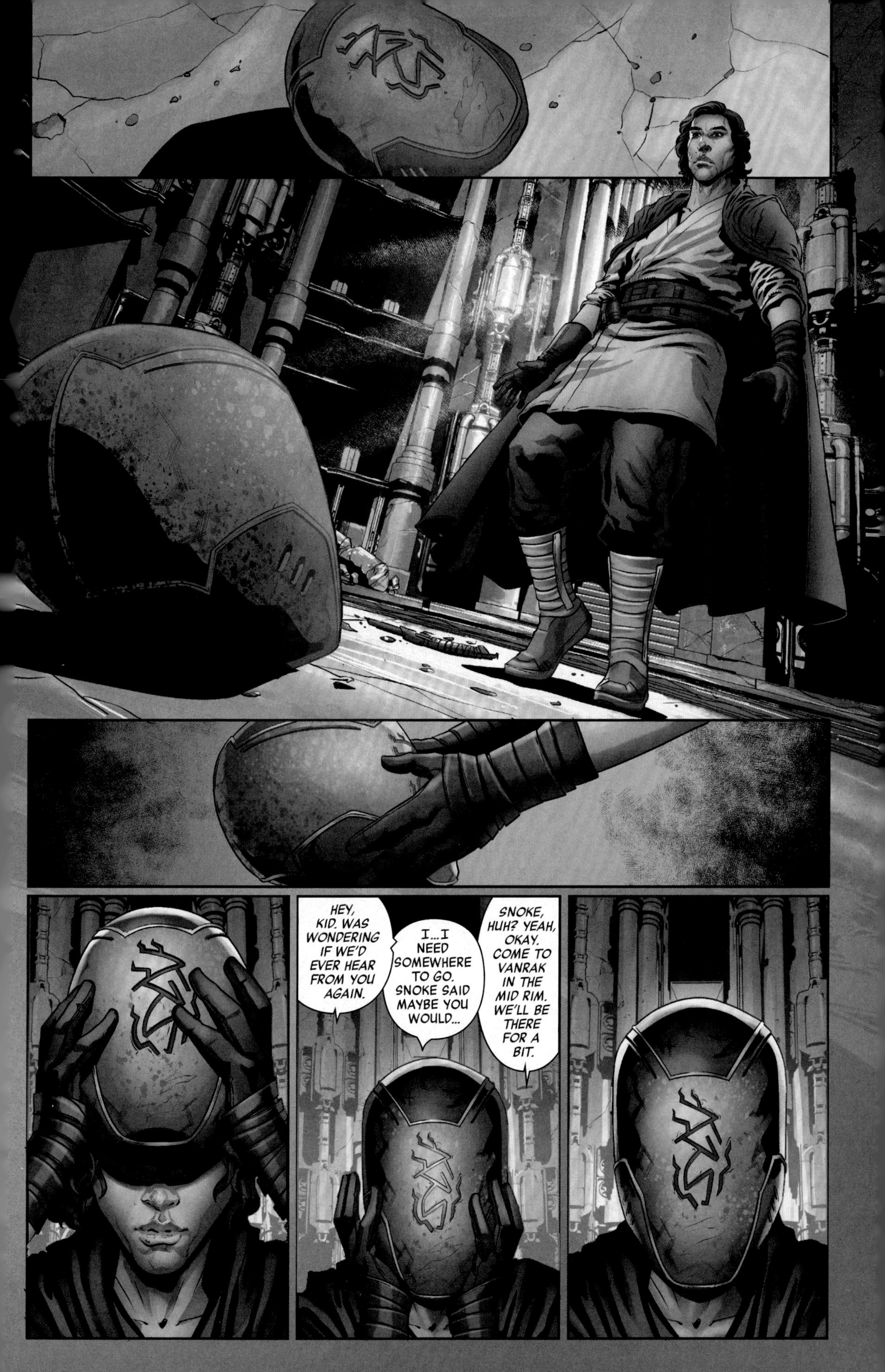
HEY, KID. WAS WONDERING IF WE'D EVER HEAR FROM YOU AGAIN.
I...I NEED SOMEWHERE TO GO. SNOKE SAID MAYBE YOU WOULD...
SNOKE, HUH? YEAH, OKAY. COME TO VANRAK IN THE MID RIM. WE'LL BE THERE FOR A BIT.

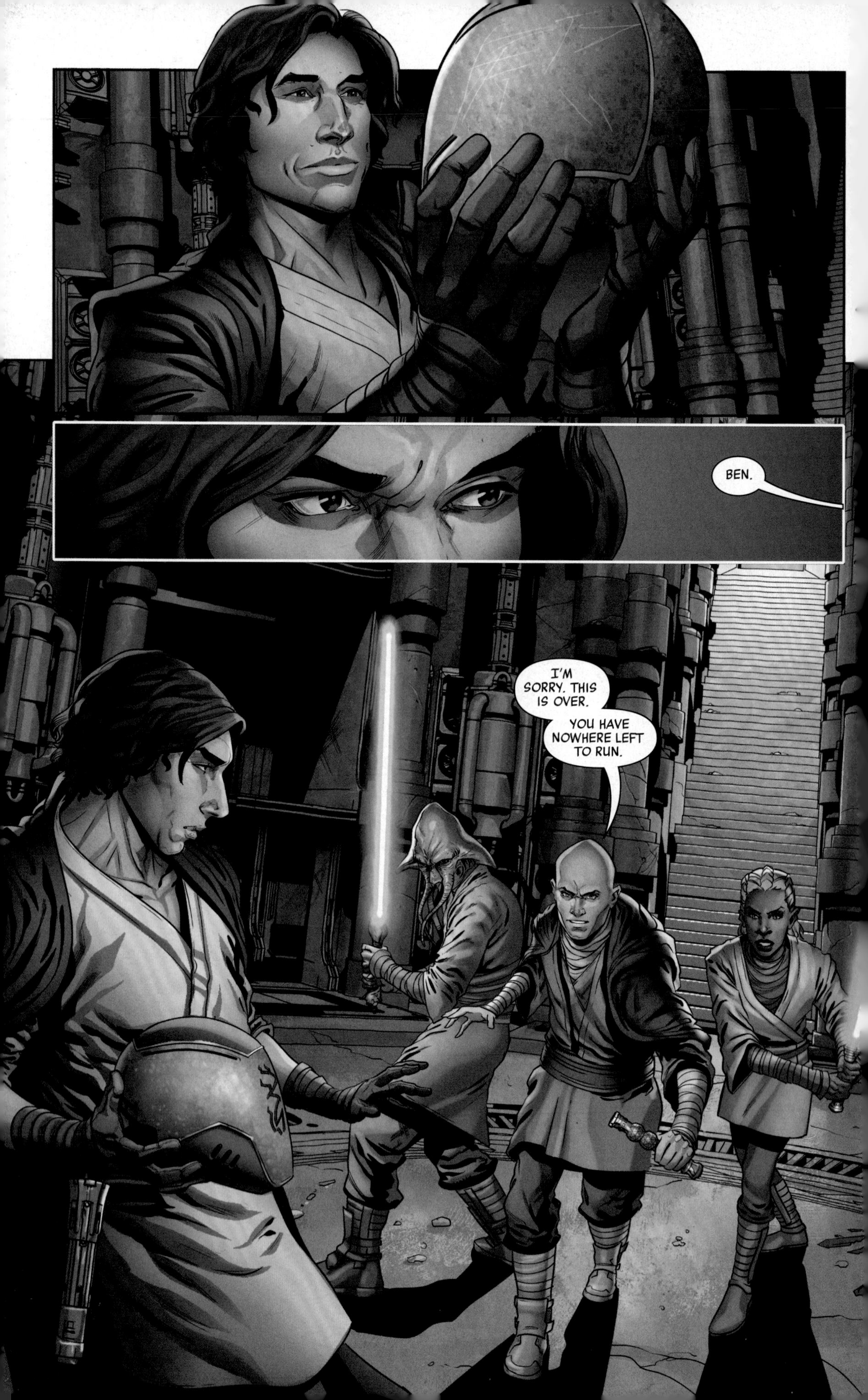
BEN.
I'M SORRY. THIS IS OVER.
YOU HAVE NOWHERE LEFT TO RUN.

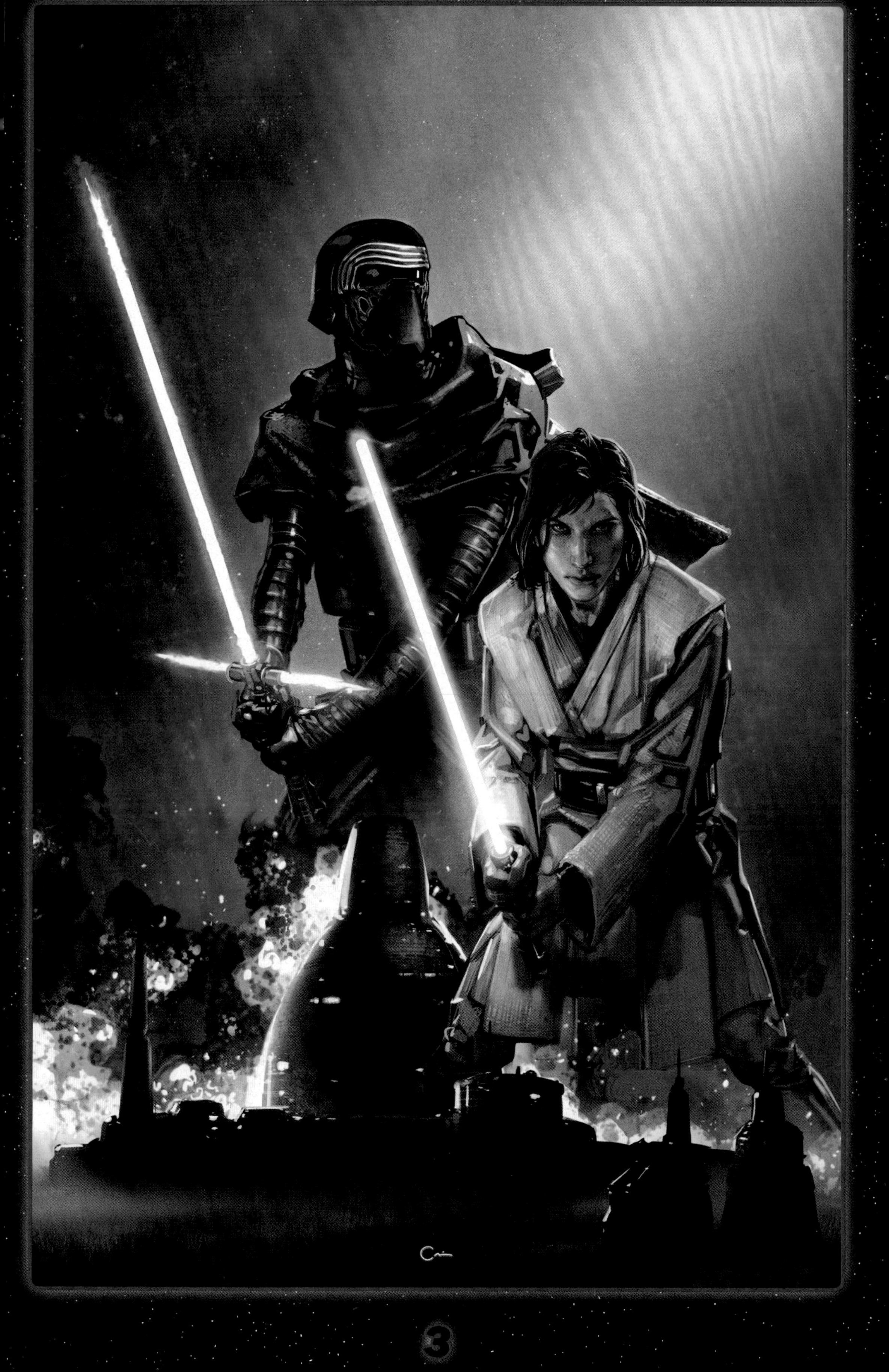

3

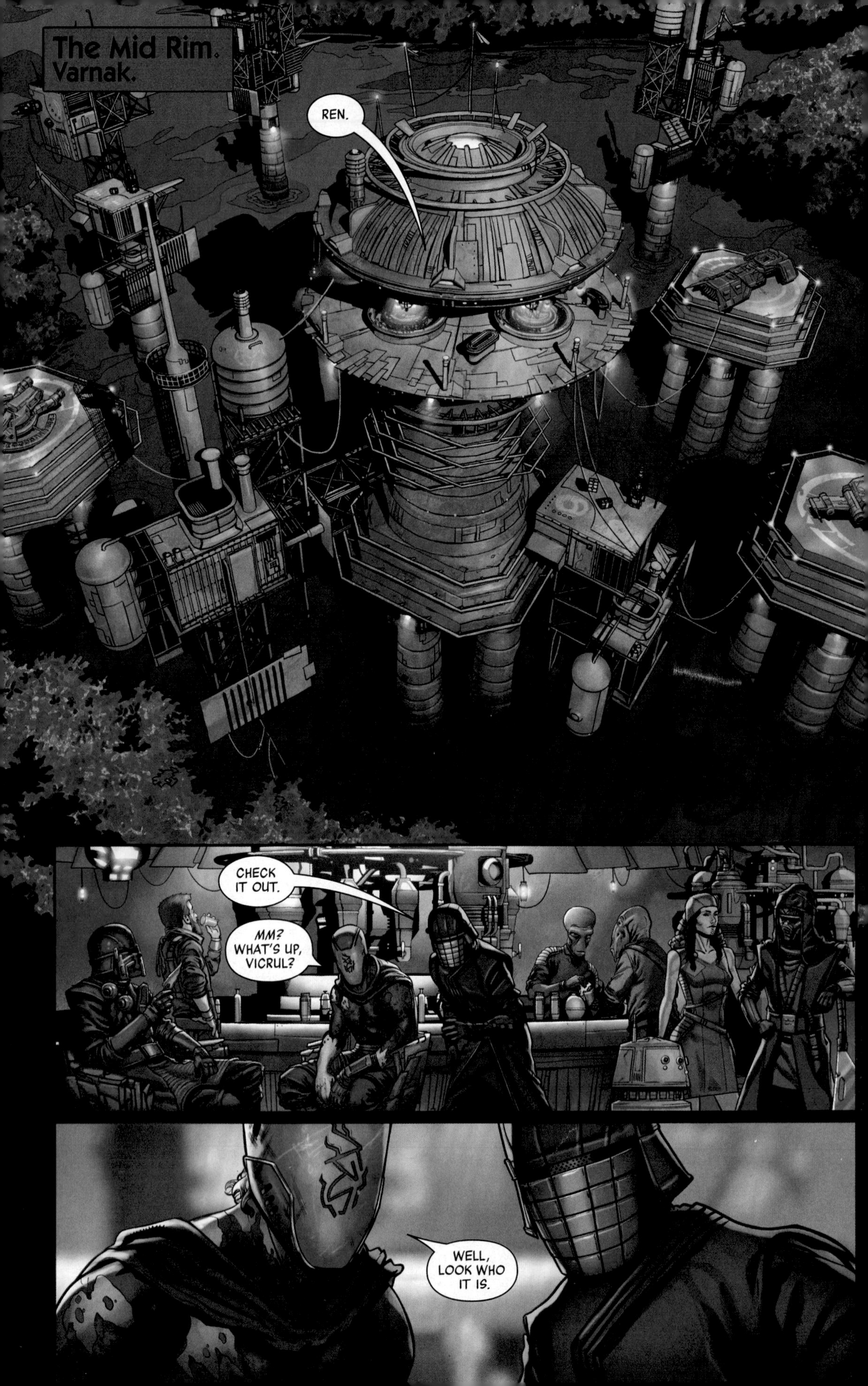
The Mid Rim.
Varnak.
REN.
CHECK IT OUT.
MM? WHAT'S UP, VICRUL?
WELL, LOOK WHO IT IS.

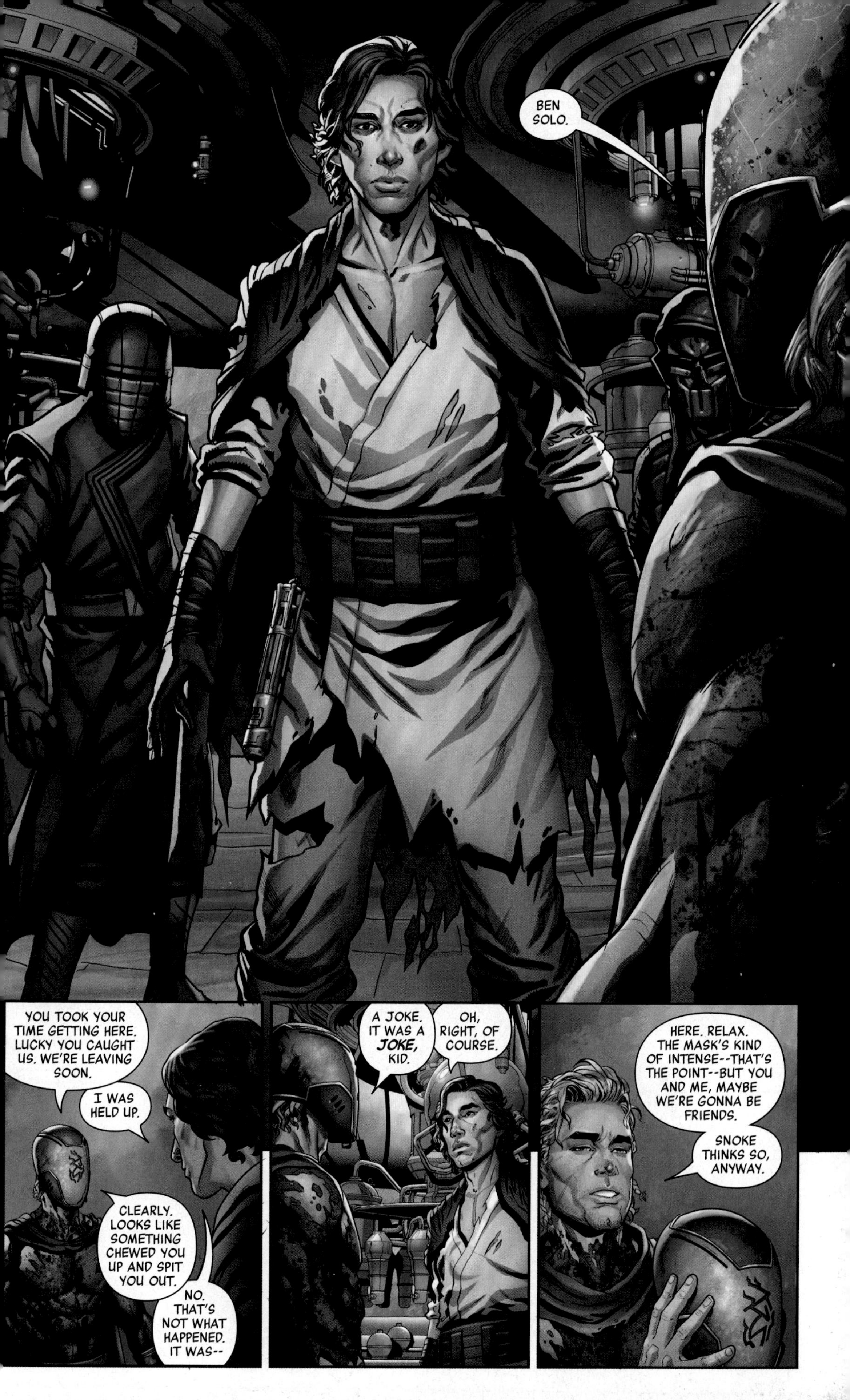
BEN SOLO.
YOU TOOK YOUR TIME GETTING HERE. LUCKY YOU CAUGHT US. WE'RE LEAVING SOON.
I WAS HELD UP.
CLEARLY. LOOKS LIKE SOMETHING CHEWED YOU UP AND SPIT YOU OUT.
NO. THAT'S NOT WHAT HAPPENED. IT WAS--
A JOKE. IT WAS A JOKE, KID.
OH, RIGHT, OF COURSE.
HERE. RELAX. THE MASK'S KIND OF INTENSE--THAT'S THE POINT--BUT YOU AND ME, MAYBE WE'RE GONNA BE FRIENDS.
SNOKE THINKS SO, ANYWAY.

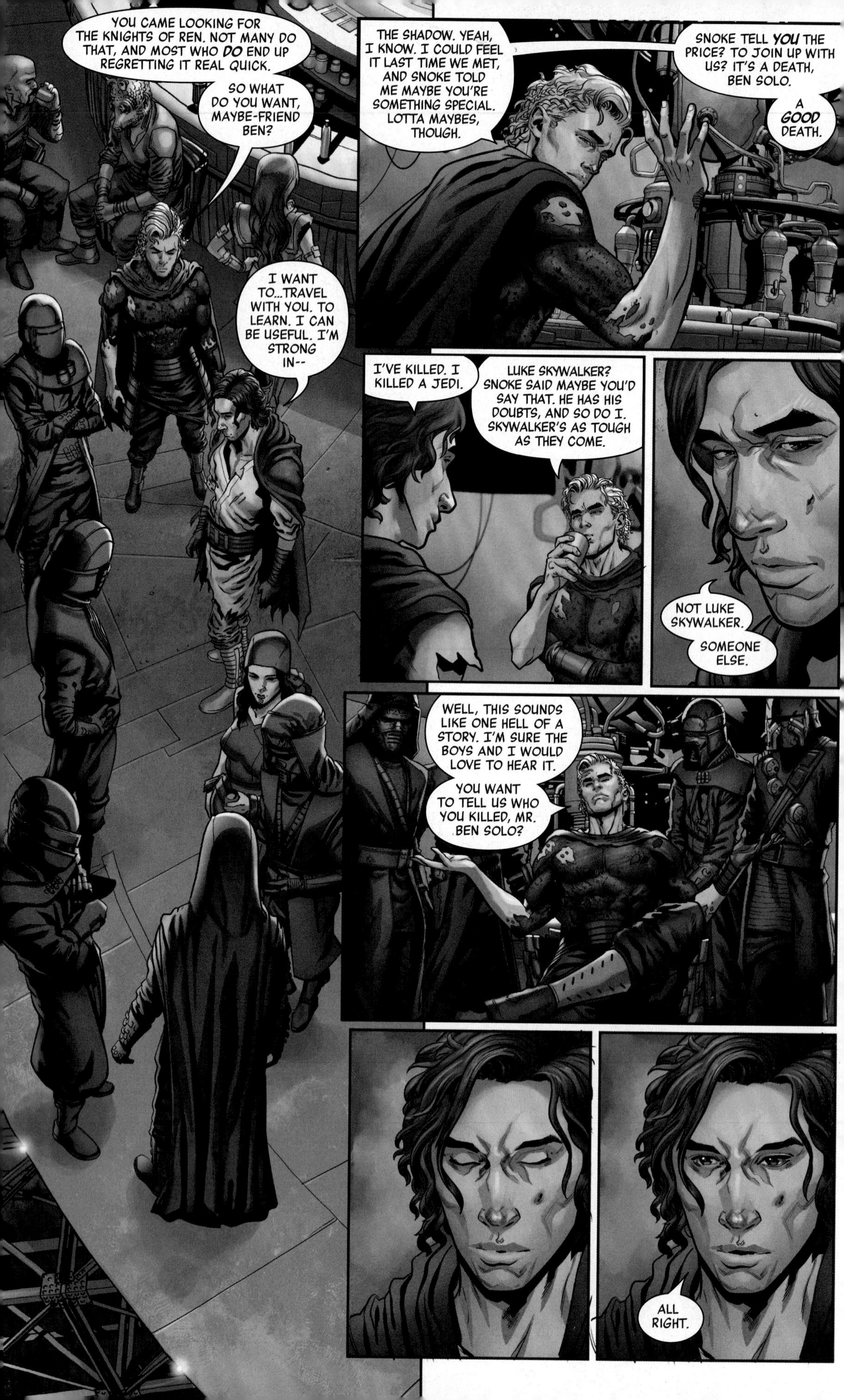
YOU CAME LOOKING FOR THE KNIGHTS OF REN. NOT MANY DO THAT, AND MOST WHO **DO** END UP REGRETTING IT REAL QUICK.
SO WHAT DO YOU WANT, MAYBE-FRIEND BEN?
I WANT TO...TRAVEL WITH YOU. TO LEARN. I CAN BE USEFUL. I'M STRONG IN--
THE SHADOW. YEAH, I KNOW. I COULD FEEL IT LAST TIME WE MET, AND SNOKE TOLD ME MAYBE YOU'RE SOMETHING SPECIAL. LOTTA MAYBES, THOUGH.
SNOKE TELL **YOU** THE PRICE? TO JOIN UP WITH US? IT'S A DEATH, BEN SOLO.
A **GOOD** DEATH.
I'VE KILLED. I KILLED A JEDI.
LUKE SKYWALKER? SNOKE SAID MAYBE YOU'D SAY THAT. HE HAS HIS DOUBTS, AND SO DO I. SKYWALKER'S AS TOUGH AS THEY COME.
NOT LUKE SKYWALKER.
SOMEONE ELSE.
WELL, THIS SOUNDS LIKE ONE HELL OF A STORY. I'M SURE THE BOYS AND I WOULD LOVE TO HEAR IT.
YOU WANT TO TELL US WHO YOU KILLED, MR. BEN SOLO?
ALL RIGHT.

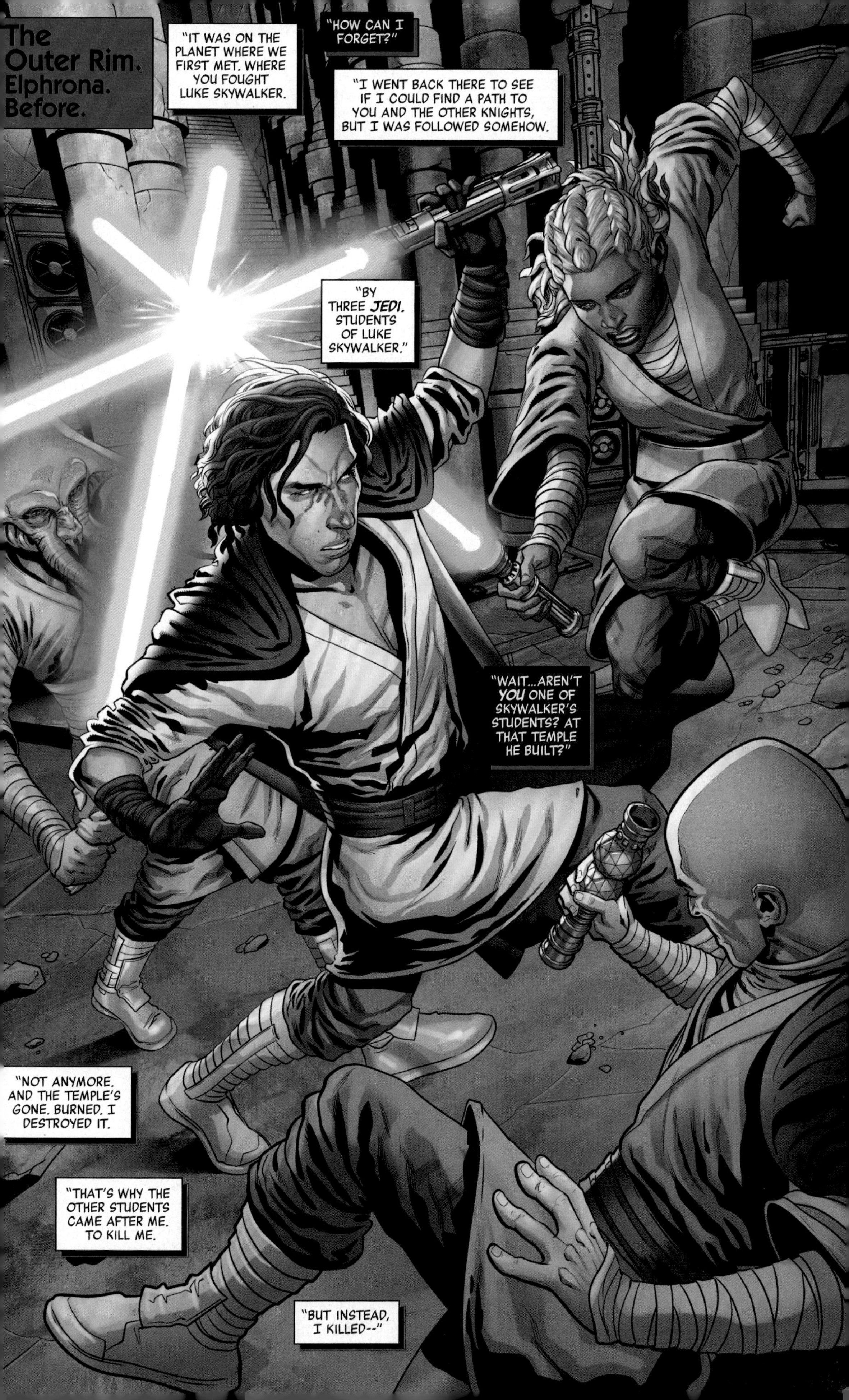
The Outer Rim. Elphrona. Before.
"IT WAS ON THE PLANET WHERE WE FIRST MET. WHERE YOU FOUGHT LUKE SKYWALKER.
"HOW CAN I FORGET?"
"I WENT BACK THERE TO SEE IF I COULD FIND A PATH TO YOU AND THE OTHER KNIGHTS, BUT I WAS FOLLOWED SOMEHOW.
"BY THREE JEDI. STUDENTS OF LUKE SKYWALKER."
"WAIT...AREN'T YOU ONE OF SKYWALKER'S STUDENTS? AT THAT TEMPLE HE BUILT?"
"NOT ANYMORE. AND THE TEMPLE'S GONE. BURNED. I DESTROYED IT.
"THAT'S WHY THE OTHER STUDENTS CAME AFTER ME. TO KILL ME.
"BUT INSTEAD, I KILLED--"

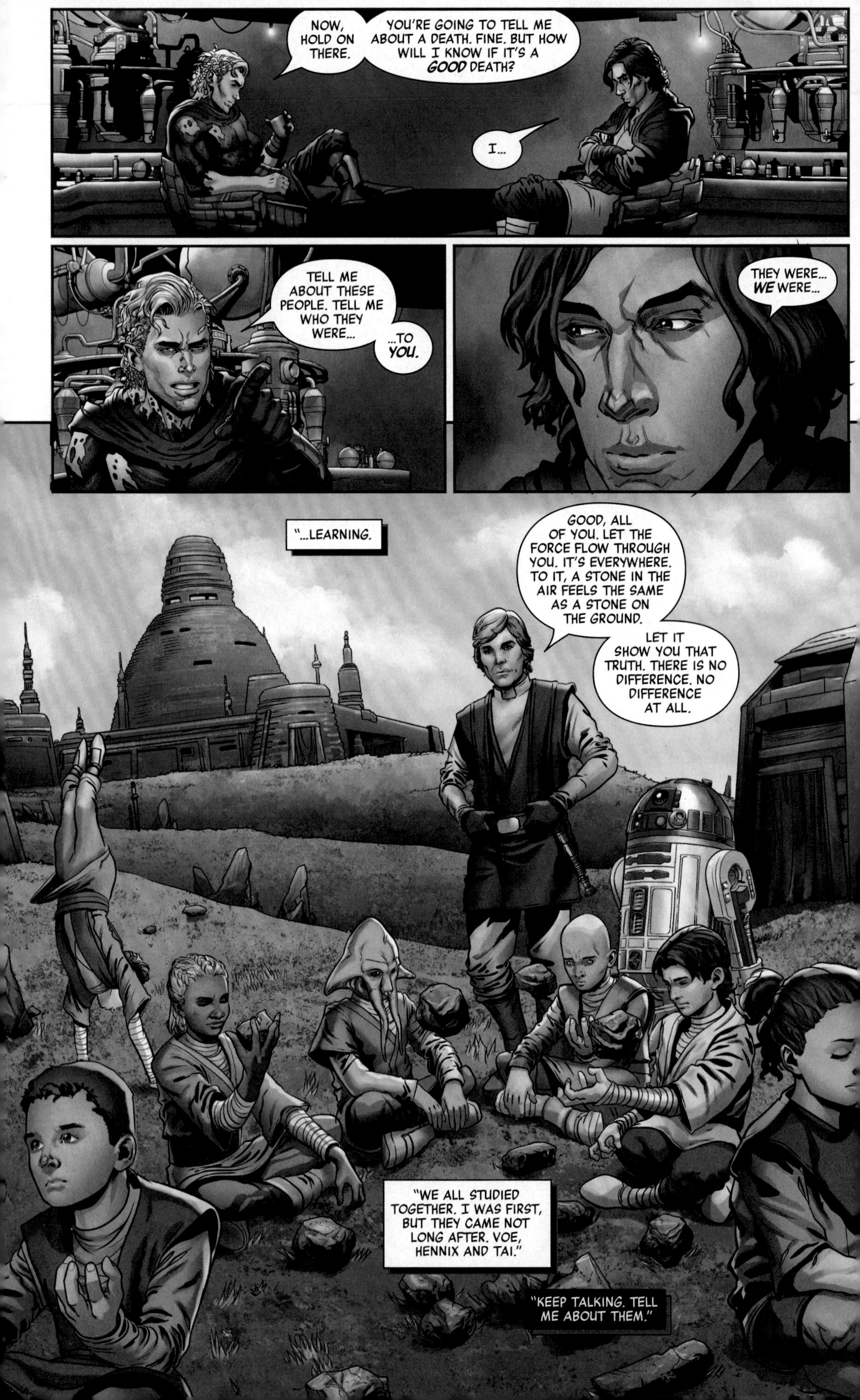
NOW, HOLD ON THERE.
YOU'RE GOING TO TELL ME ABOUT A DEATH. FINE. BUT HOW WILL I KNOW IF IT'S A *GOOD* DEATH?
I...
TELL ME ABOUT THESE PEOPLE. TELL ME WHO THEY WERE...
...TO *YOU.*
THEY WERE... *WE* WERE...
"...LEARNING.
GOOD, ALL OF YOU. LET THE FORCE FLOW THROUGH YOU. IT'S EVERYWHERE. TO IT, A STONE IN THE AIR FEELS THE SAME AS A STONE ON THE GROUND.
LET IT SHOW YOU THAT TRUTH. THERE IS NO DIFFERENCE. NO DIFFERENCE AT ALL.
"WE ALL STUDIED TOGETHER. I WAS FIRST, BUT THEY CAME NOT LONG AFTER. VOE, HENNIX AND TAI."
"KEEP TALKING. TELL ME ABOUT THEM."

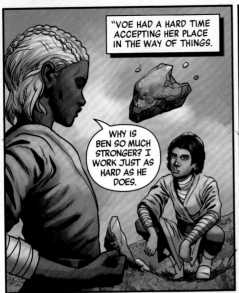

"VOE HAD A HARD TIME ACCEPTING HER PLACE IN THE WAY OF THINGS."

WHY IS BEN SO MUCH STRONGER? I WORK JUST AS HARD AS HE DOES.

BEN ISN'T STRONGER, VOE. THAT'S NOT HOW IT WORKS.

THE FORCE CAN BE A TRICKLE, A STREAM, A RIVER, A FLOOD...FOR *ANYONE* WHO CAN SENSE IT.

THINK OF YOURSELF AS A DOOR. THE WIDER YOU OPEN, THE MORE EASILY THE FORCE FLOWS THROUGH YOU.

SOME PEOPLE JUST START OUT WITH THEIR DOOR A BIT MORE OPEN. BUT ANY DOOR CAN OPEN WIDE.

"THROUGH OUR ENTIRE TIME TOGETHER AS STUDENTS, VOE TRIED TO MEASURE UP TO ME."

KRK

"LIGHTSABERS, MEDITATION, ANY OF THE JEDI TECHNIQUES..."

"SHE TRIED TO BEAT ME. SHE COULDN'T."

"THAT WAS HER WHOLE PROBLEM. SHE COULDN'T JUST BE HERSELF. SHE WANTED TO BE ME. OR BETTER THAN ME."

"I THINK THAT MADE HER ANGRY, AND THAT MADE HER ASHAMED. JEDI AREN'T SUPPOSED TO GET MAD ABOUT THINGS."

"ANYWAY. THAT'S VOE."

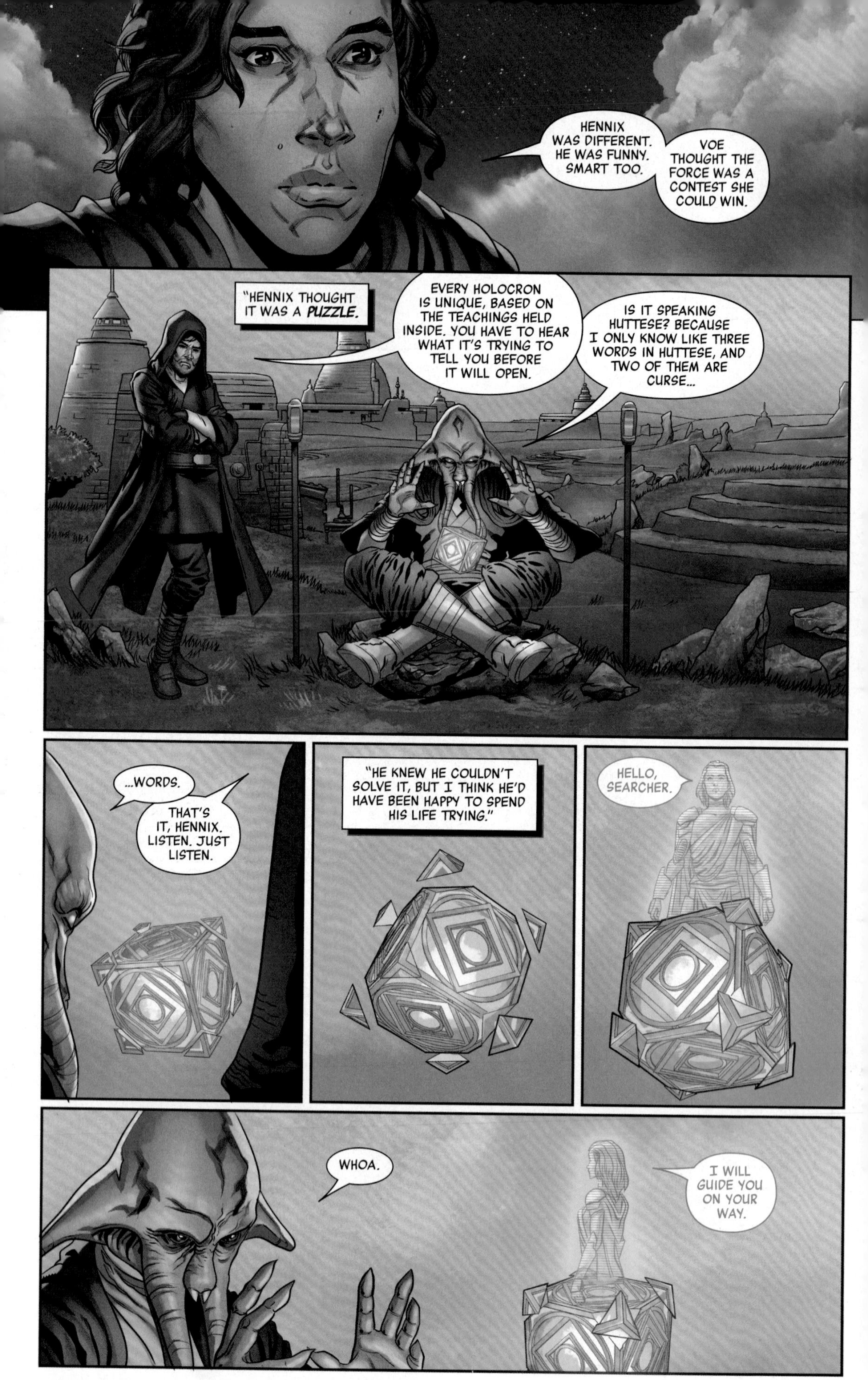
HENNIX WAS DIFFERENT. HE WAS FUNNY. SMART TOO.
VOE THOUGHT THE FORCE WAS A CONTEST SHE COULD WIN.
"HENNIX THOUGHT IT WAS A PUZZLE.
EVERY HOLOCRON IS UNIQUE, BASED ON THE TEACHINGS HELD INSIDE. YOU HAVE TO HEAR WHAT IT'S TRYING TO TELL YOU BEFORE IT WILL OPEN.
IS IT SPEAKING HUTTESE? BECAUSE I ONLY KNOW LIKE THREE WORDS IN HUTTESE, AND TWO OF THEM ARE CURSE...
...WORDS.
THAT'S IT, HENNIX. LISTEN. JUST LISTEN.
"HE KNEW HE COULDN'T SOLVE IT, BUT I THINK HE'D HAVE BEEN HAPPY TO SPEND HIS LIFE TRYING."
HELLO, SEARCHER.
WHOA.
I WILL GUIDE YOU ON YOUR WAY.

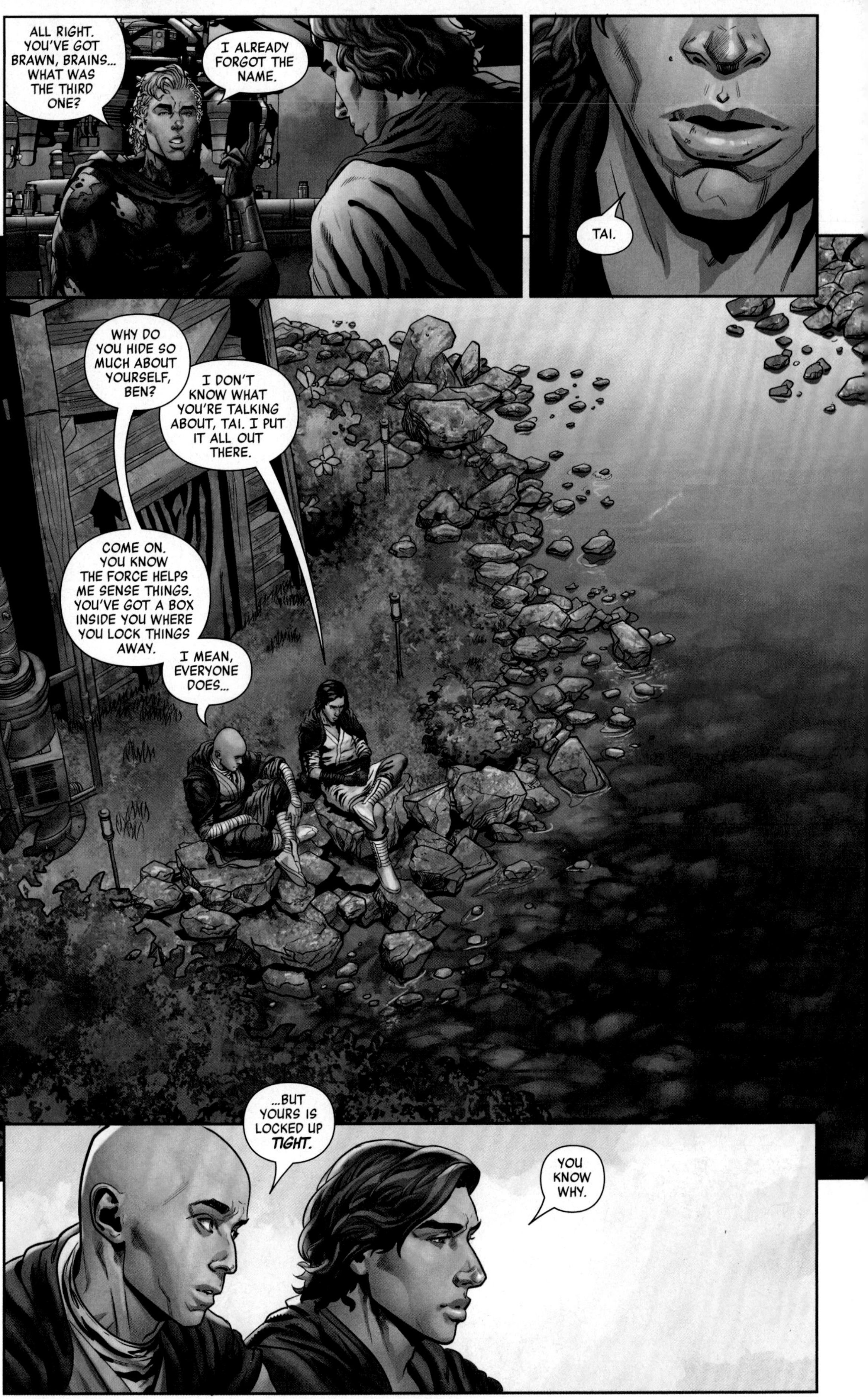
ALL RIGHT. YOU'VE GOT BRAWN, BRAINS... WHAT WAS THE THIRD ONE?
I ALREADY FORGOT THE NAME.
TAI.
WHY DO YOU HIDE SO MUCH ABOUT YOURSELF, BEN?
I DON'T KNOW WHAT YOU'RE TALKING ABOUT, TAI. I PUT IT ALL OUT THERE.
COME ON. YOU KNOW THE FORCE HELPS ME SENSE THINGS. YOU'VE GOT A BOX INSIDE YOU WHERE YOU LOCK THINGS AWAY.
I MEAN, EVERYONE DOES...
...BUT YOURS IS LOCKED UP ***TIGHT.***
YOU KNOW WHY.

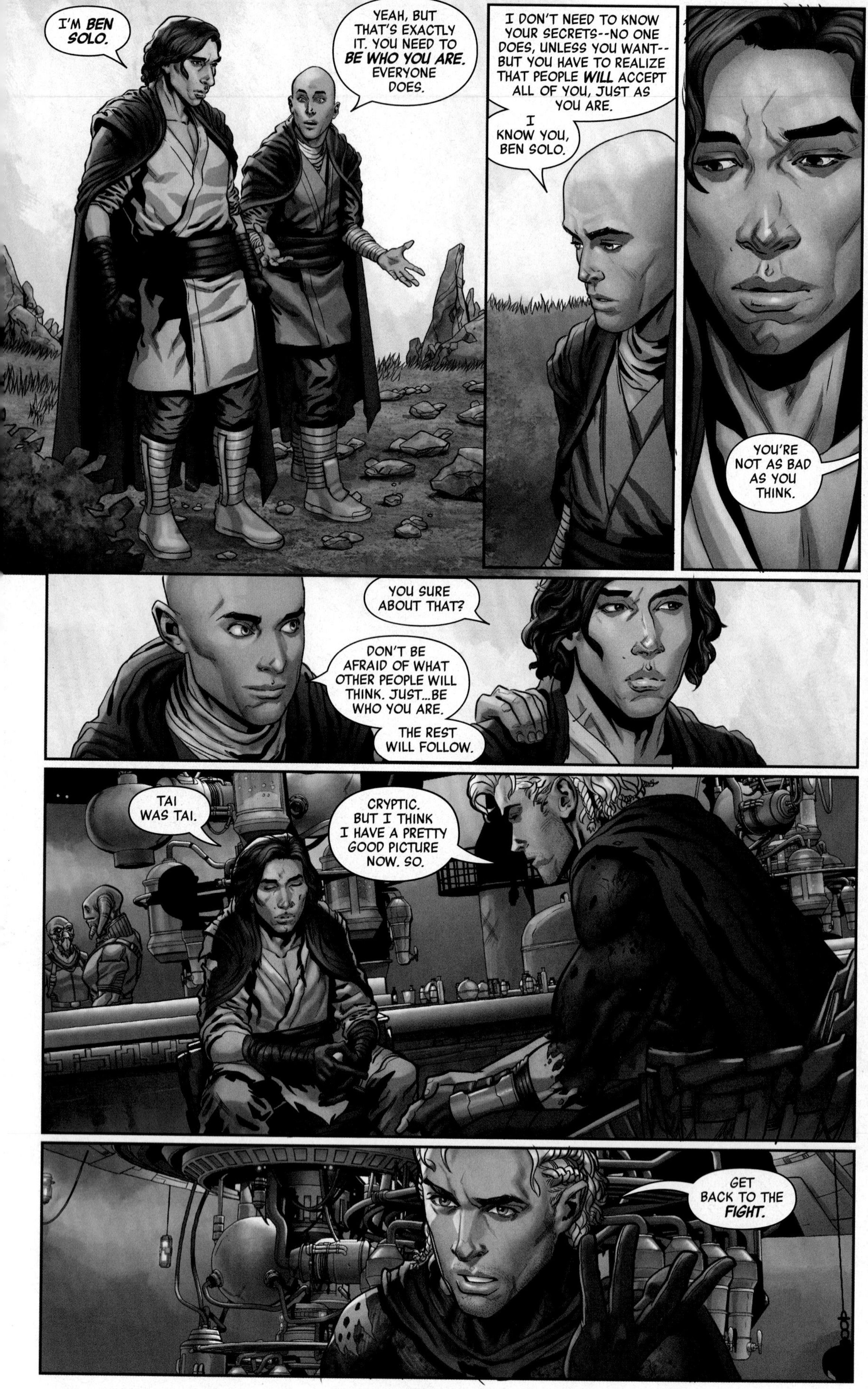
I'M **BEN SOLO.**
YEAH, BUT THAT'S EXACTLY IT. YOU NEED TO ***BE WHO YOU ARE.*** EVERYONE DOES.
I DON'T NEED TO KNOW YOUR SECRETS--NO ONE DOES, UNLESS YOU WANT--BUT YOU HAVE TO REALIZE THAT PEOPLE ***WILL*** ACCEPT ALL OF YOU, JUST AS YOU ARE.
I KNOW YOU, BEN SOLO.
YOU'RE NOT AS BAD AS YOU THINK.
YOU SURE ABOUT THAT?
DON'T BE AFRAID OF WHAT OTHER PEOPLE WILL THINK. JUST...BE WHO YOU ARE.
THE REST WILL FOLLOW.
TAI WAS TAI.
CRYPTIC. BUT I THINK I HAVE A PRETTY GOOD PICTURE NOW. SO.
GET BACK TO THE ***FIGHT.***

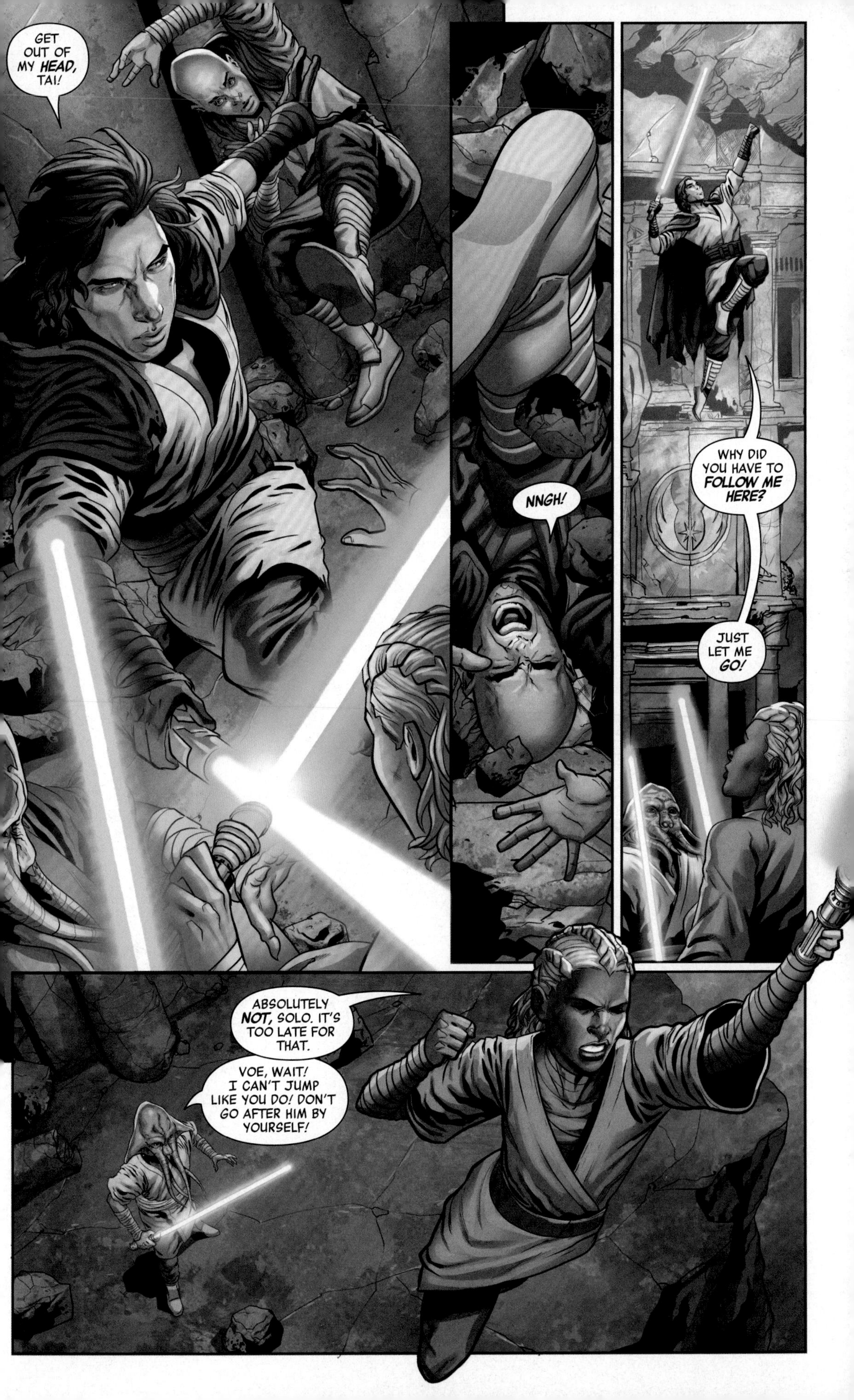
GET OUT OF MY HEAD, TAI!
NNGH!
WHY DID YOU HAVE TO FOLLOW ME HERE?
JUST LET ME GO!
ABSOLUTELY NOT, SOLO. IT'S TOO LATE FOR THAT.
VOE, WAIT! I CAN'T JUMP LIKE YOU DO! DON'T GO AFTER HIM BY YOURSELF!

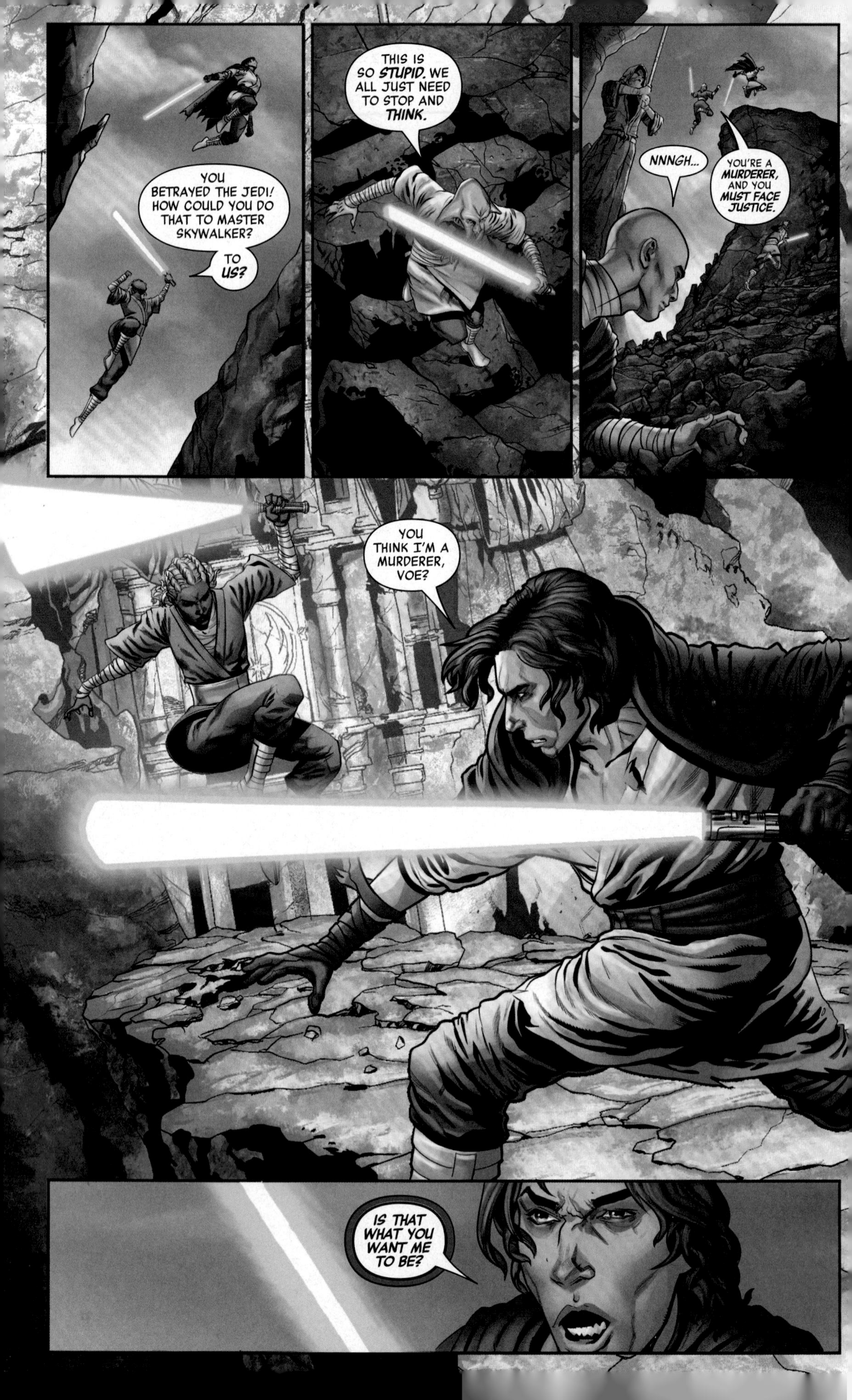
YOU BETRAYED THE JEDI! HOW COULD YOU DO THAT TO MASTER SKYWALKER?
TO US?
THIS IS SO STUPID. WE ALL JUST NEED TO STOP AND THINK.
NNNGH...
YOU'RE A MURDERER, AND YOU MUST FACE JUSTICE.
YOU THINK I'M A MURDERER, VOE?
IS THAT WHAT YOU WANT ME TO BE?

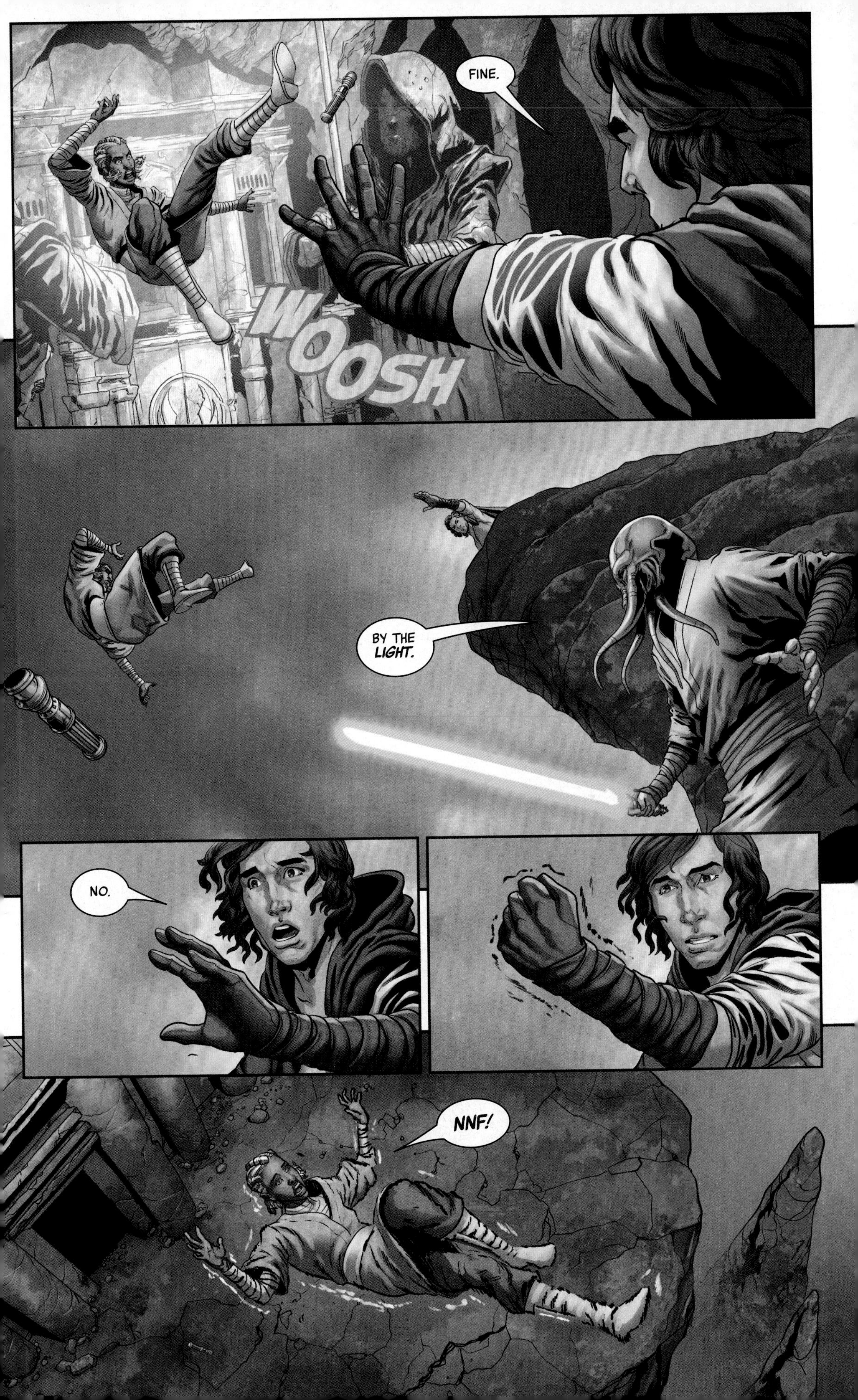

FINE.
WOOSH
BY THE LIGHT.
NO.
NNF!

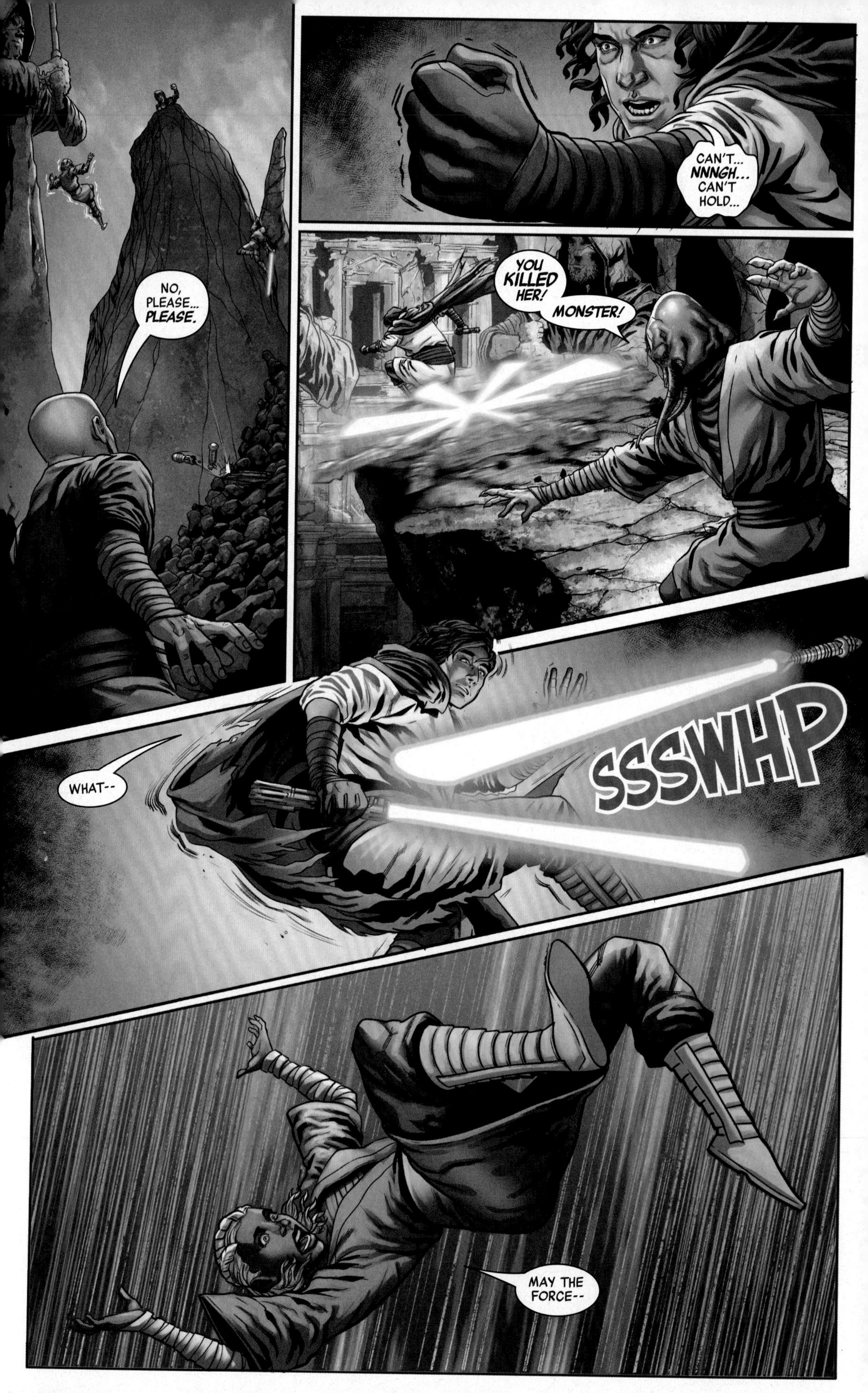
NO, PLEASE... PLEASE.
CAN'T... NNNGH... CAN'T HOLD...
YOU KILLED HER!
MONSTER!
WHAT--
SSSWHP
MAY THE FORCE--

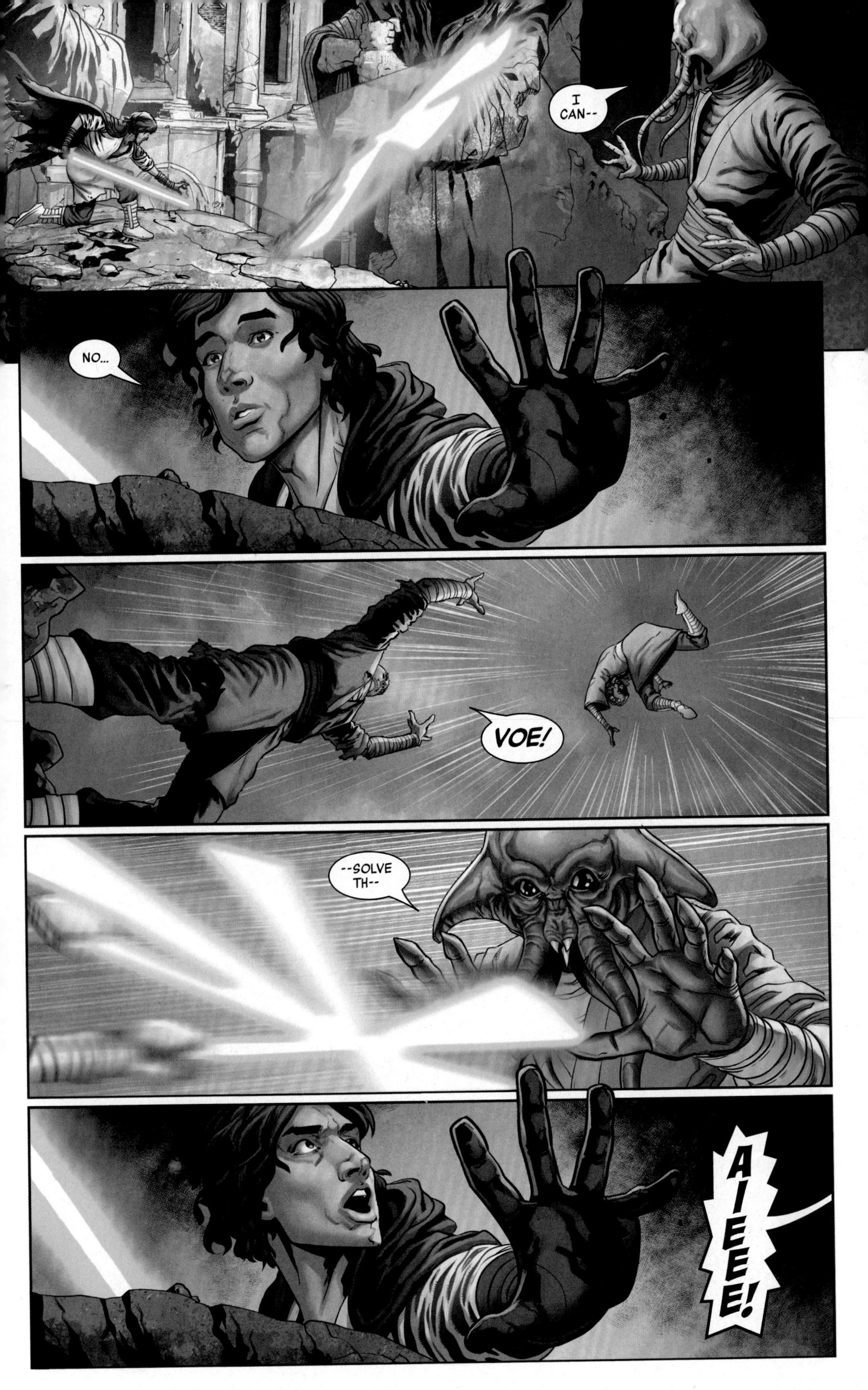
I CAN--
NO...
VOE!
--SOLVE TH--
AIEEE!

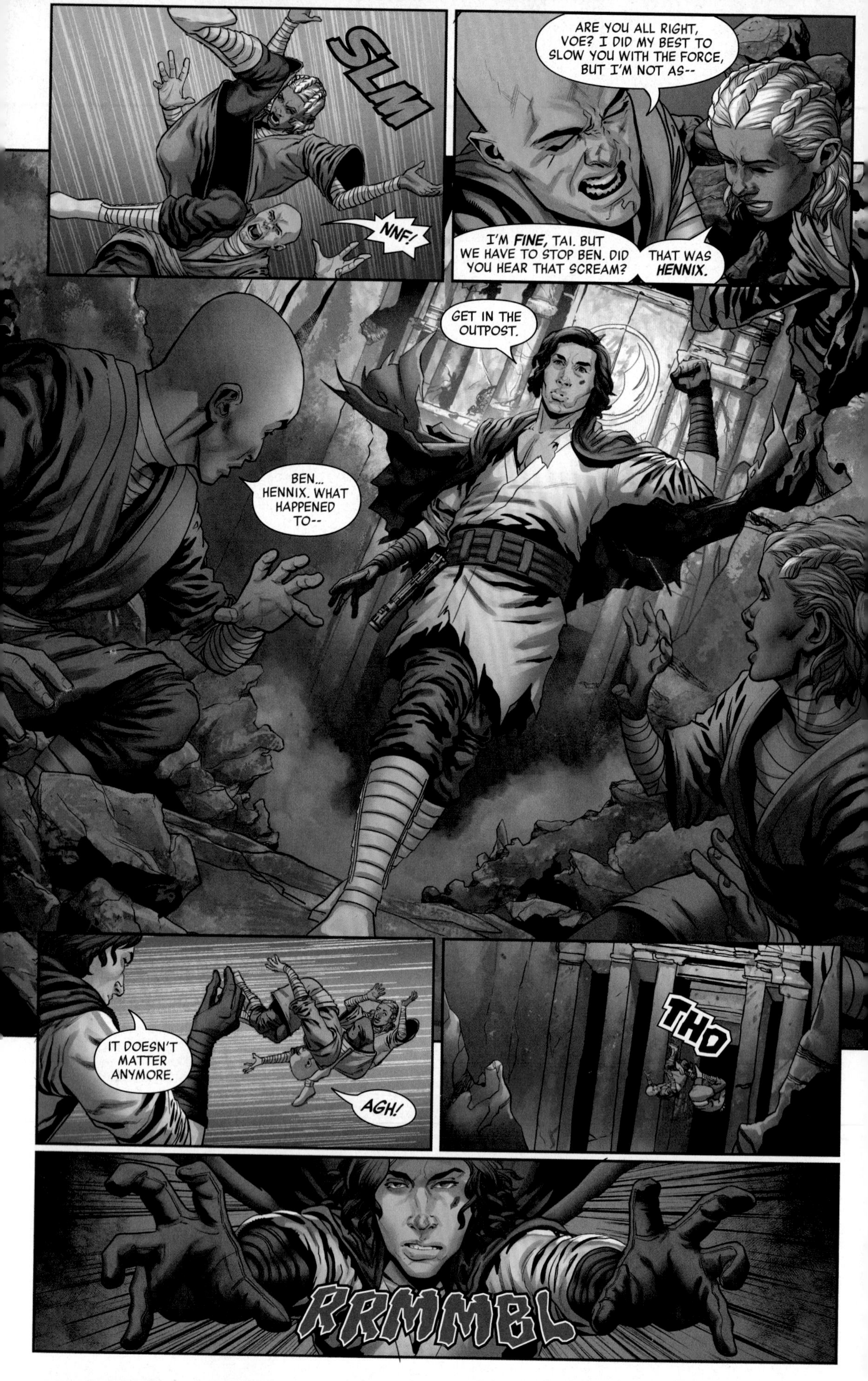
SLM
NNF!
ARE YOU ALL RIGHT, VOE? I DID MY BEST TO SLOW YOU WITH THE FORCE, BUT I'M NOT AS--
I'M FINE, TAI. BUT WE HAVE TO STOP BEN. DID YOU HEAR THAT SCREAM?
THAT WAS HENNIX.
GET IN THE OUTPOST.
BEN... HENNIX. WHAT HAPPENED TO--
IT DOESN'T MATTER ANYMORE.
AGH!
THD
RRMMBL

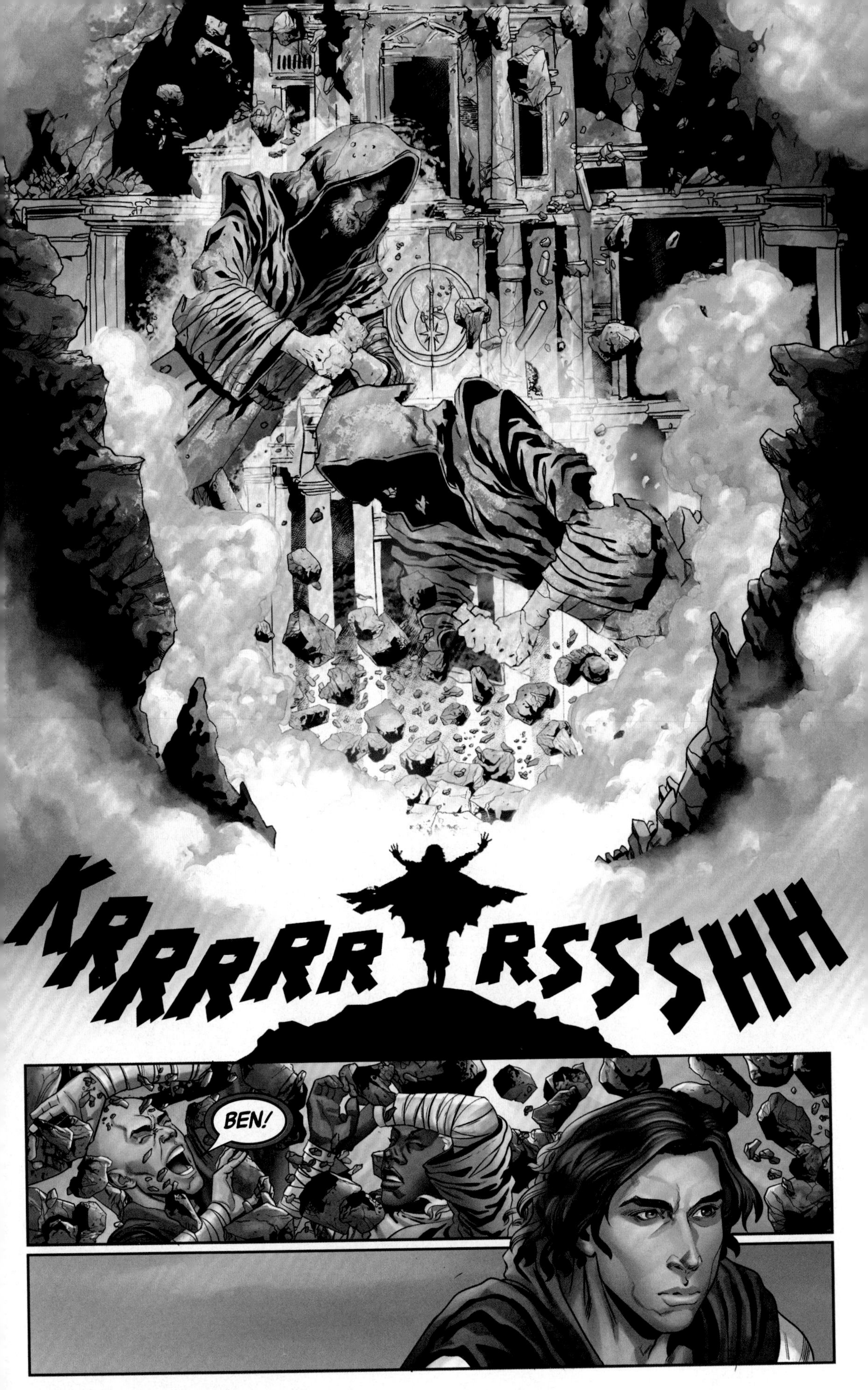
KRRRRR RSSSHH
BEN!

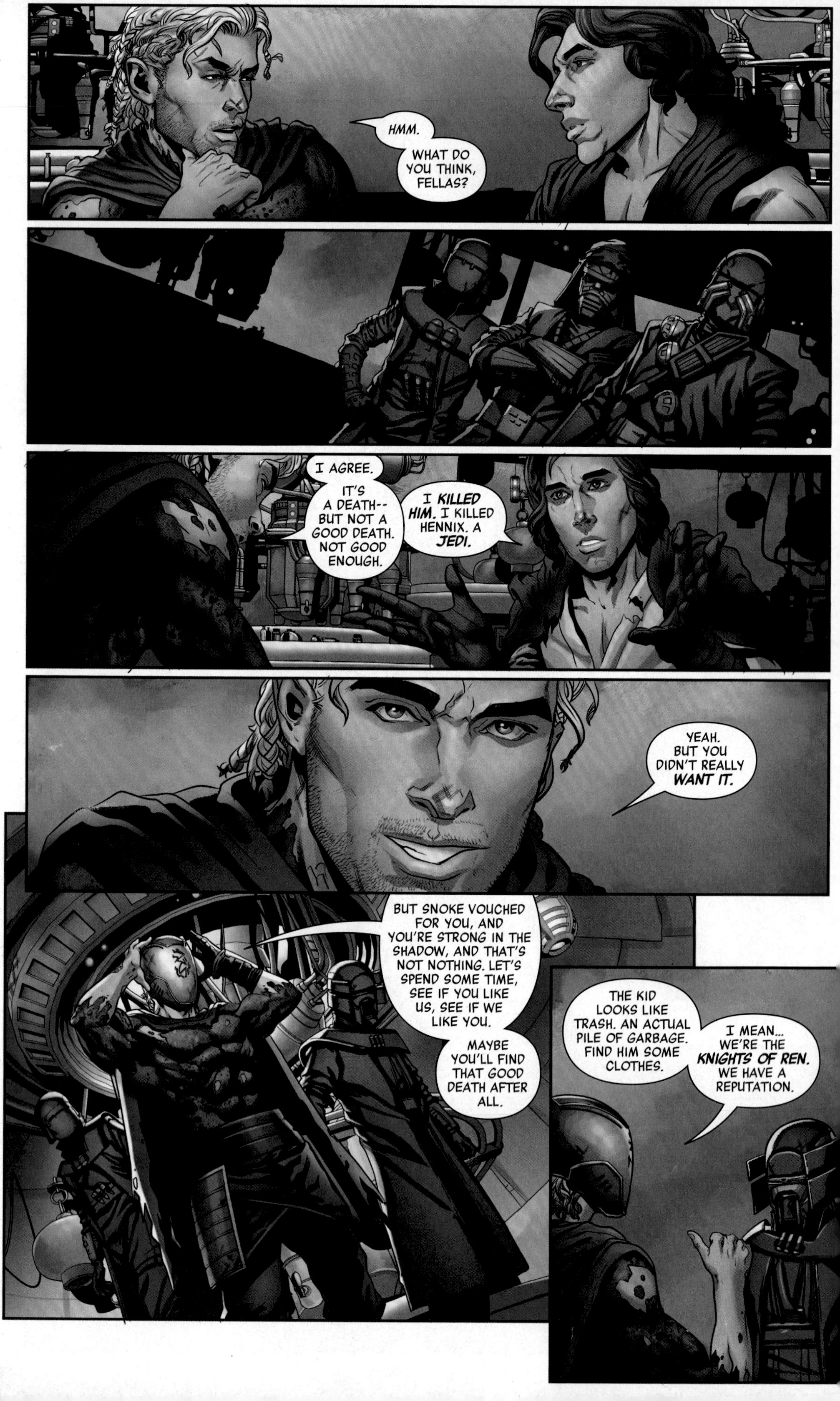
HMM.
WHAT DO YOU THINK, FELLAS?
I AGREE.
IT'S A DEATH-- BUT NOT A GOOD DEATH. NOT GOOD ENOUGH.
I **KILLED HIM.** I KILLED HENNIX. A **JEDI.**
YEAH. BUT YOU DIDN'T REALLY **WANT IT.**
BUT SNOKE VOUCHED FOR YOU, AND YOU'RE STRONG IN THE SHADOW, AND THAT'S NOT NOTHING. LET'S SPEND SOME TIME, SEE IF YOU LIKE US, SEE IF WE LIKE YOU.
MAYBE YOU'LL FIND THAT GOOD DEATH AFTER ALL.
THE KID LOOKS LIKE TRASH. AN ACTUAL PILE OF GARBAGE. FIND HIM SOME CLOTHES.
I MEAN... WE'RE THE **KNIGHTS OF REN.** WE HAVE A REPUTATION.

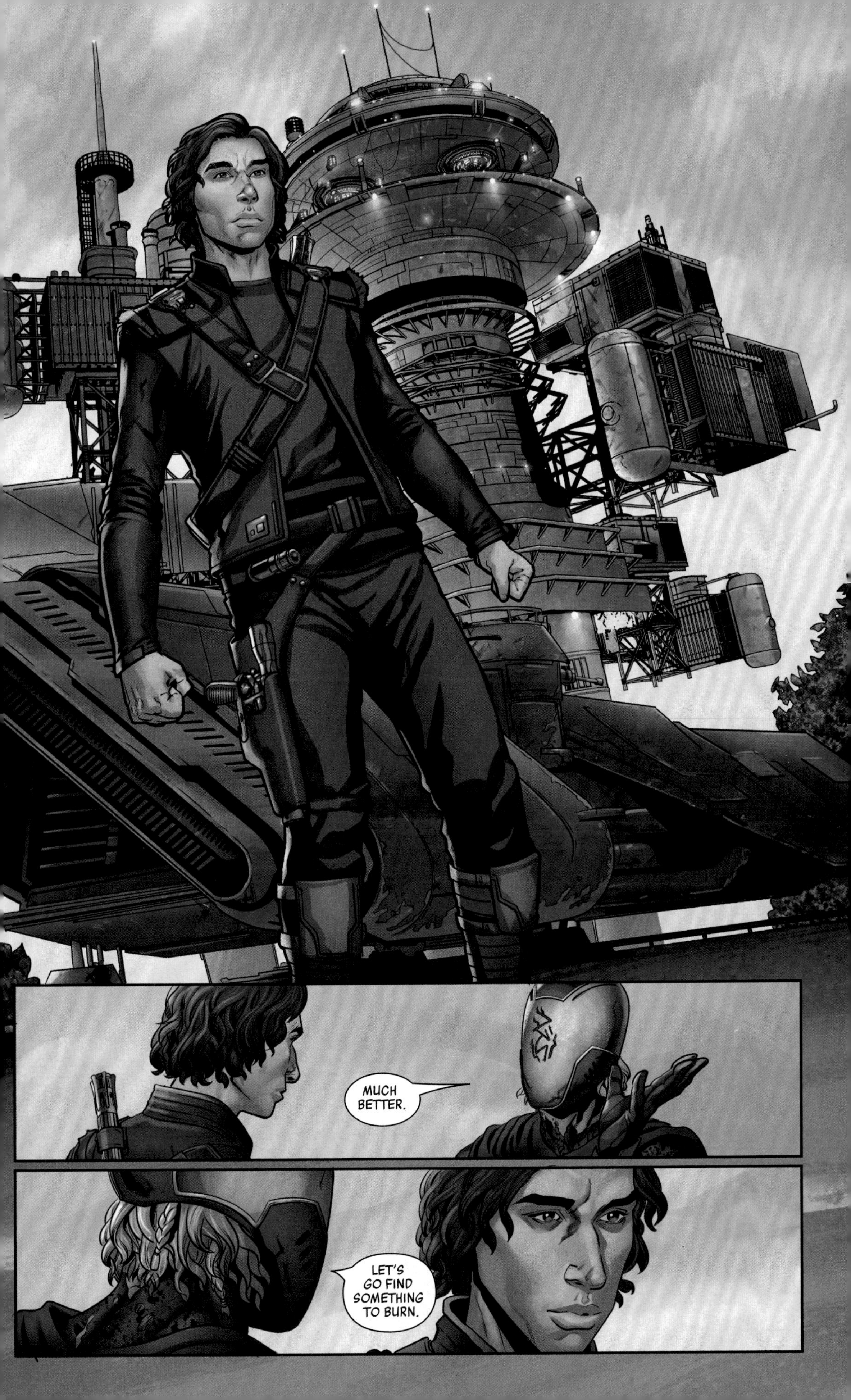
MUCH BETTER.
LET'S GO FIND SOMETHING TO BURN.

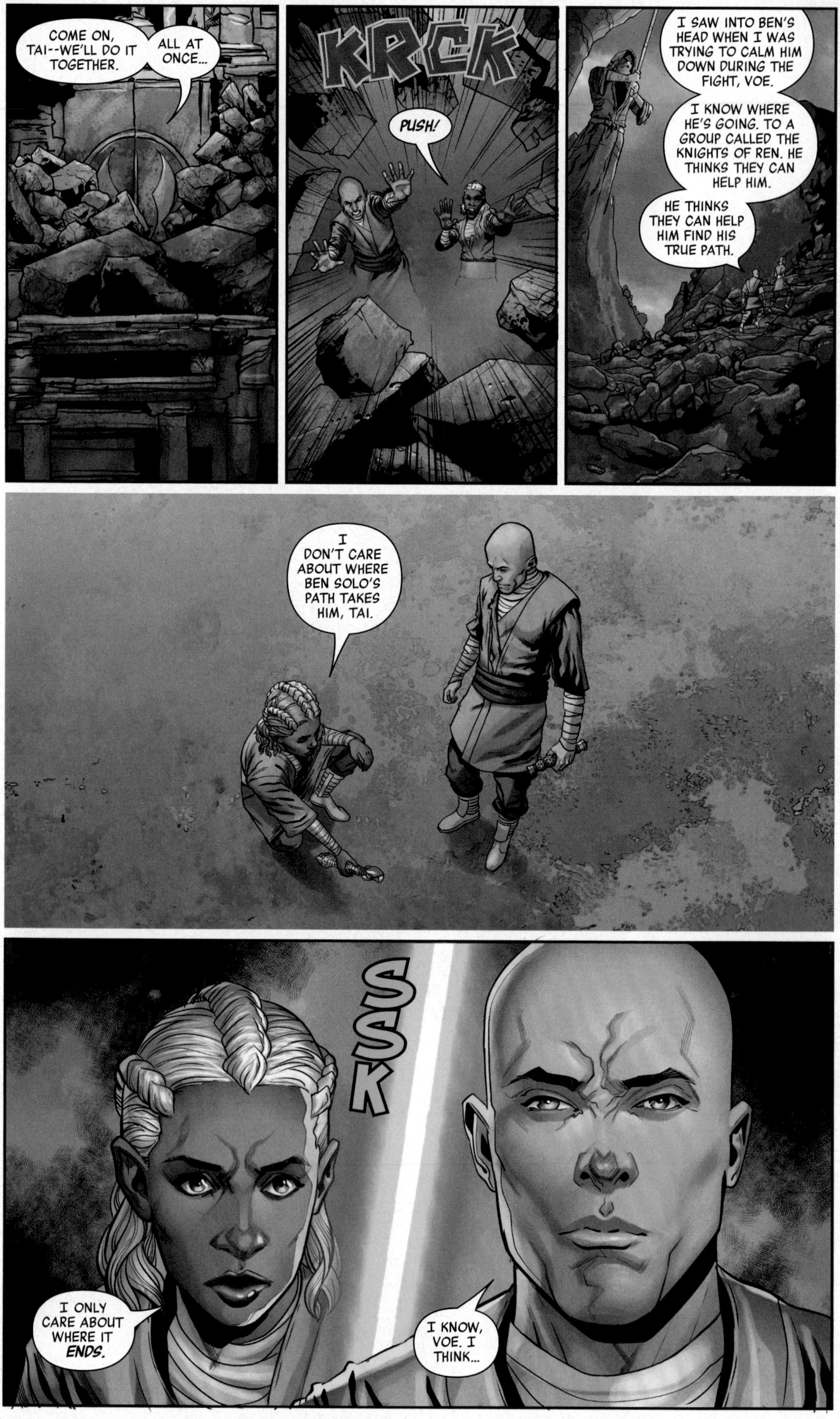
COME ON, TAI--WE'LL DO IT TOGETHER.
ALL AT ONCE...
KRCK
PUSH!
I SAW INTO BEN'S HEAD WHEN I WAS TRYING TO CALM HIM DOWN DURING THE FIGHT, VOE.
I KNOW WHERE HE'S GOING. TO A GROUP CALLED THE KNIGHTS OF REN. HE THINKS THEY CAN HELP HIM.
HE THINKS THEY CAN HELP HIM FIND HIS TRUE PATH.
I DON'T CARE ABOUT WHERE BEN SOLO'S PATH TAKES HIM, TAI.
SSSK
I ONLY CARE ABOUT WHERE IT *ENDS.*
I KNOW, VOE. I THINK...

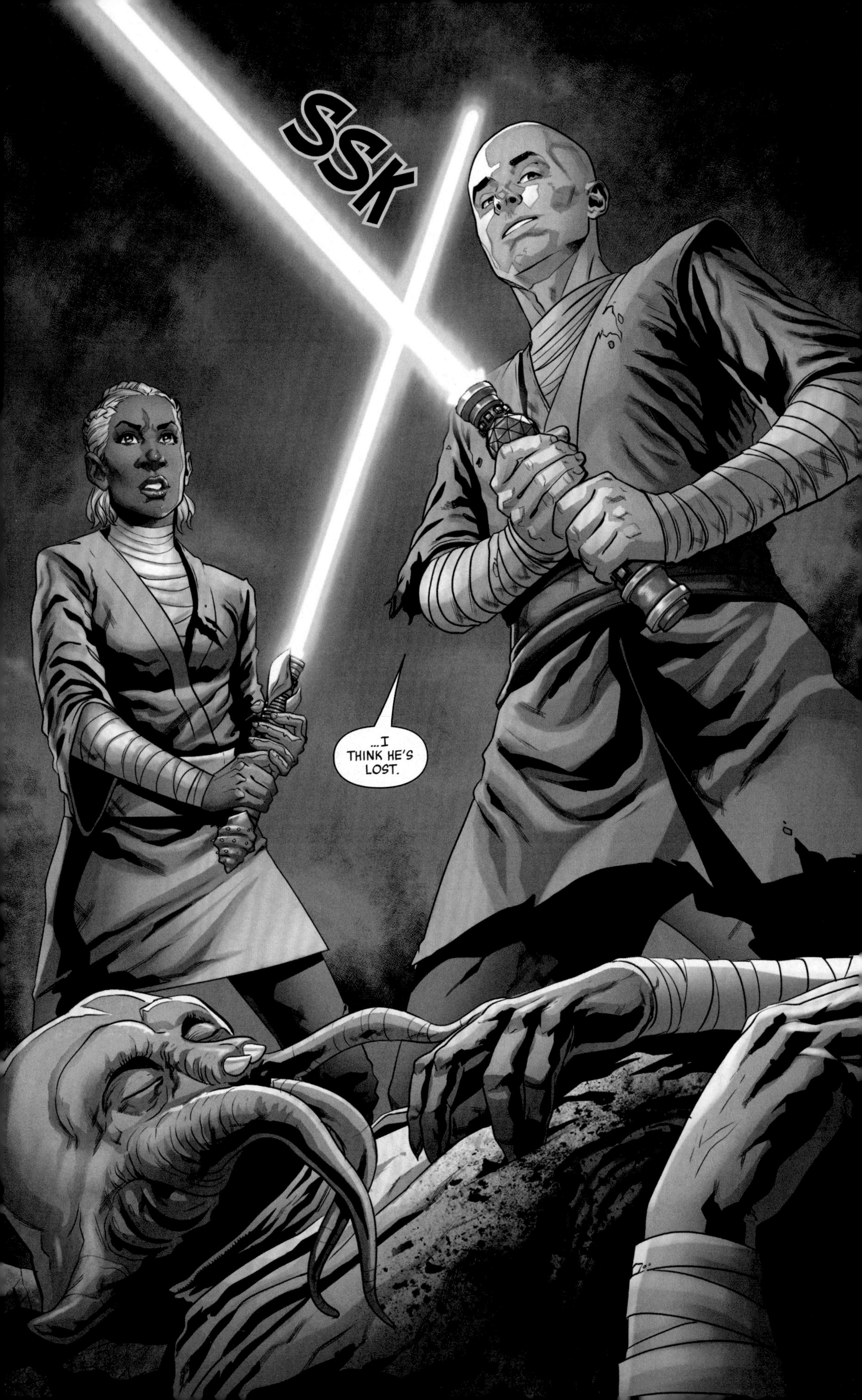
SSK
...I THINK HE'S LOST.

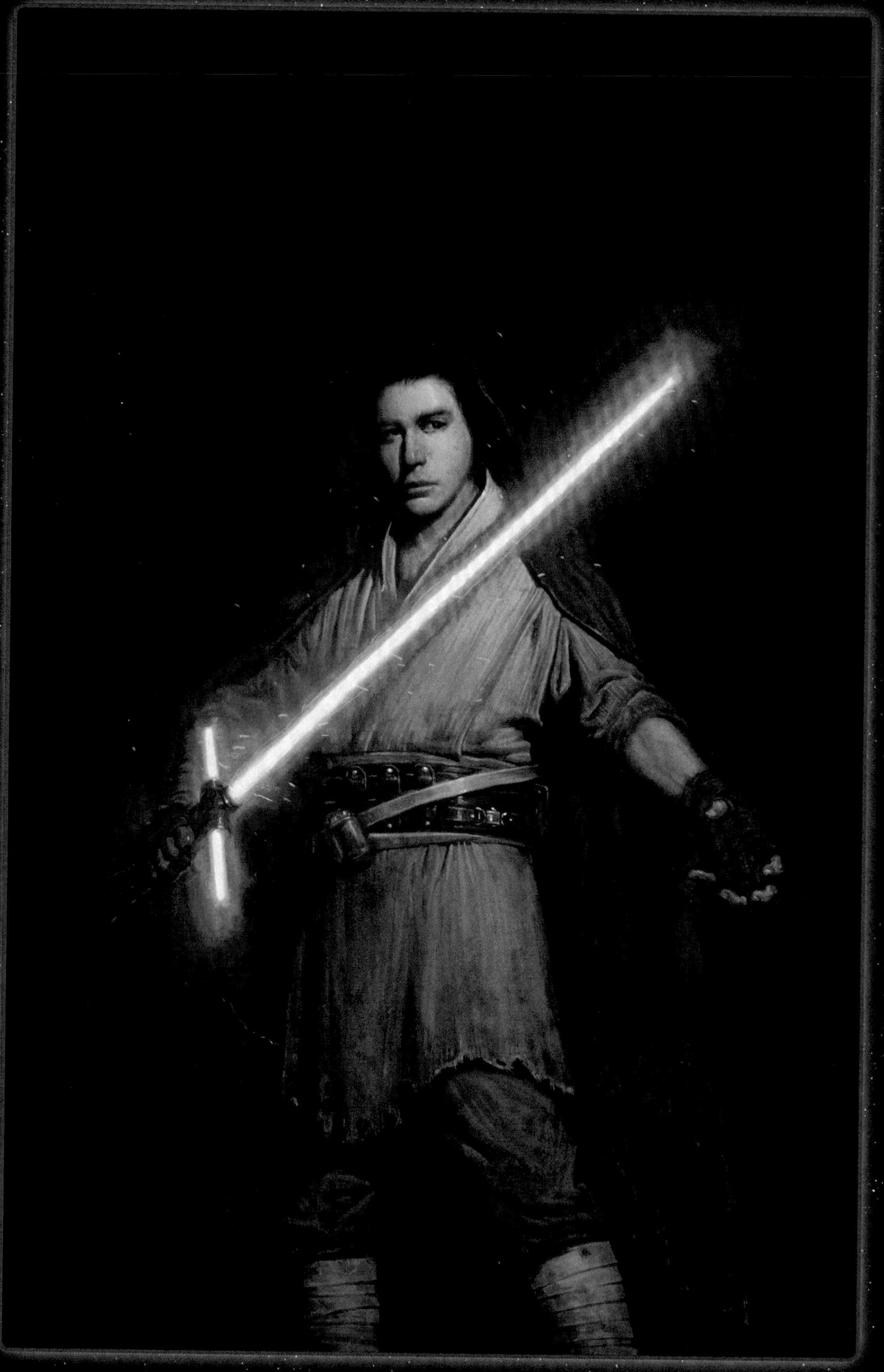

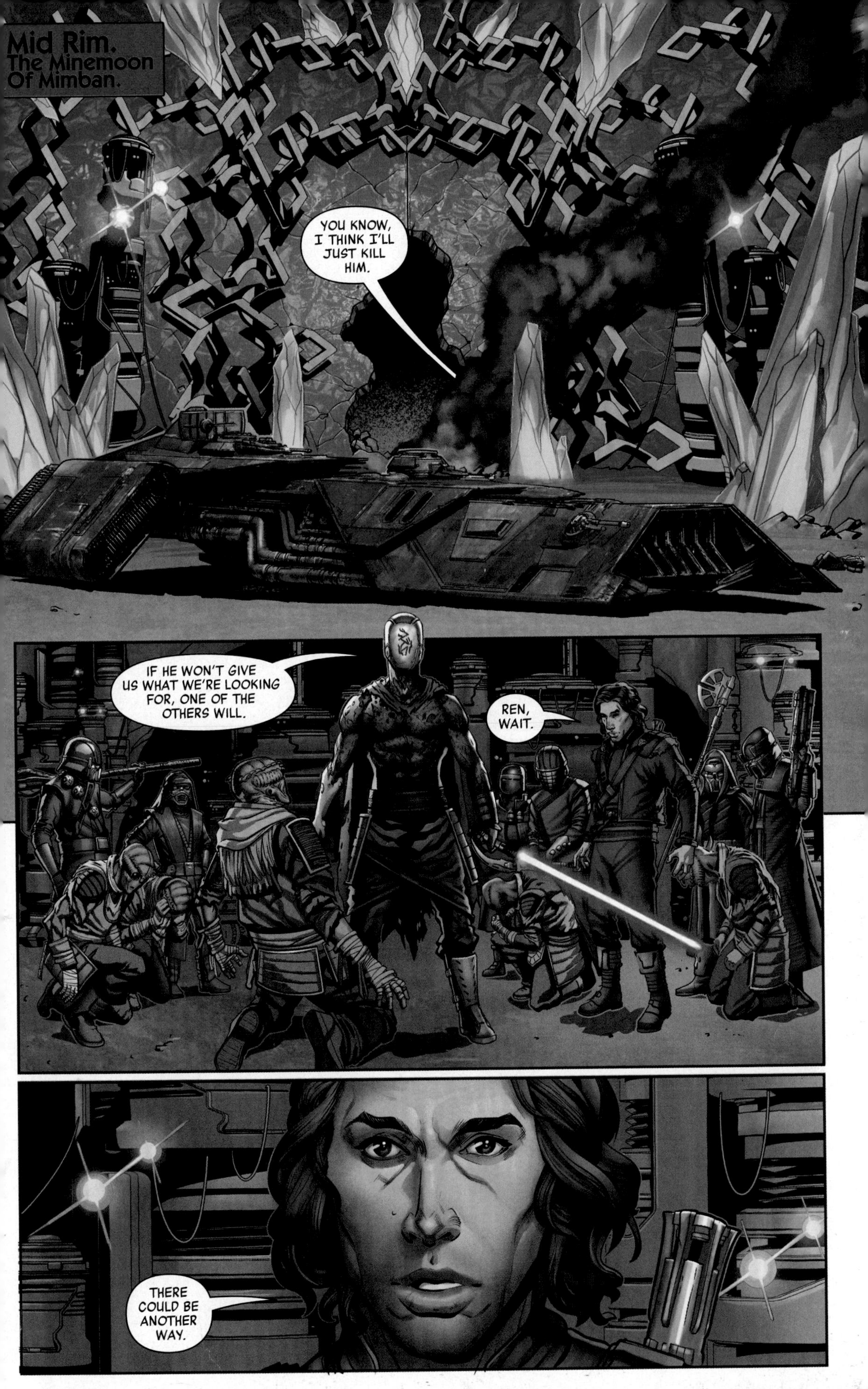

Mid Rim. The Minemoon Of Mimban.
YOU KNOW, I THINK I'LL JUST KILL HIM.
IF HE WON'T GIVE US WHAT WE'RE LOOKING FOR, ONE OF THE OTHERS WILL.
REN, WAIT.
THERE COULD BE ANOTHER WAY.

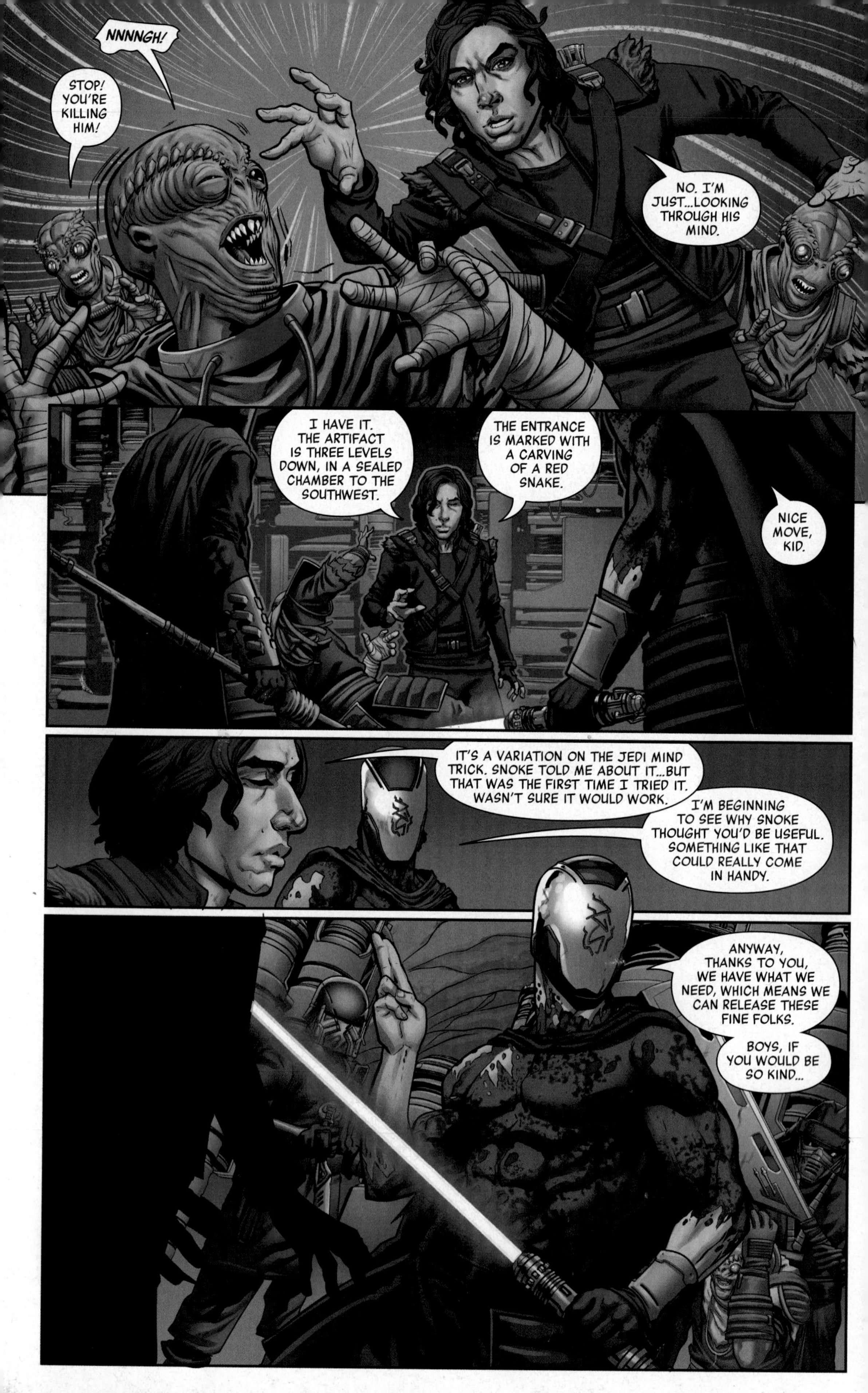
NNNNGH!
STOP! YOU'RE KILLING HIM!
NO. I'M JUST...LOOKING THROUGH HIS MIND.
I HAVE IT. THE ARTIFACT IS THREE LEVELS DOWN, IN A SEALED CHAMBER TO THE SOUTHWEST.
THE ENTRANCE IS MARKED WITH A CARVING OF A RED SNAKE.
NICE MOVE, KID.
IT'S A VARIATION ON THE JEDI MIND TRICK. SNOKE TOLD ME ABOUT IT...BUT THAT WAS THE FIRST TIME I TRIED IT. WASN'T SURE IT WOULD WORK.
I'M BEGINNING TO SEE WHY SNOKE THOUGHT YOU'D BE USEFUL. SOMETHING LIKE THAT COULD REALLY COME IN HANDY.
ANYWAY, THANKS TO YOU, WE HAVE WHAT WE NEED, WHICH MEANS WE CAN RELEASE THESE FINE FOLKS.
BOYS, IF YOU WOULD BE SO KIND...

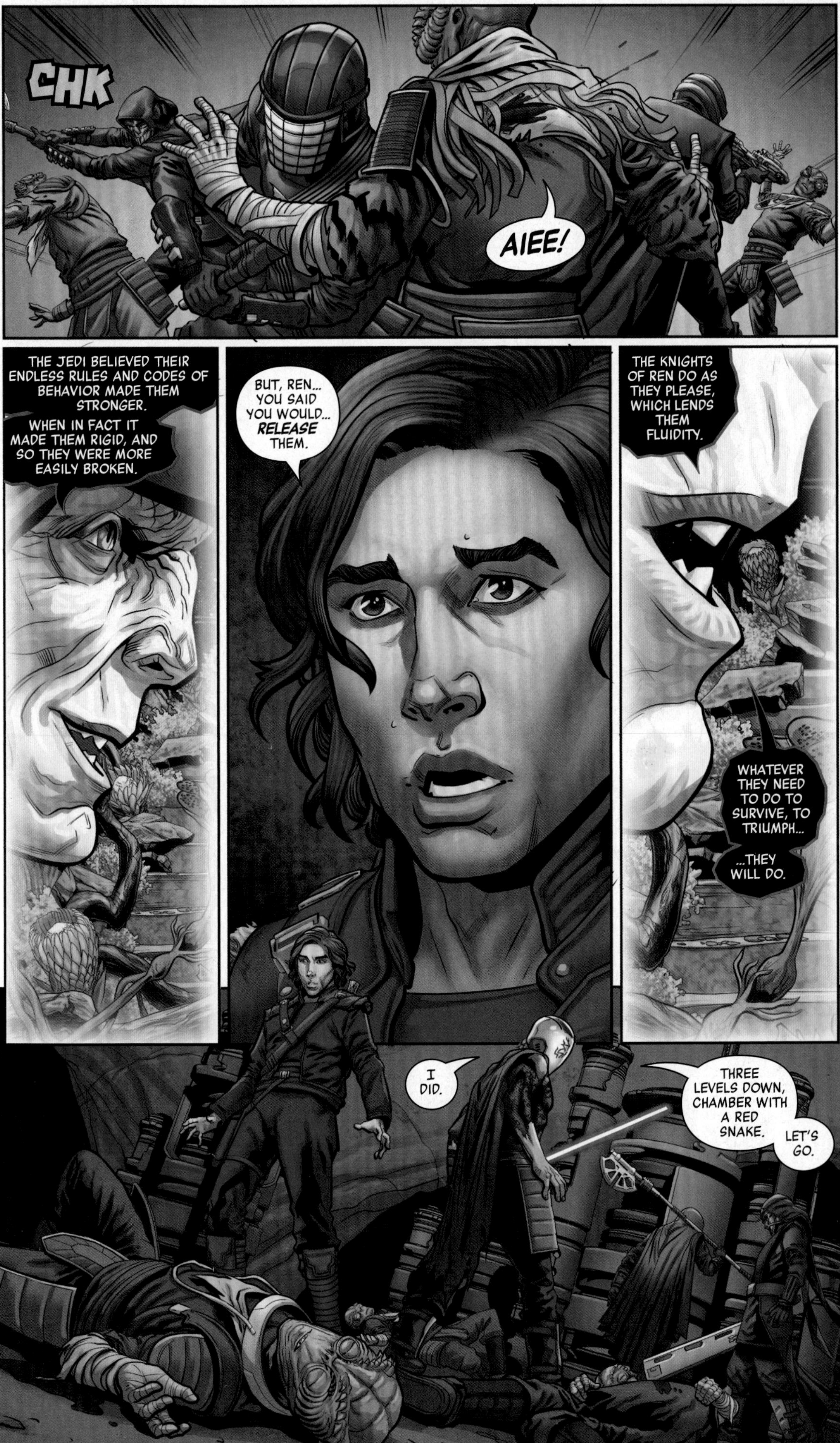
CHK
AIEE!
THE JEDI BELIEVED THEIR ENDLESS RULES AND CODES OF BEHAVIOR MADE THEM STRONGER.
WHEN IN FACT IT MADE THEM RIGID, AND SO THEY WERE MORE EASILY BROKEN.
BUT, REN... YOU SAID YOU WOULD... RELEASE THEM.
THE KNIGHTS OF REN DO AS THEY PLEASE, WHICH LENDS THEM FLUIDITY.
WHATEVER THEY NEED TO DO TO SURVIVE, TO TRIUMPH...
...THEY WILL DO.
I DID.
THREE LEVELS DOWN, CHAMBER WITH A RED SNAKE.
LET'S GO.

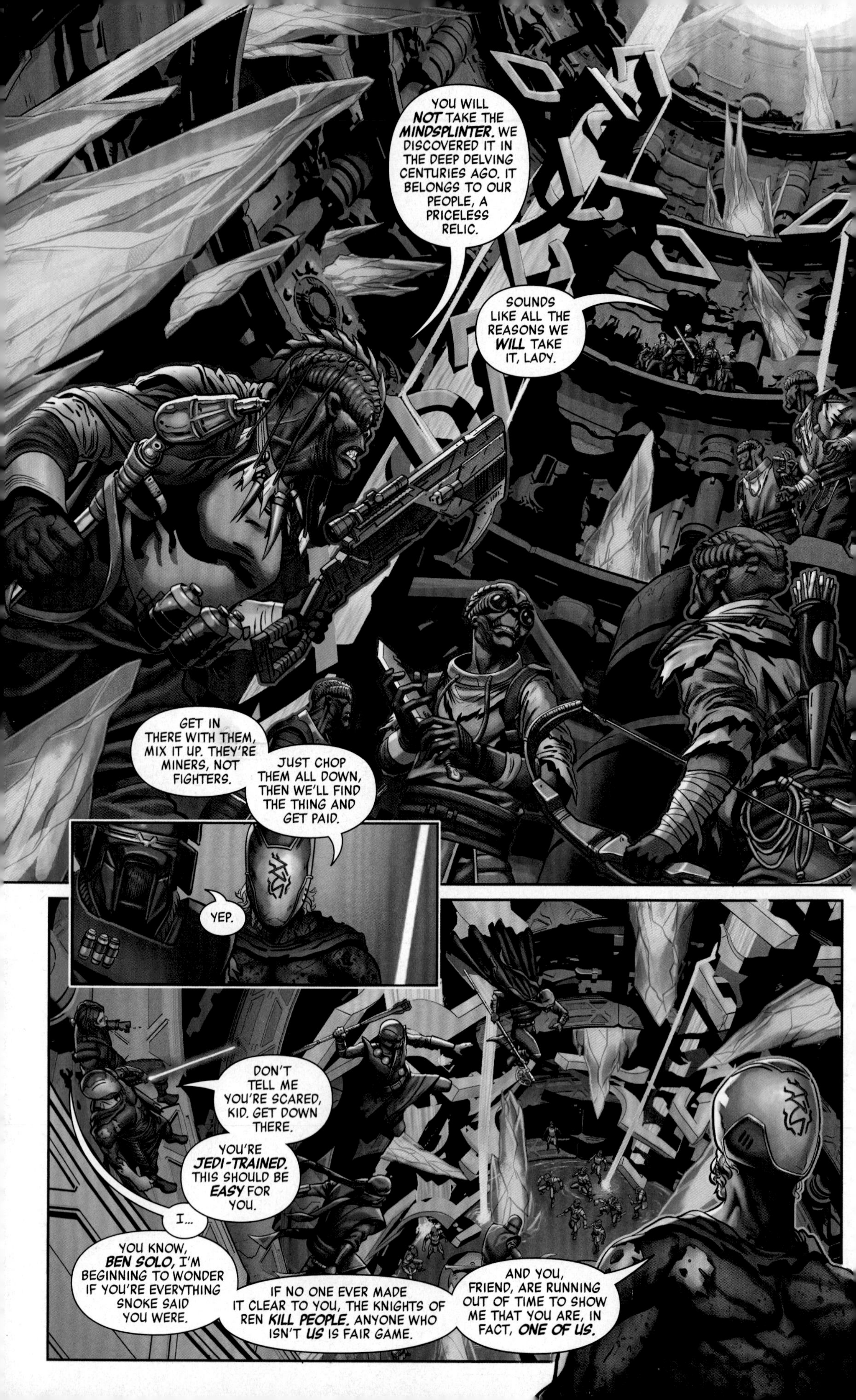
YOU WILL NOT TAKE THE MINDSPLINTER. WE DISCOVERED IT IN THE DEEP DELVING CENTURIES AGO. IT BELONGS TO OUR PEOPLE, A PRICELESS RELIC.
SOUNDS LIKE ALL THE REASONS WE WILL TAKE IT, LADY.
GET IN THERE WITH THEM, MIX IT UP. THEY'RE MINERS, NOT FIGHTERS.
JUST CHOP THEM ALL DOWN, THEN WE'LL FIND THE THING AND GET PAID.
YEP.
DON'T TELL ME YOU'RE SCARED, KID. GET DOWN THERE.
YOU'RE JEDI-TRAINED. THIS SHOULD BE EASY FOR YOU.
I...
YOU KNOW, BEN SOLO, I'M BEGINNING TO WONDER IF YOU'RE EVERYTHING SNOKE SAID YOU WERE.
IF NO ONE EVER MADE IT CLEAR TO YOU, THE KNIGHTS OF REN KILL PEOPLE. ANYONE WHO ISN'T US IS FAIR GAME.
AND YOU, FRIEND, ARE RUNNING OUT OF TIME TO SHOW ME THAT YOU ARE, IN FACT, ONE OF US.

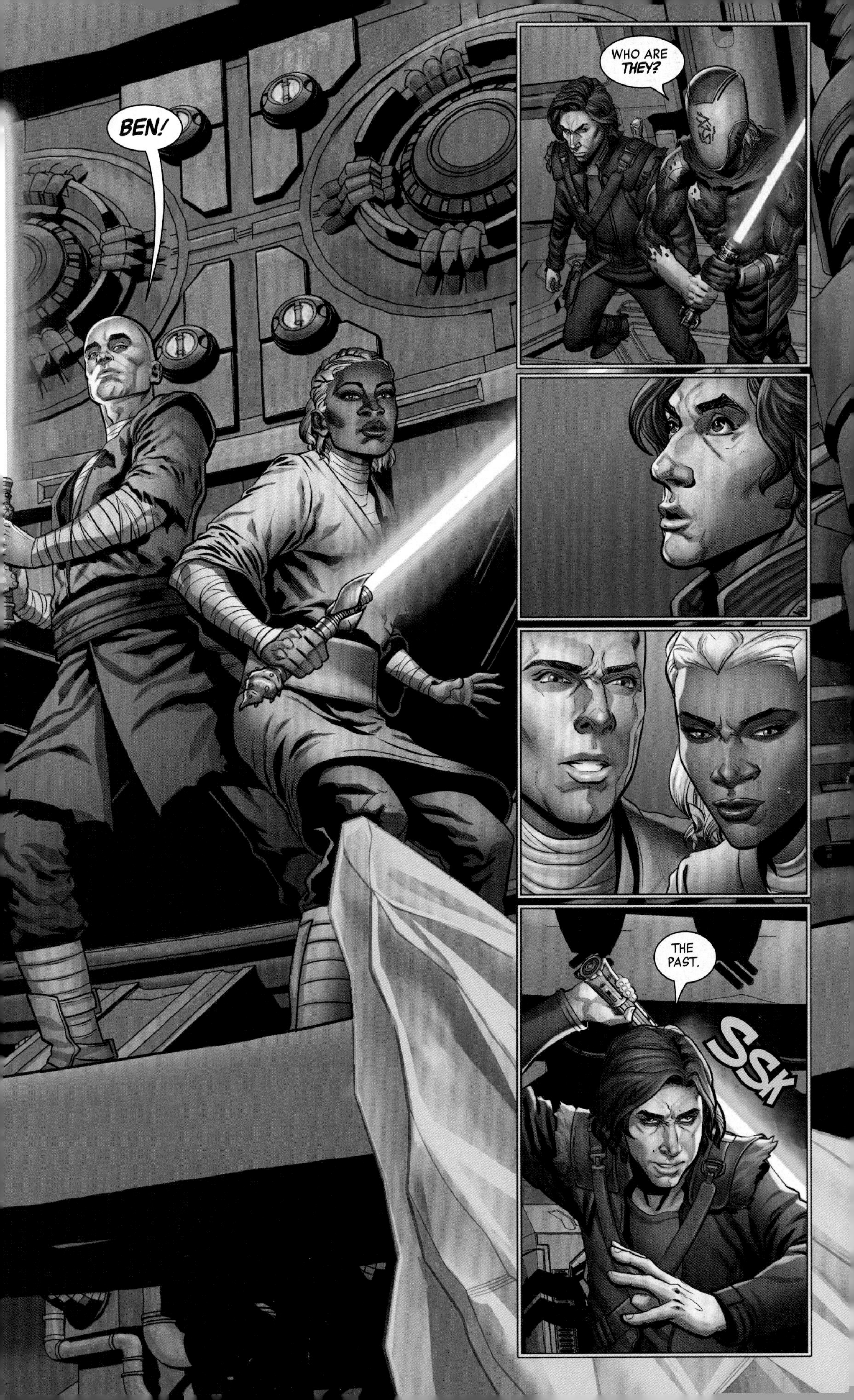
BEN!
WHO ARE THEY?
THE PAST.
SSK

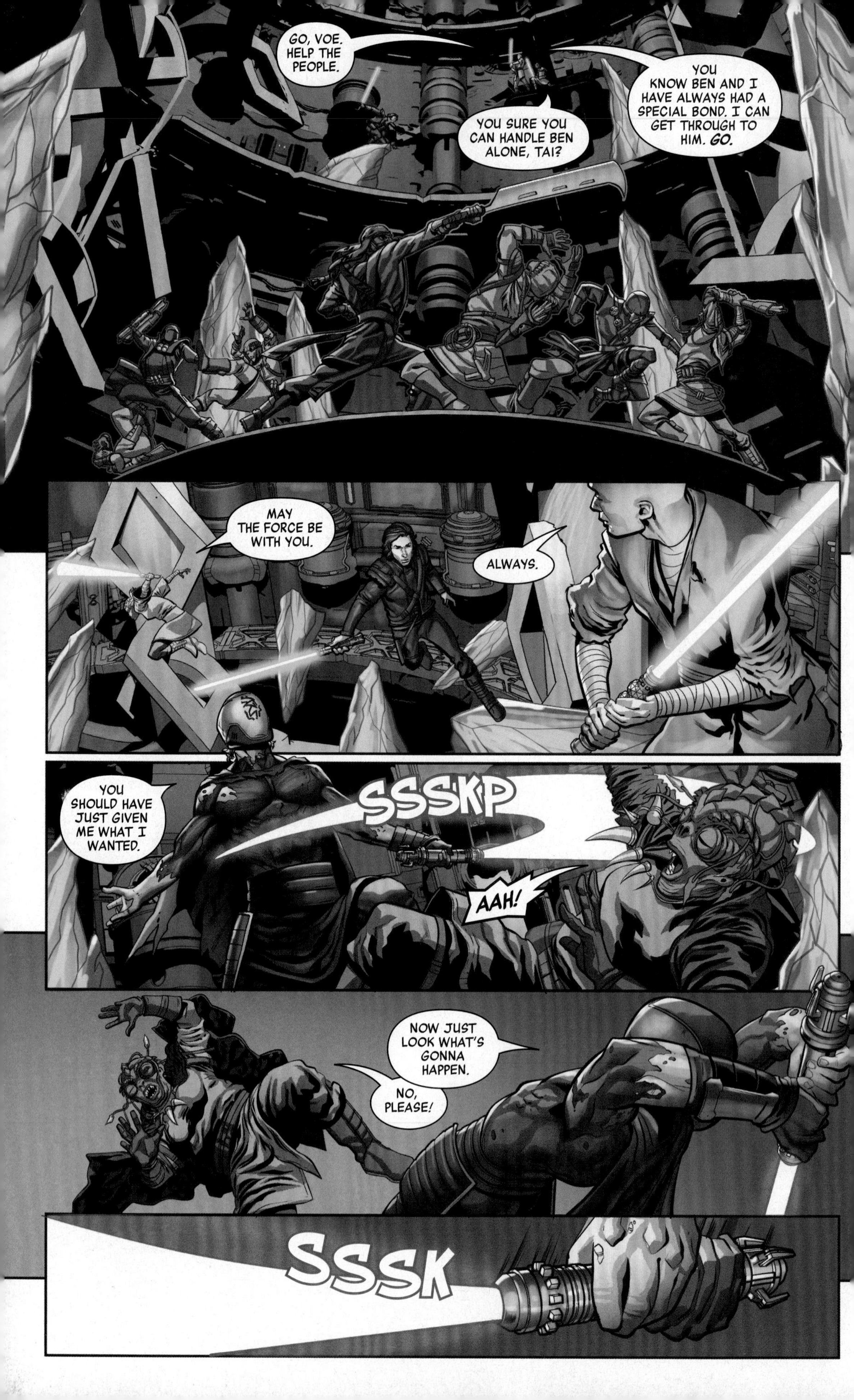
GO, VOE. HELP THE PEOPLE.
YOU SURE YOU CAN HANDLE BEN ALONE, TAI?
YOU KNOW BEN AND I HAVE ALWAYS HAD A SPECIAL BOND. I CAN GET THROUGH TO HIM. GO.
MAY THE FORCE BE WITH YOU.
ALWAYS.
YOU SHOULD HAVE JUST GIVEN ME WHAT I WANTED.
SSSKP
AAH!
NOW JUST LOOK WHAT'S GONNA HAPPEN.
NO, PLEASE!
SSSK

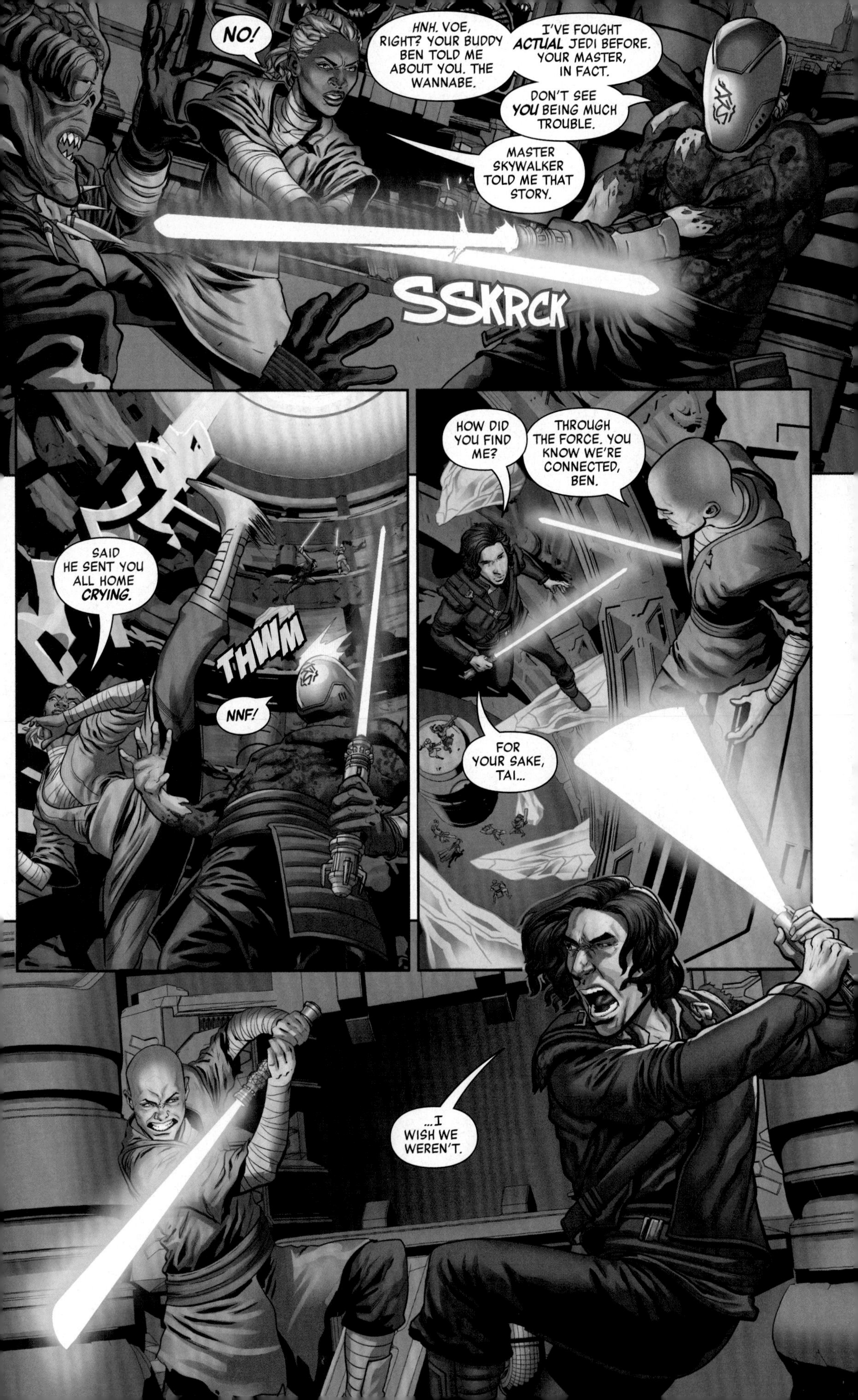
NO!
HNH. VOE, RIGHT? YOUR BUDDY BEN TOLD ME ABOUT YOU. THE WANNABE.
I'VE FOUGHT ACTUAL JEDI BEFORE. YOUR MASTER, IN FACT.
DON'T SEE YOU BEING MUCH TROUBLE.
MASTER SKYWALKER TOLD ME THAT STORY.
SSKRCK
SAID HE SENT YOU ALL HOME CRYING.
THWM
NNF!
HOW DID YOU FIND ME?
THROUGH THE FORCE. YOU KNOW WE'RE CONNECTED, BEN.
FOR YOUR SAKE, TAI...
...I WISH WE WEREN'T.

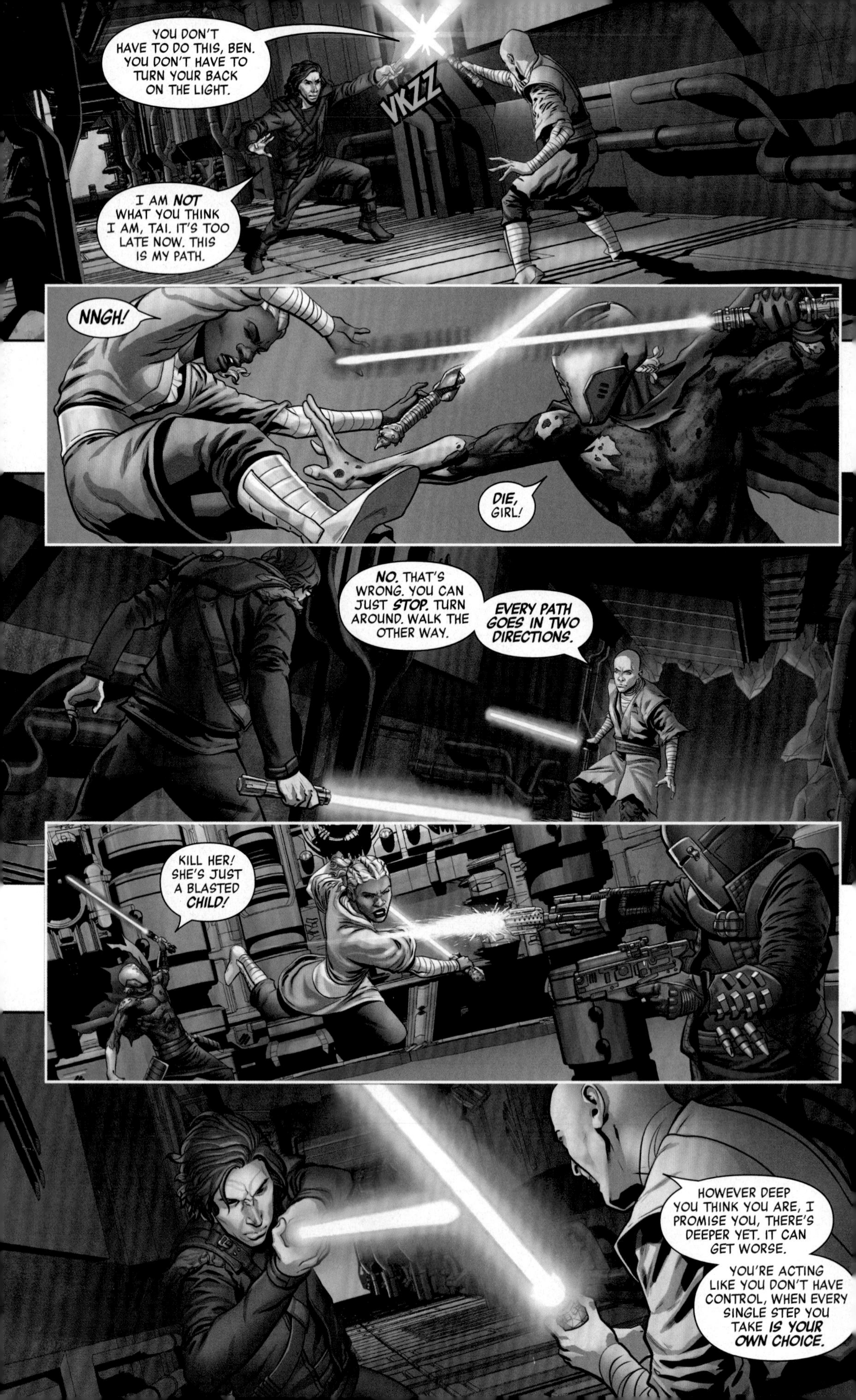
YOU DON'T HAVE TO DO THIS, BEN. YOU DON'T HAVE TO TURN YOUR BACK ON THE LIGHT.
VKZZ
I AM NOT WHAT YOU THINK I AM, TAI. IT'S TOO LATE NOW. THIS IS MY PATH.
NNGH!
DIE, GIRL!
NO. THAT'S WRONG. YOU CAN JUST STOP. TURN AROUND. WALK THE OTHER WAY.
EVERY PATH GOES IN TWO DIRECTIONS.
KILL HER! SHE'S JUST A BLASTED CHILD!
HOWEVER DEEP YOU THINK YOU ARE, I PROMISE YOU, THERE'S DEEPER YET. IT CAN GET WORSE.
YOU'RE ACTING LIKE YOU DON'T HAVE CONTROL, WHEN EVERY SINGLE STEP YOU TAKE IS YOUR OWN CHOICE.

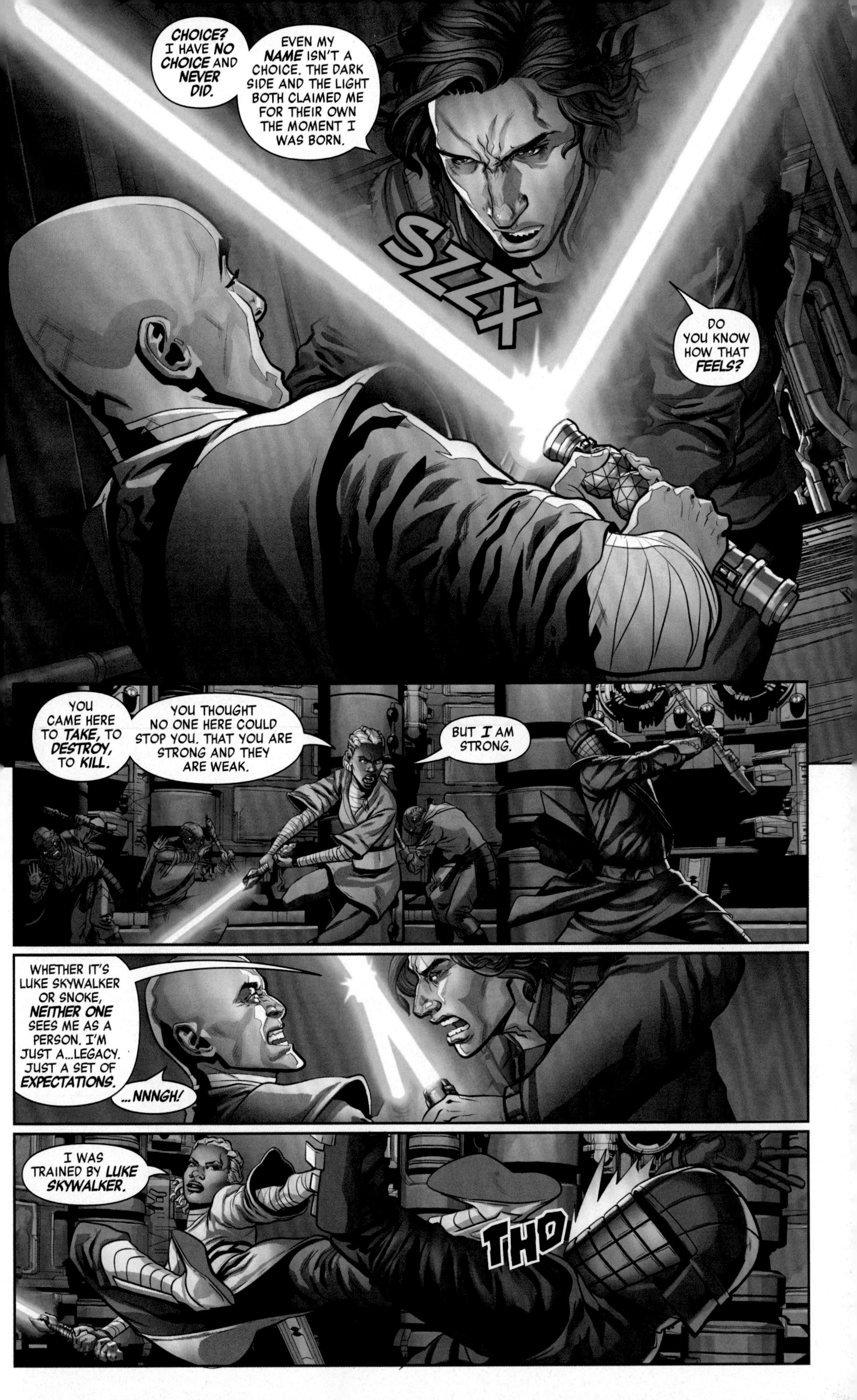
CHOICE? I HAVE NO CHOICE AND NEVER DID.
EVEN MY NAME ISN'T A CHOICE. THE DARK SIDE AND THE LIGHT BOTH CLAIMED ME FOR THEIR OWN THE MOMENT I WAS BORN.
SZZX
DO YOU KNOW HOW THAT FEELS?
YOU CAME HERE TO TAKE, TO DESTROY, TO KILL.
YOU THOUGHT NO ONE HERE COULD STOP YOU. THAT YOU ARE STRONG AND THEY ARE WEAK.
BUT I AM STRONG.
WHETHER IT'S LUKE SKYWALKER OR SNOKE, NEITHER ONE SEES ME AS A PERSON. I'M JUST A...LEGACY. JUST A SET OF EXPECTATIONS.
...NNNGH!
I WAS TRAINED BY LUKE SKYWALKER.
THD

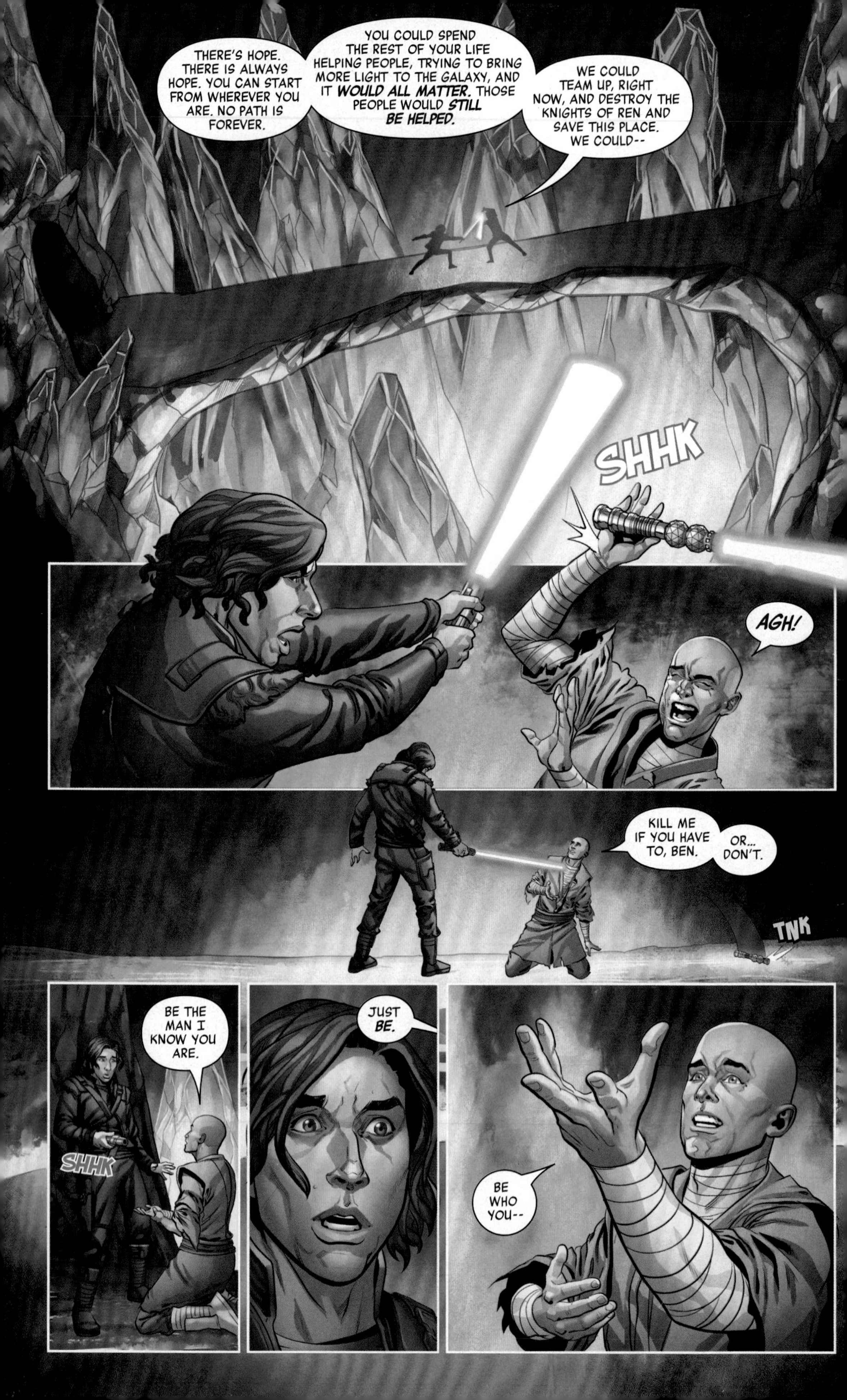
THERE'S HOPE. THERE IS ALWAYS HOPE. YOU CAN START FROM WHEREVER YOU ARE. NO PATH IS FOREVER.
YOU COULD SPEND THE REST OF YOUR LIFE HELPING PEOPLE, TRYING TO BRING MORE LIGHT TO THE GALAXY, AND IT WOULD ALL MATTER. THOSE PEOPLE WOULD STILL BE HELPED.
WE COULD TEAM UP, RIGHT NOW, AND DESTROY THE KNIGHTS OF REN AND SAVE THIS PLACE. WE COULD--
SHHK
AGH!
KILL ME IF YOU HAVE TO, BEN.
OR... DON'T.
TNK
BE THE MAN I KNOW YOU ARE.
SHHK
JUST BE.
BE WHO YOU--

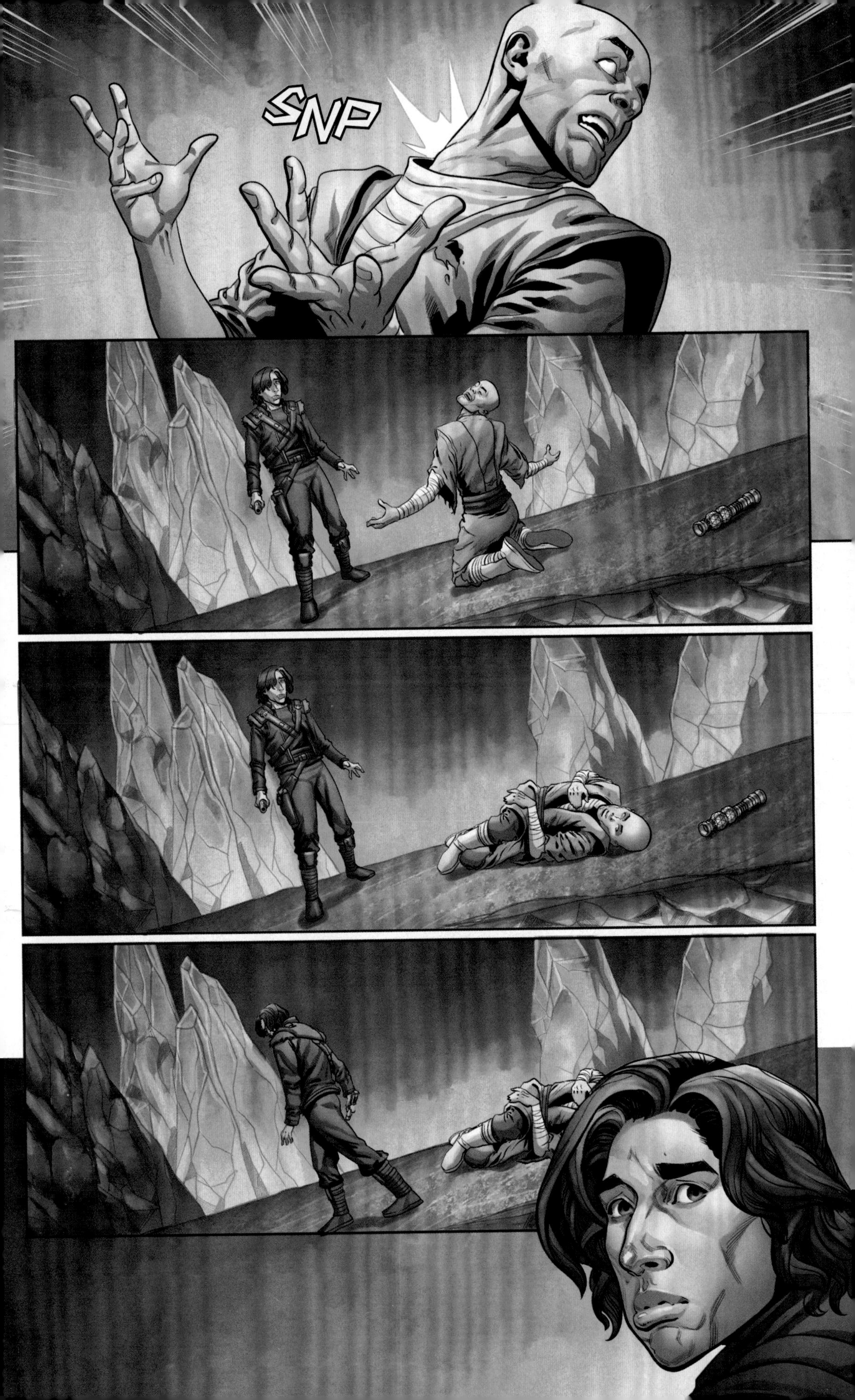
SNP

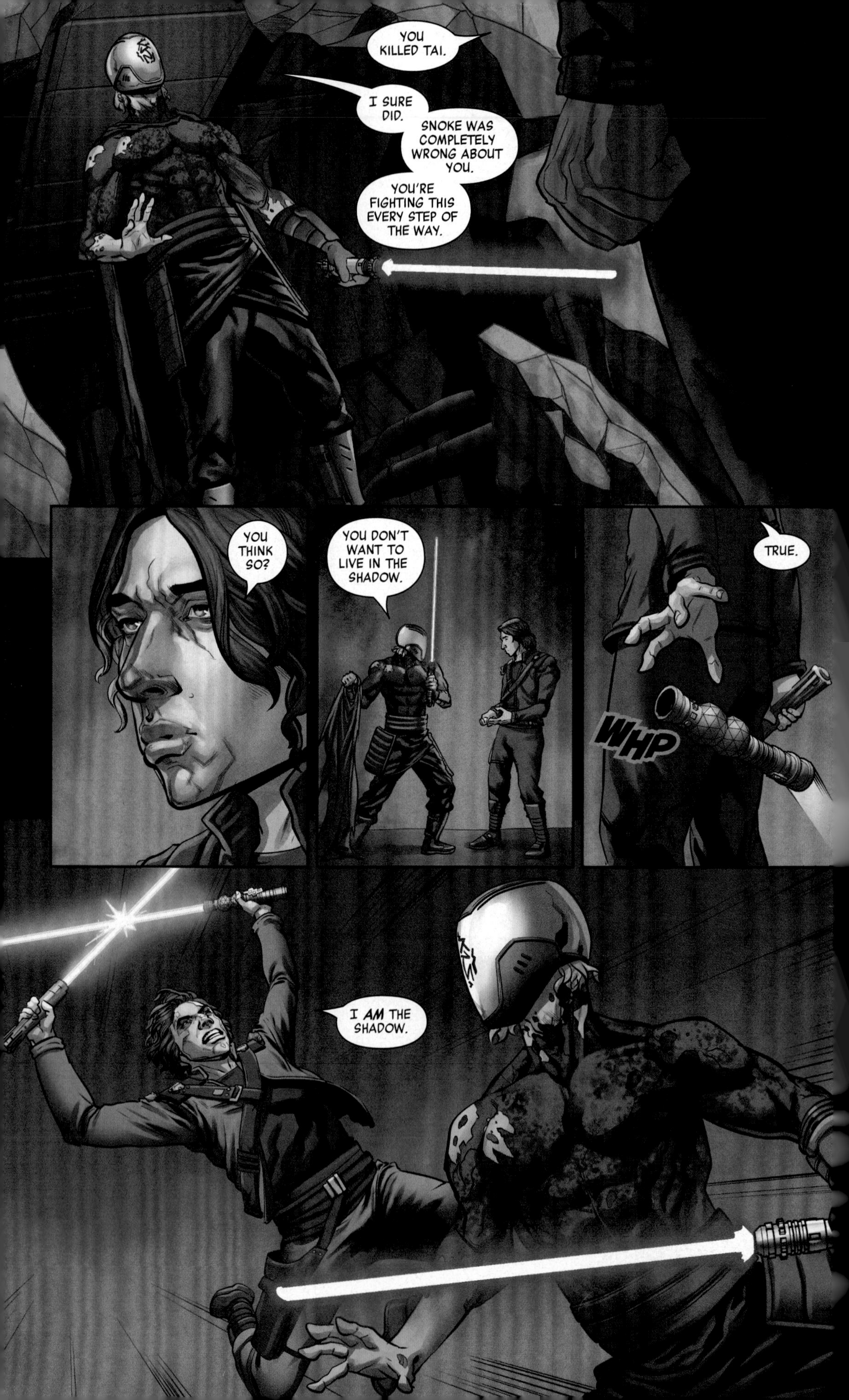
YOU KILLED TAI.
I SURE DID.
SNOKE WAS COMPLETELY WRONG ABOUT YOU.
YOU'RE FIGHTING THIS EVERY STEP OF THE WAY.
YOU THINK SO?
YOU DON'T WANT TO LIVE IN THE SHADOW.
TRUE.
WHP
I *AM* THE SHADOW.

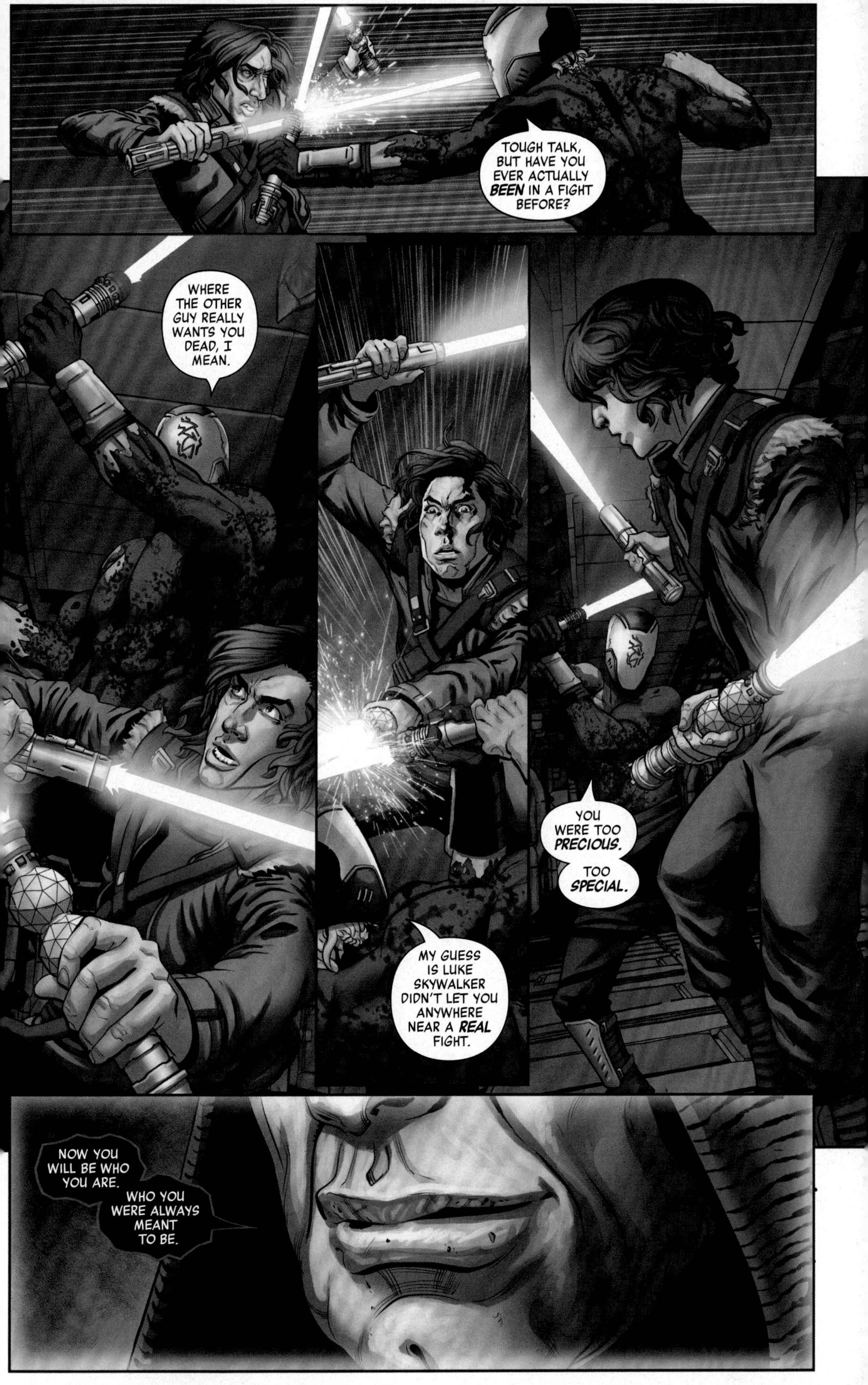

TOUGH TALK, BUT HAVE YOU EVER ACTUALLY ***BEEN*** IN A FIGHT BEFORE?
WHERE THE OTHER GUY REALLY WANTS YOU DEAD, I MEAN.
MY GUESS IS LUKE SKYWALKER DIDN'T LET YOU ANYWHERE NEAR A ***REAL*** FIGHT.
YOU WERE TOO ***PRECIOUS.***
TOO ***SPECIAL.***
NOW YOU WILL BE WHO YOU ARE.
WHO YOU WERE ALWAYS MEANT TO BE.

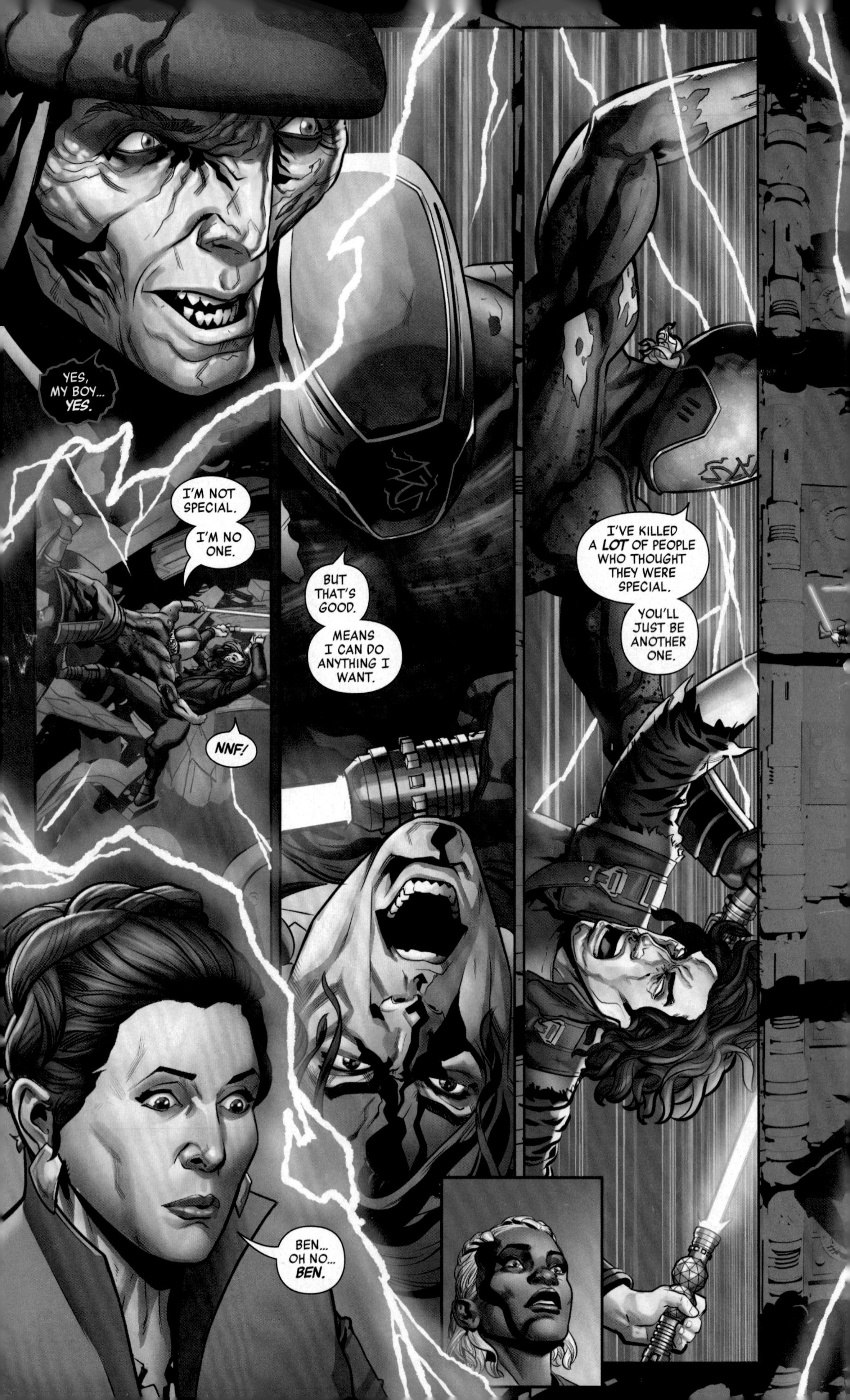
YES, MY BOY... YES.
I'M NOT SPECIAL.
I'M NO ONE.
NNF!
BUT THAT'S GOOD.
MEANS I CAN DO ANYTHING I WANT.
I'VE KILLED A LOT OF PEOPLE WHO THOUGHT THEY WERE SPECIAL.
YOU'LL JUST BE ANOTHER ONE.
BEN... OH NO... BEN.

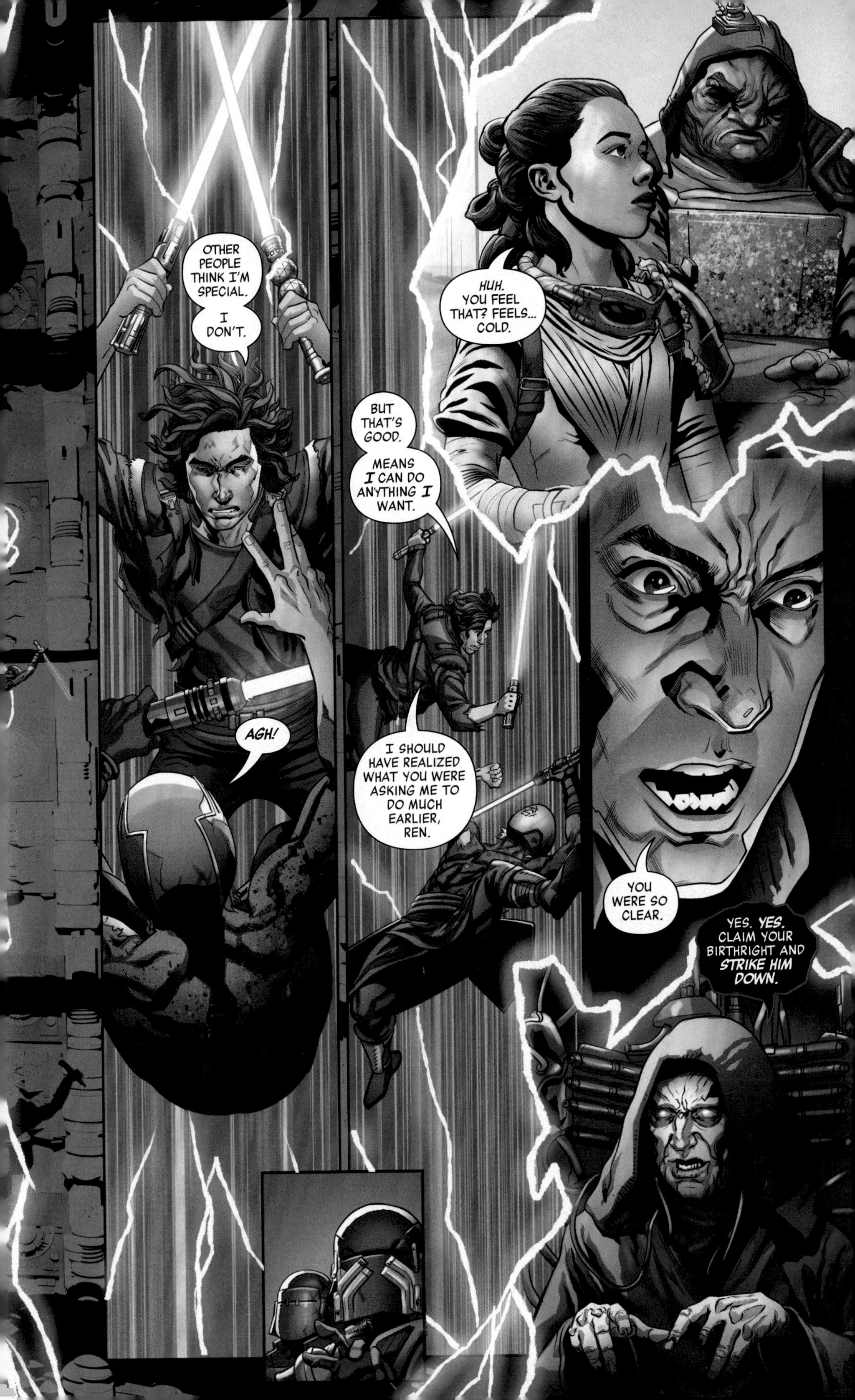
OTHER PEOPLE THINK I'M SPECIAL.
I DON'T.
AGH!
HUH. YOU FEEL THAT? FEELS... COLD.
BUT THAT'S GOOD.
MEANS I CAN DO ANYTHING I WANT.
I SHOULD HAVE REALIZED WHAT YOU WERE ASKING ME TO DO MUCH EARLIER, REN.
YOU WERE SO CLEAR.
YES. YES. CLAIM YOUR BIRTHRIGHT AND STRIKE HIM DOWN.

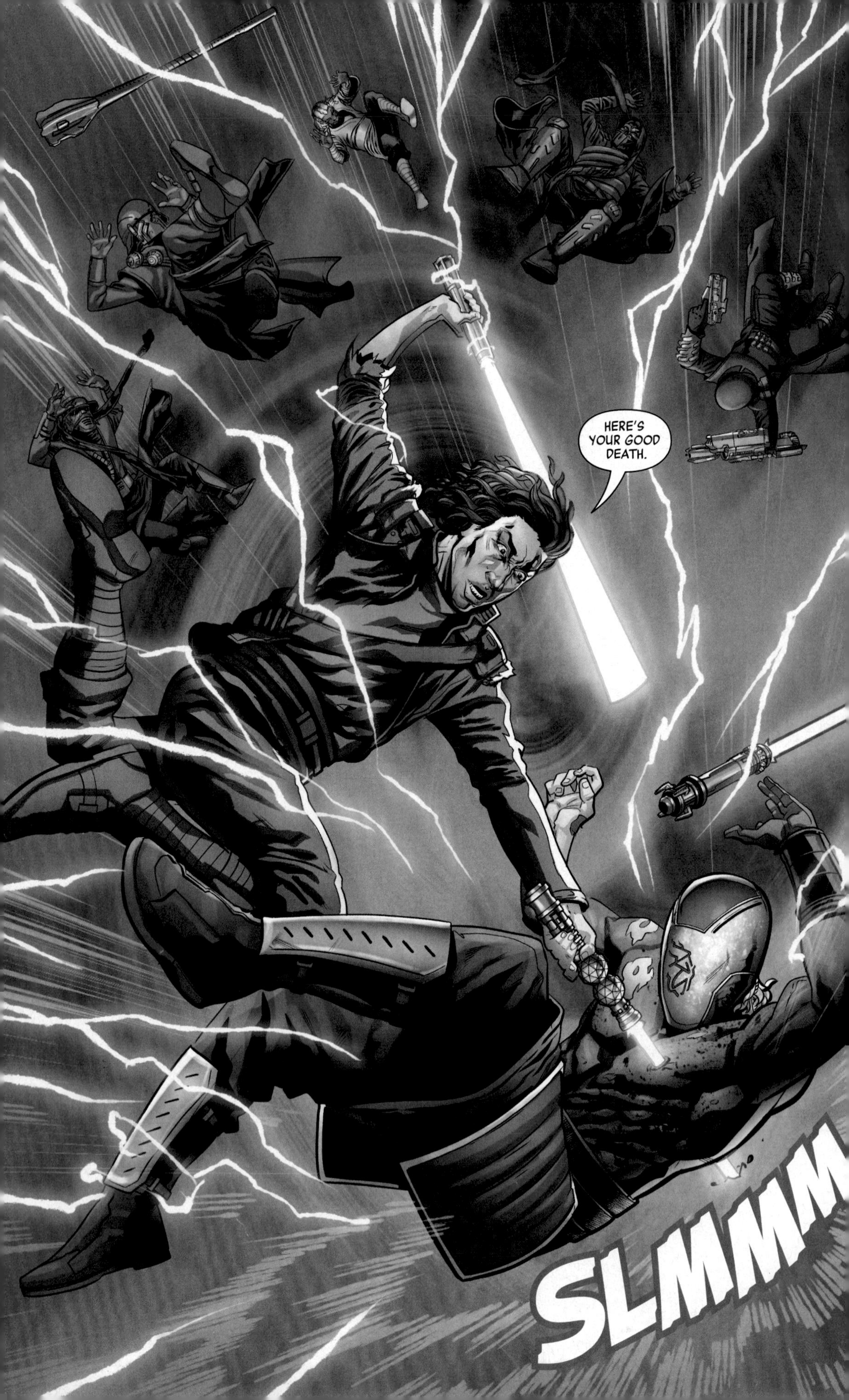
HERE'S YOUR GOOD DEATH.
SLMMM

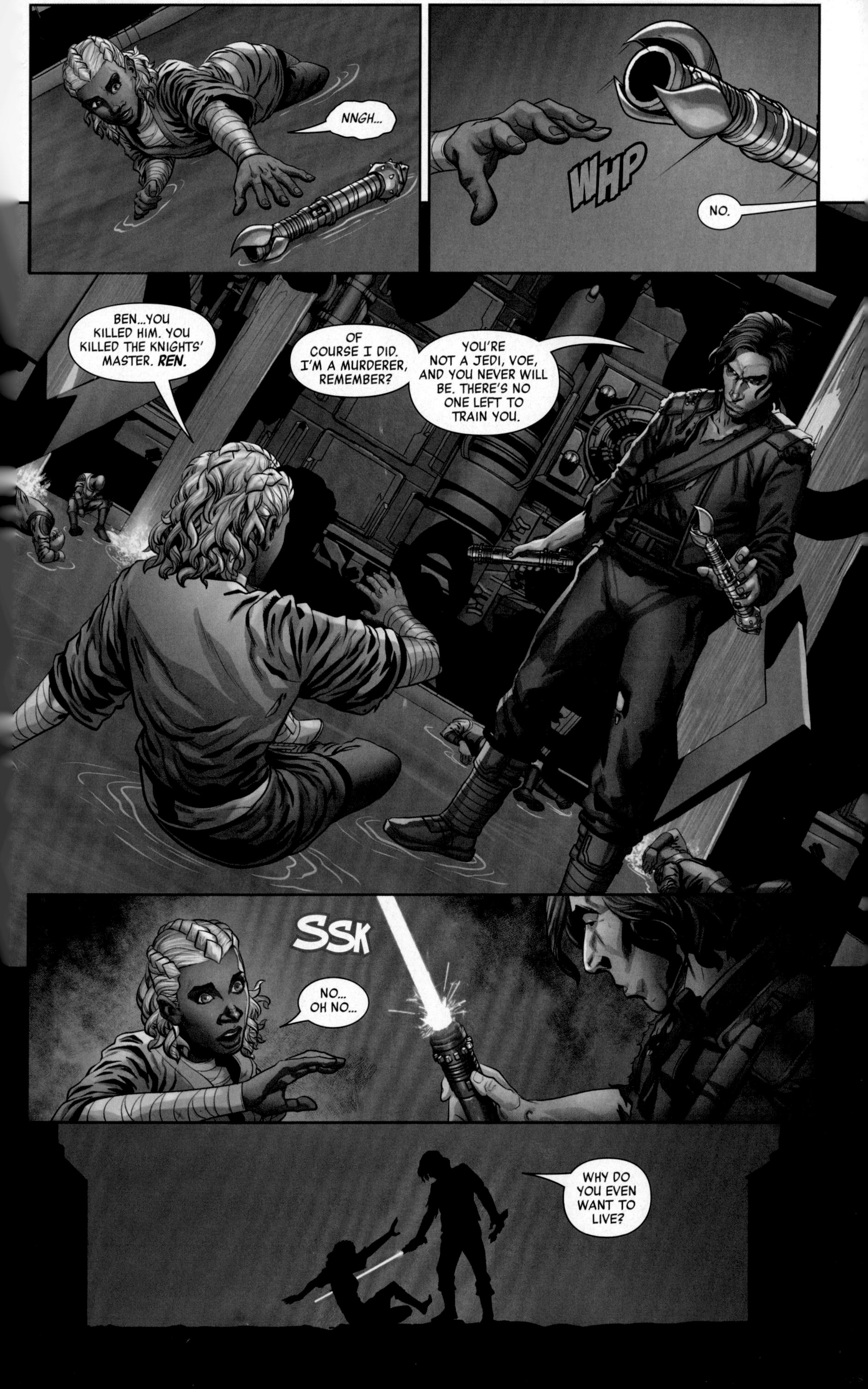
NNGH...
WHP
NO.
BEN...YOU KILLED HIM. YOU KILLED THE KNIGHTS' MASTER. REN.
OF COURSE I DID. I'M A MURDERER, REMEMBER?
YOU'RE NOT A JEDI, VOE, AND YOU NEVER WILL BE. THERE'S NO ONE LEFT TO TRAIN YOU.
SSK
NO... OH NO...
WHY DO YOU EVEN WANT TO LIVE?

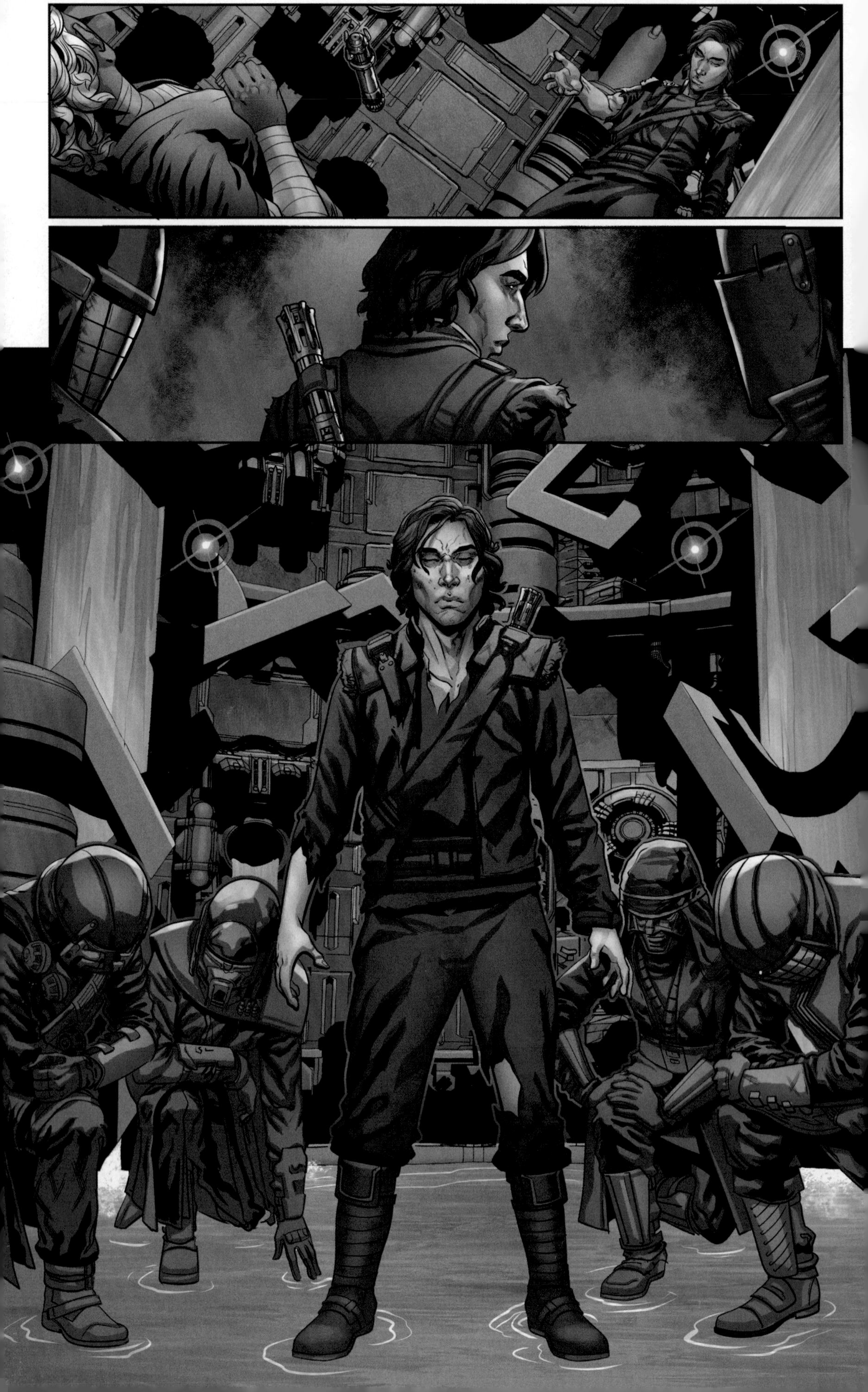

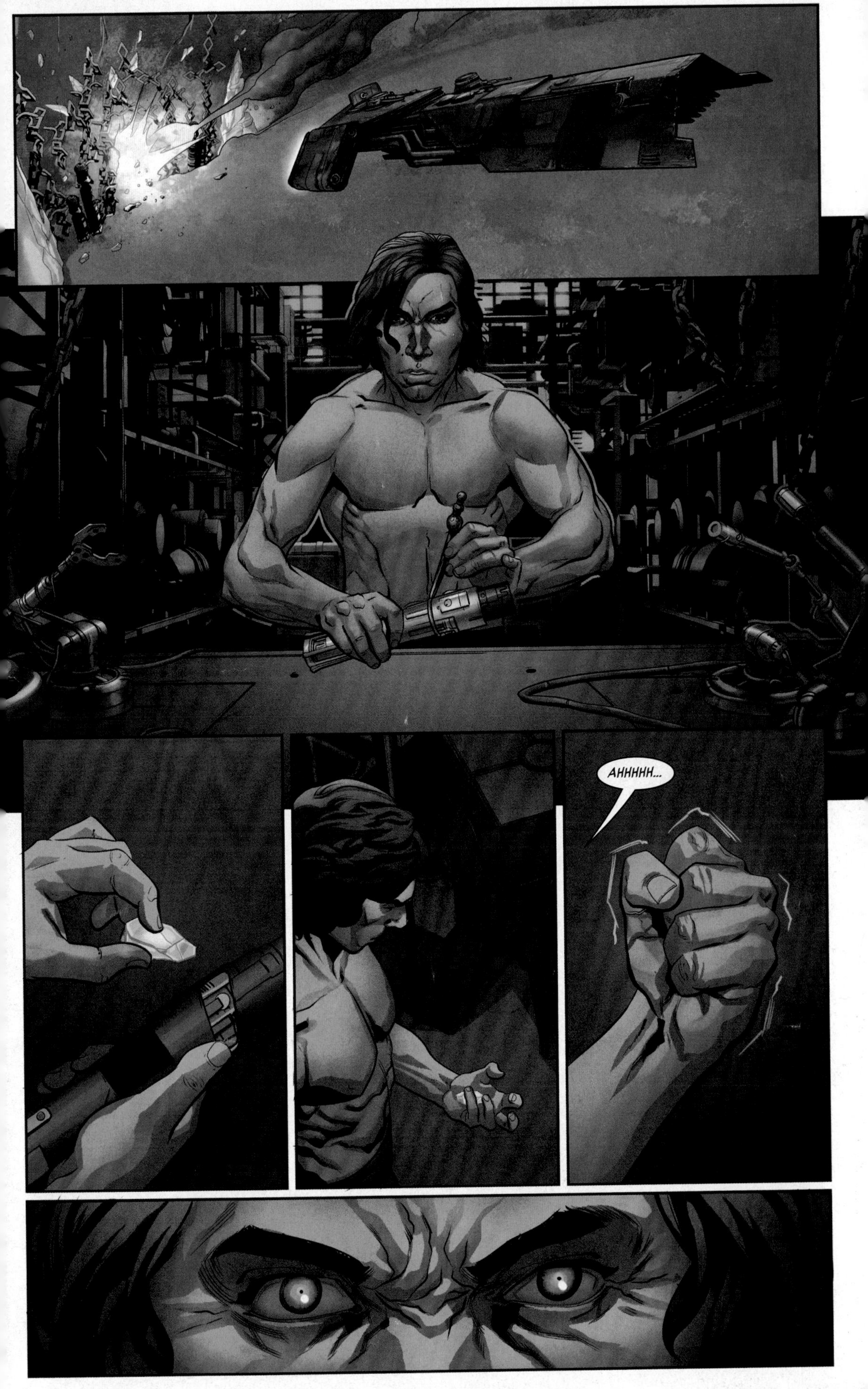
AHHHHH...

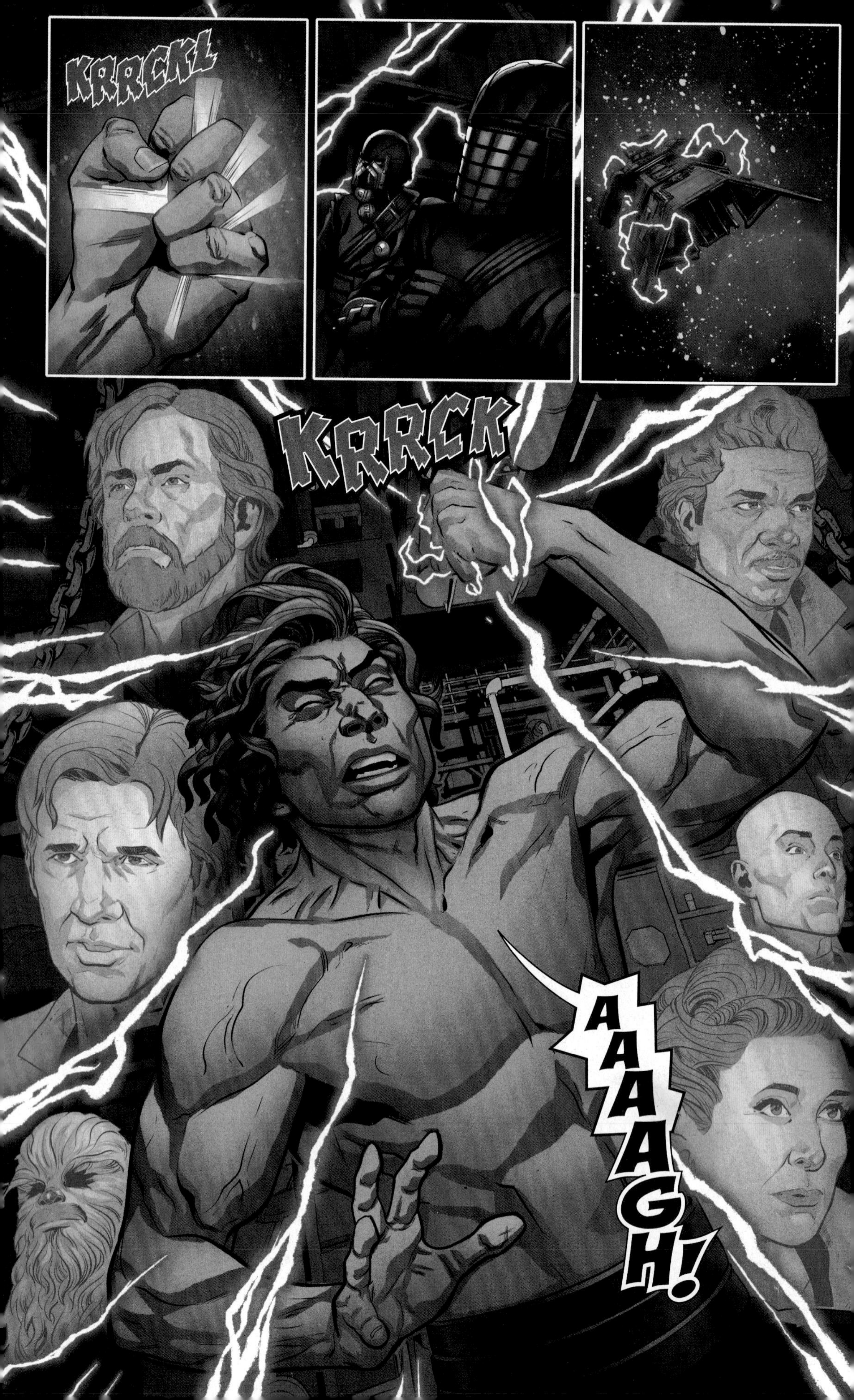
KRRCKL
KRRCK
AAAAAGH!

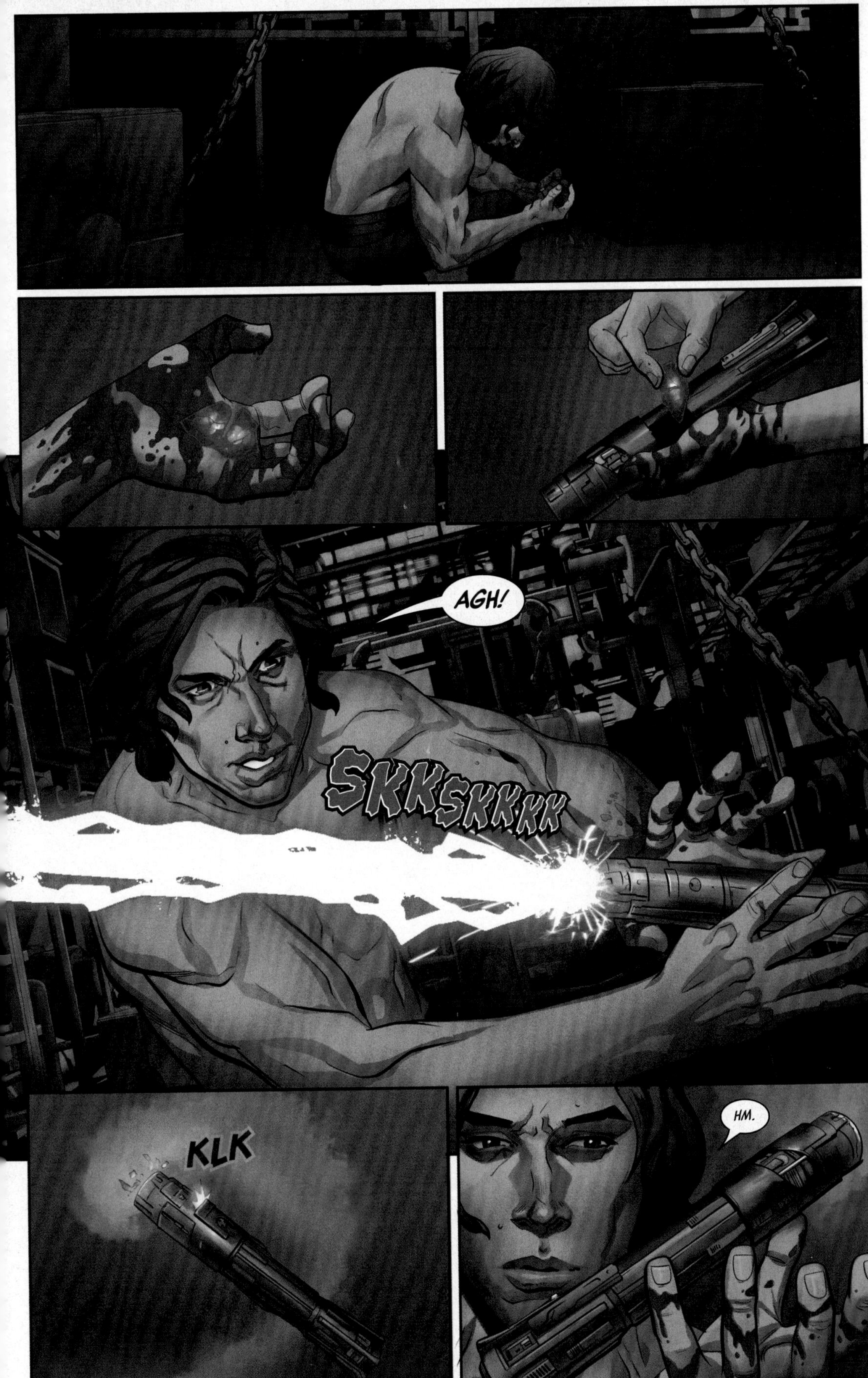
AGH!
SKKSKKKK
KLK
HM.

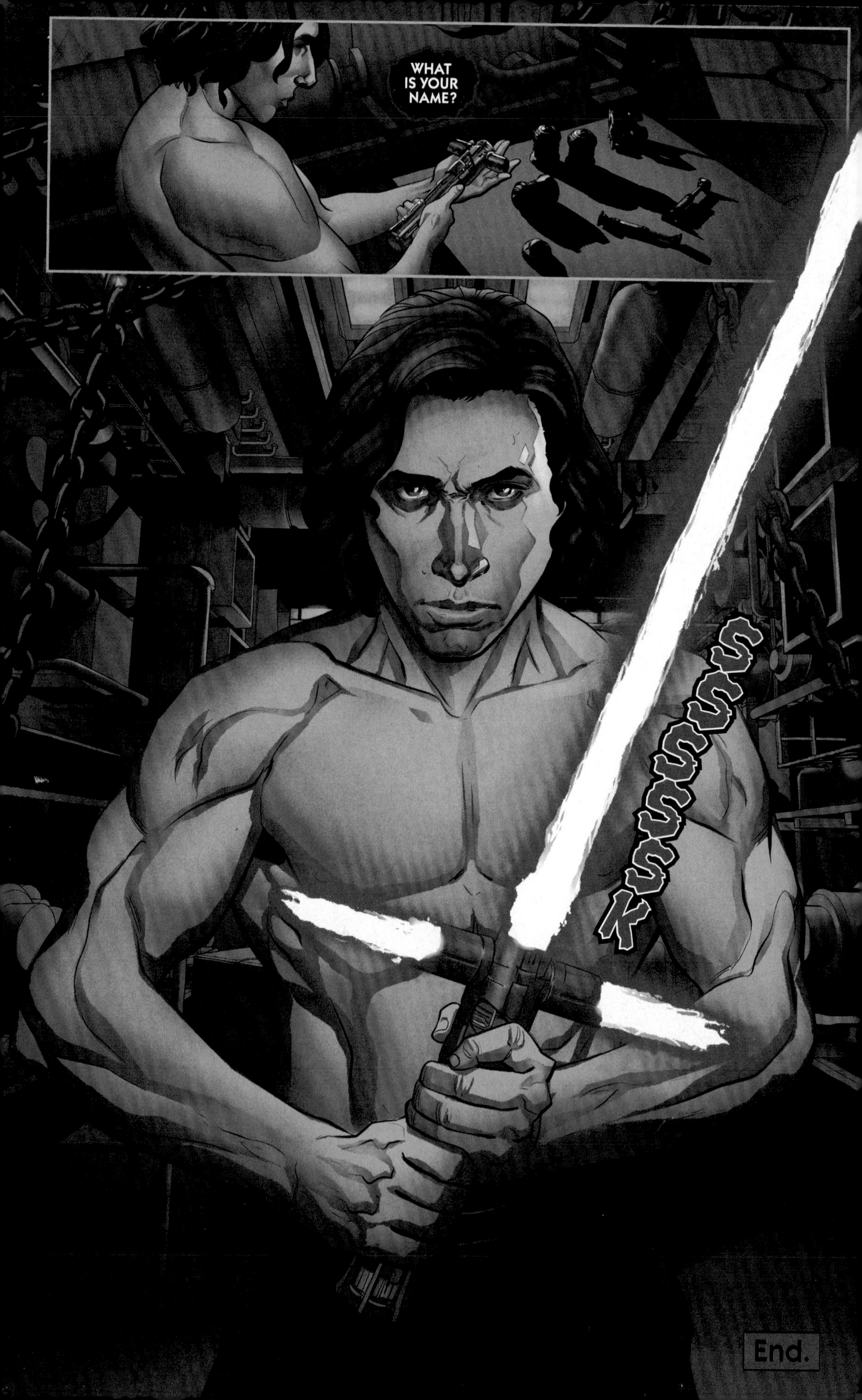
WHAT IS YOUR NAME?
SSSSSSSK
End.

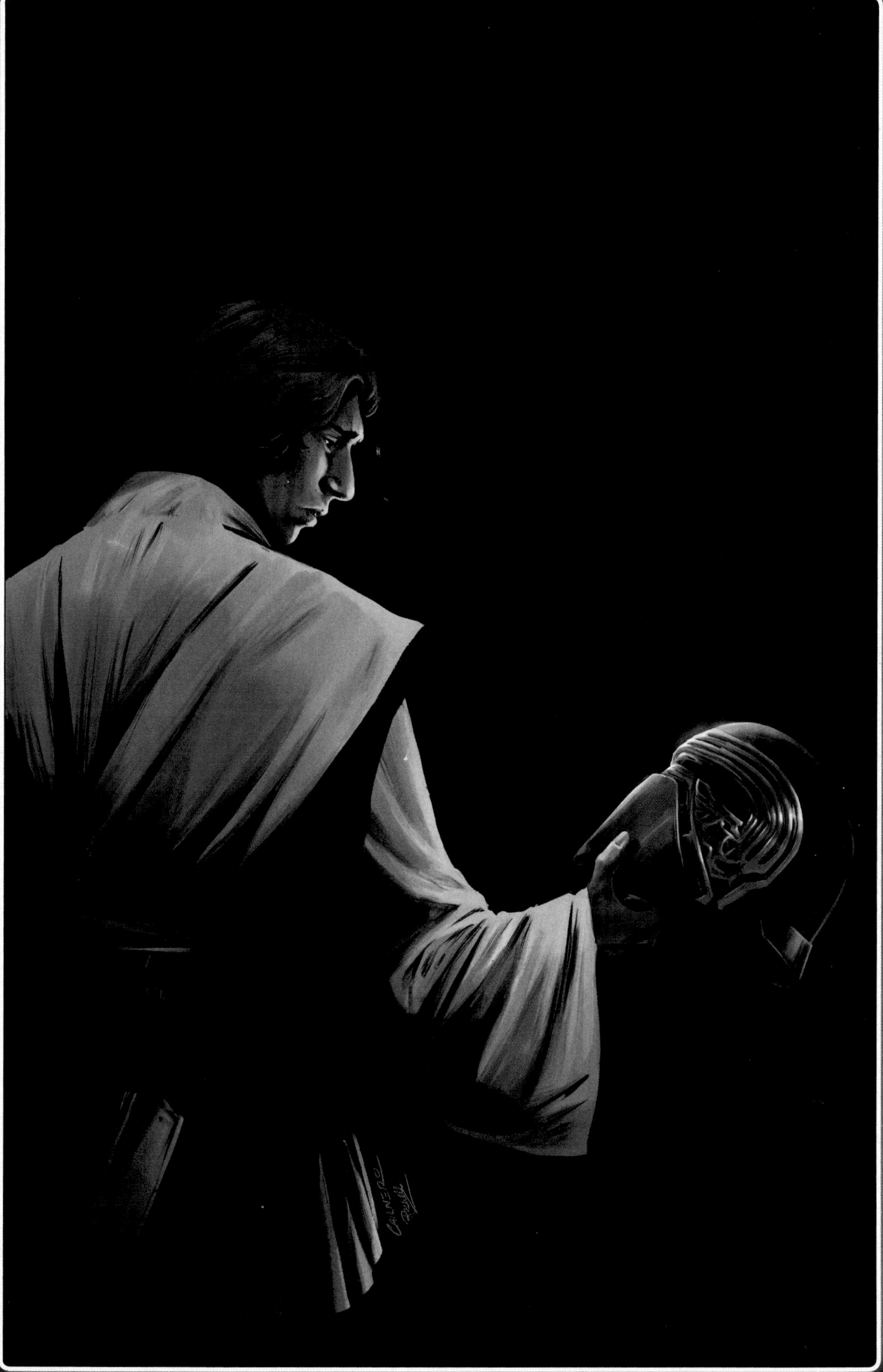

STAR WARS: THE RISE OF KYLO REN 1 **Variant by**
CARMEN CARNERO & RACHELLE ROSENBERG

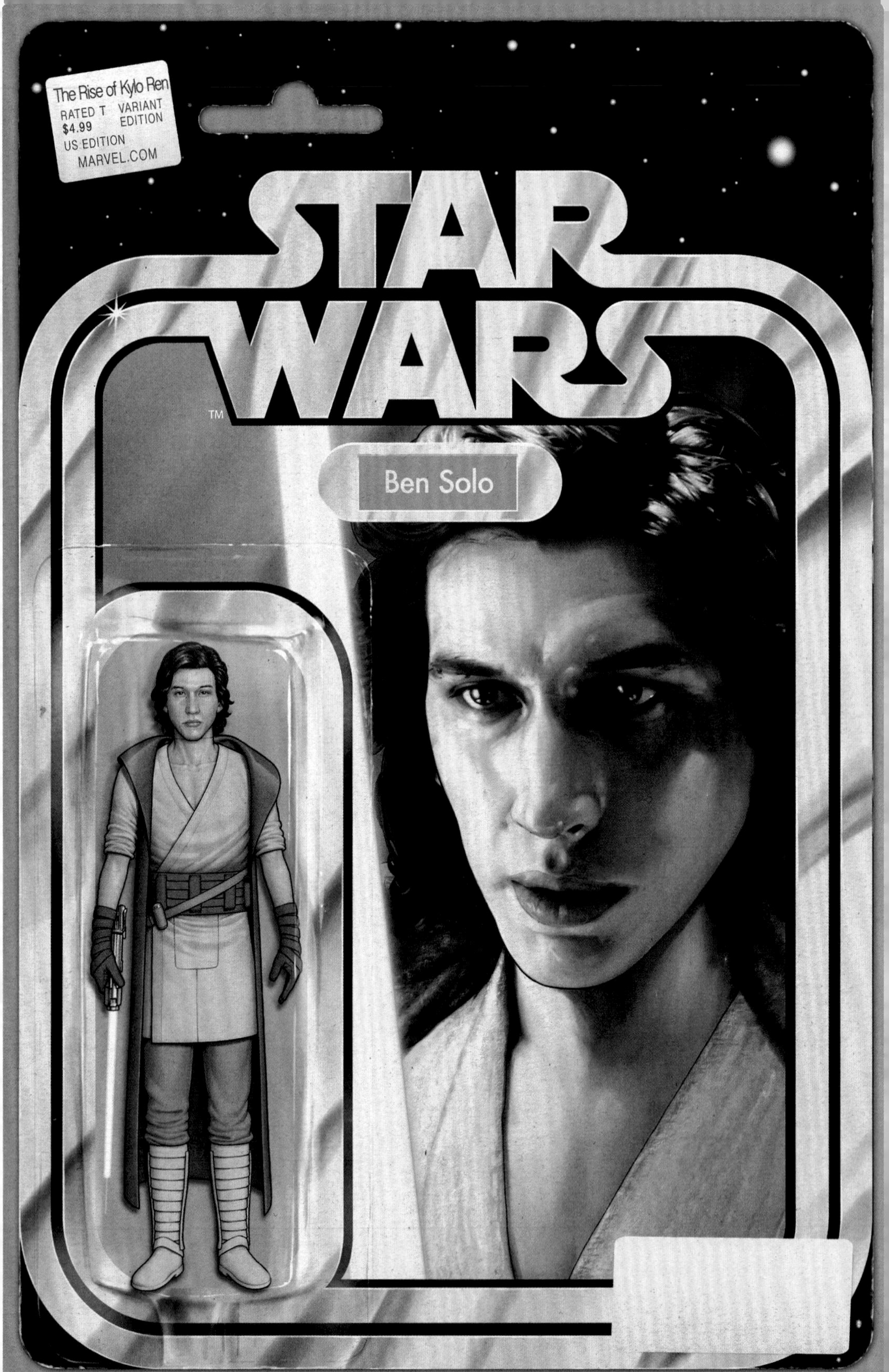
The Rise of Kylo Ren
RATED T
$4.99
VARIANT EDITION
US EDITION
MARVEL.COM
STAR WARS
TM
Ben Solo

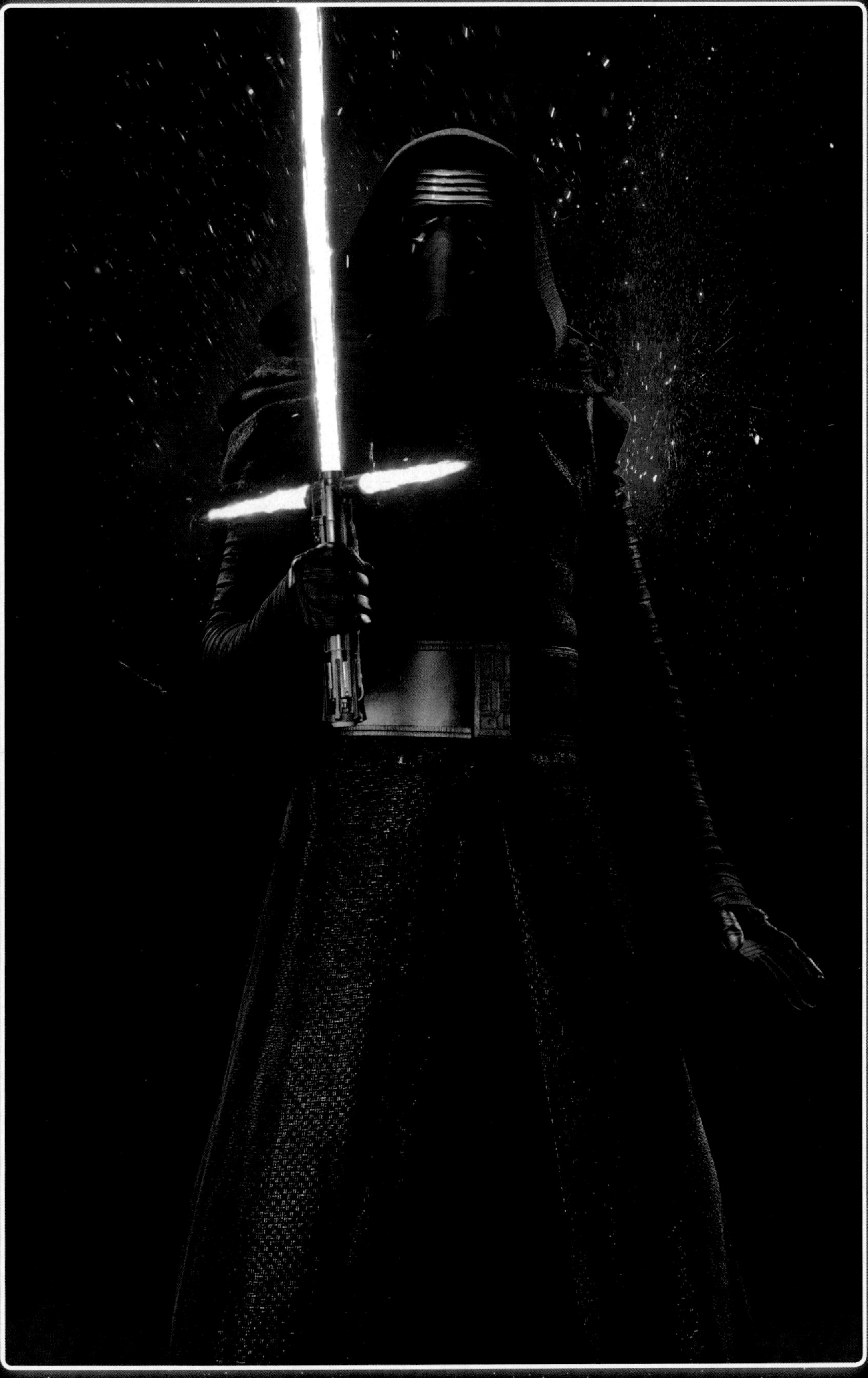

***STAR WARS: THE RISE OF KYLO REN 1* Movie Variant**

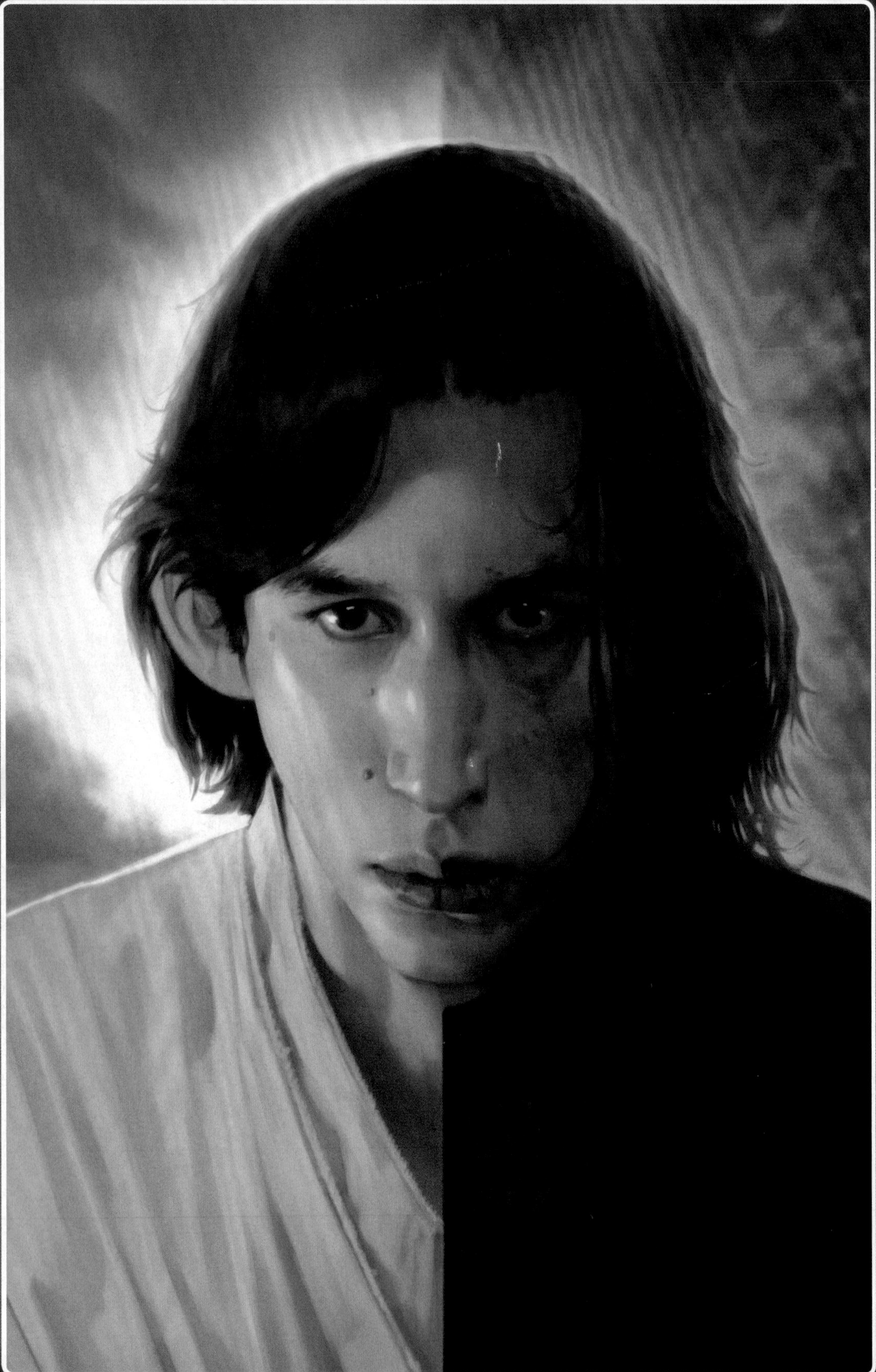

STAR WARS: THE RISE OF KYLO REN 2 **Variant by**
JODIE MUIR

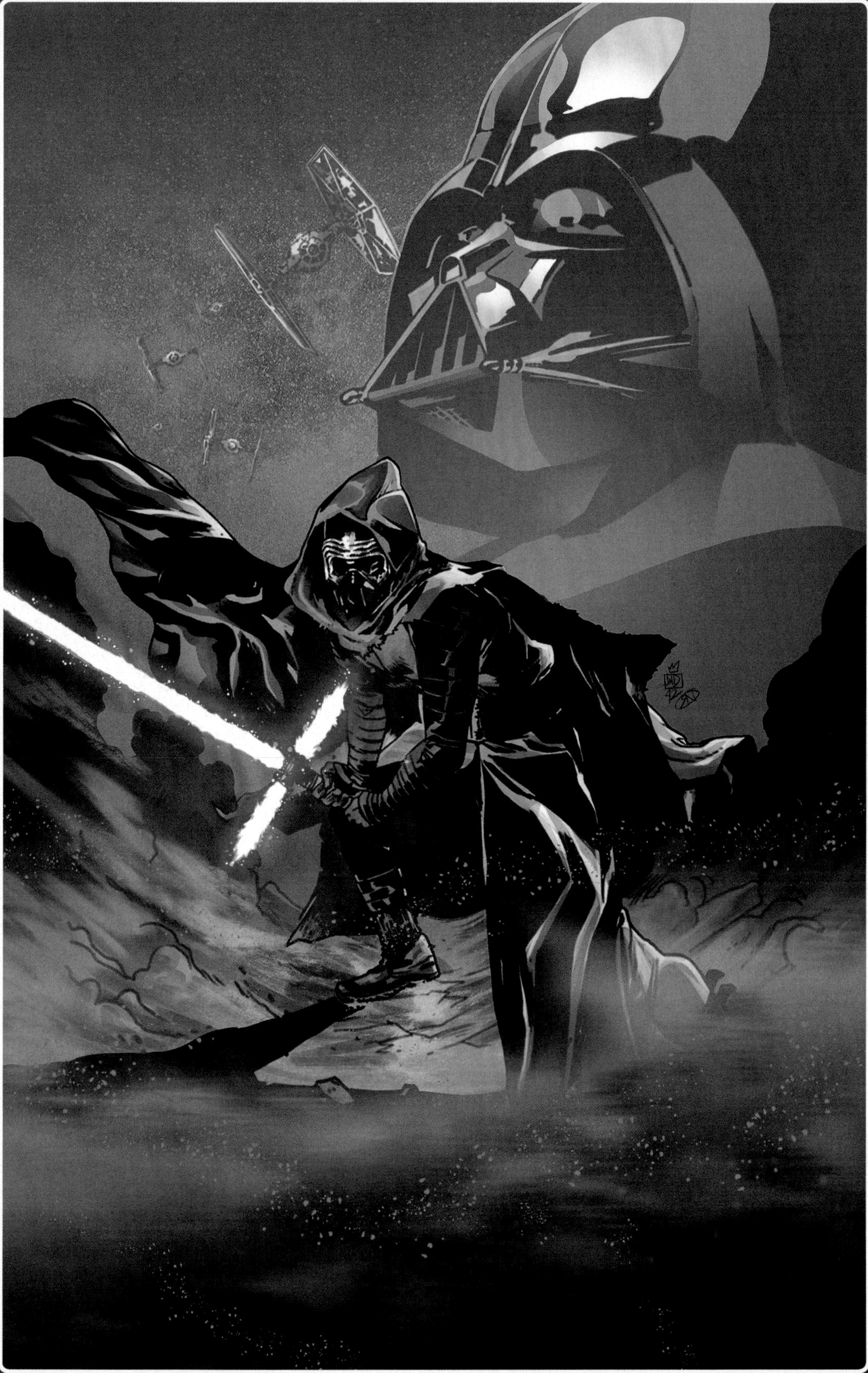

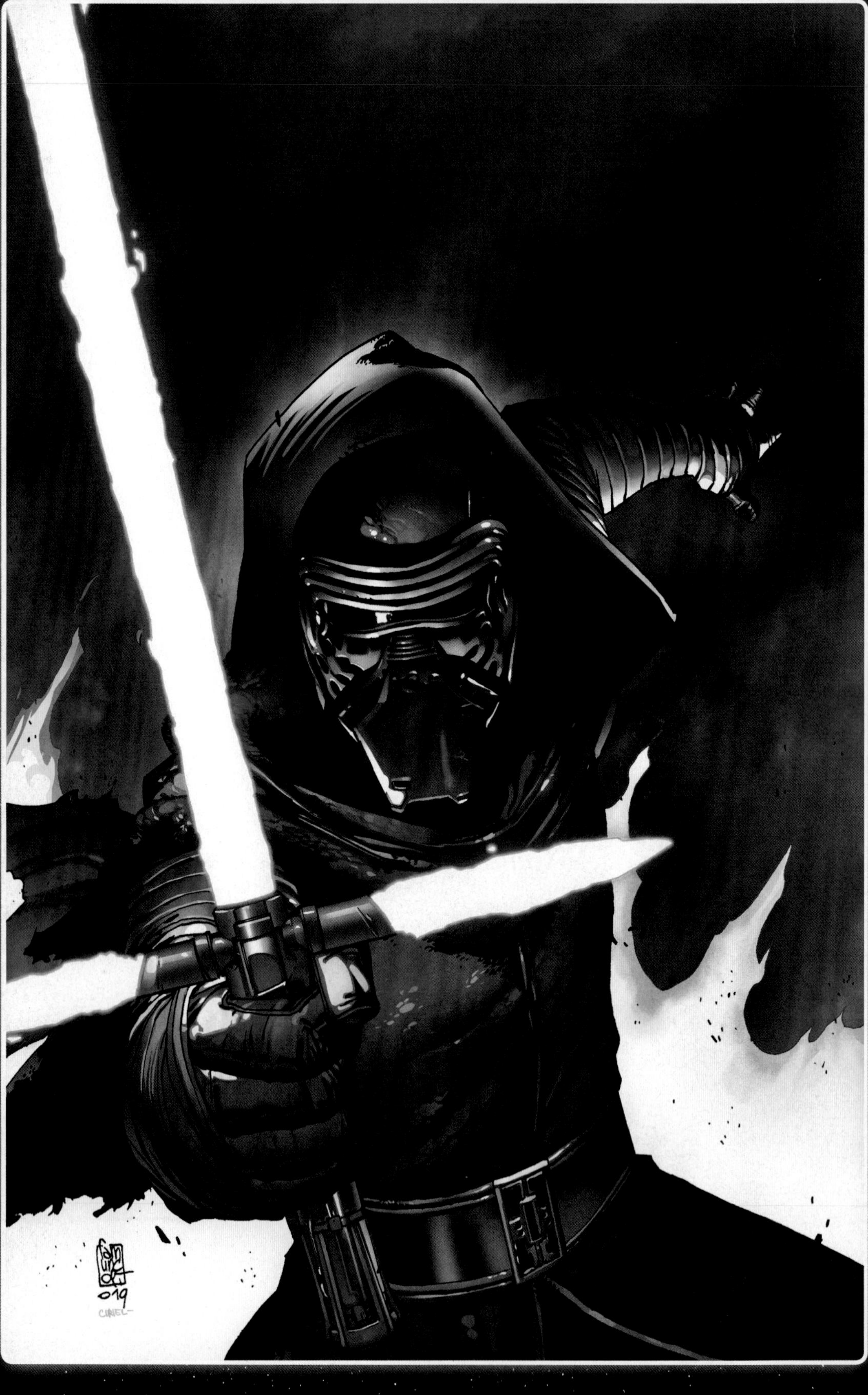

STAR WARS: THE RISE OF KYLO REN 4 **Variant by**
GIUSEPPE CAMUNCOLI & DAVID CURIEL

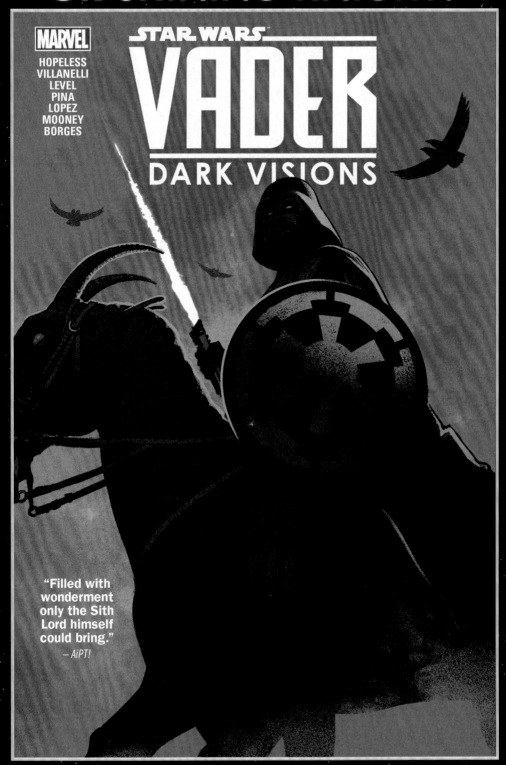

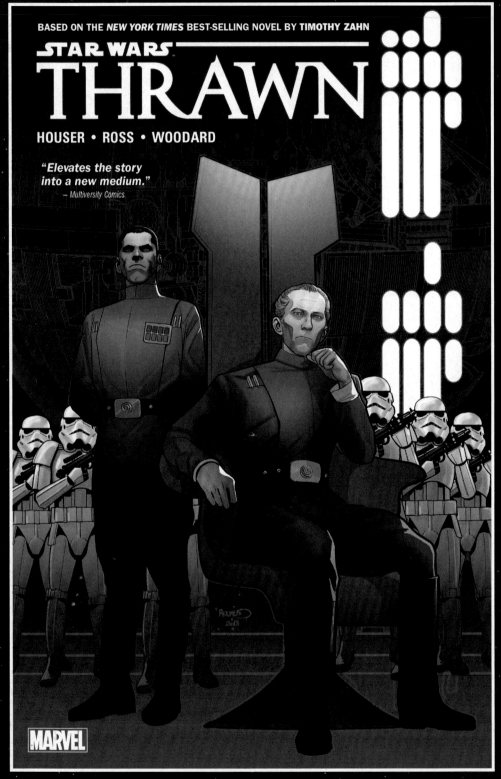

ROGUE ARCHAEOLOGIST DOCTOR APHRA THIEVES HER WAY ACROSS THE GALAXY!

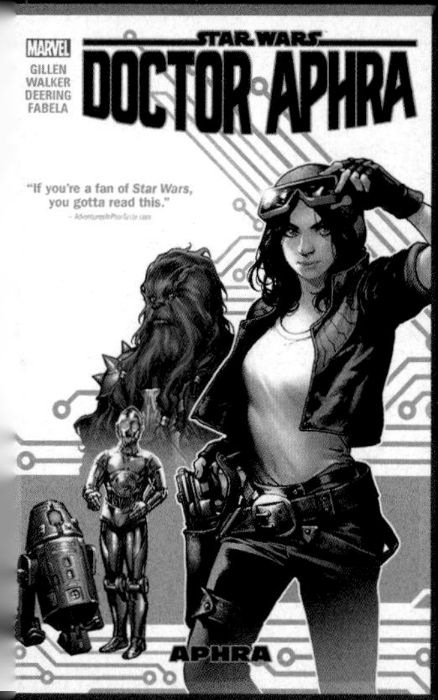
MARVEL
GILLEN
WALKER
DEERING
FABELA
STAR WARS
DOCTOR APHRA
"If you're a fan of Star Wars, you gotta read this."
APHRA

STAR WARS: DOCTOR APHRA VOL. 1 – APHRA TPB

ISBN: 978-1302913212

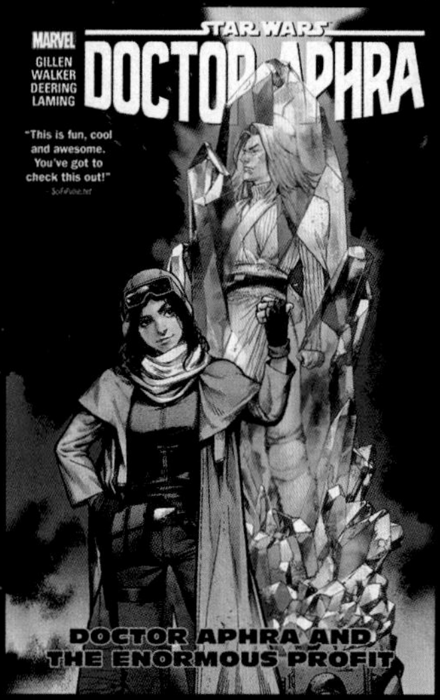
MARVEL
GILLEN
WALKER
DEERING
LAMING
STAR WARS
DOCTOR APHRA
"This is fun, cool and awesome. You've got to check this out!"
DOCTOR APHRA AND THE ENORMOUS PROFIT

STAR WARS: DOCTOR APHRA VOL. 2 – DOCTOR APHRA AND THE ENORMOUS PROFIT TPB

ISBN: 978-1302907631

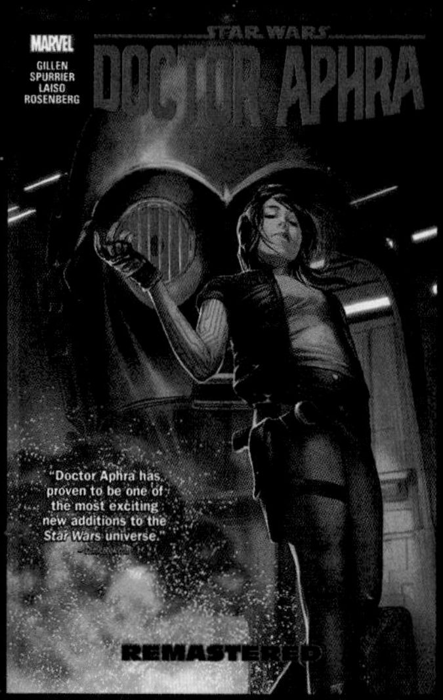
MARVEL
GILLEN
SPURRIER
LAISO
ROSENBERG
STAR WARS
DOCTOR APHRA
"Doctor Aphra has proven to be one of the most exciting new additions to the Star Wars universe."
REMASTERED

STAR WARS: DOCTOR APHRA VOL. 3 – REMASTERED TPB

ISBN: 978-1302911522

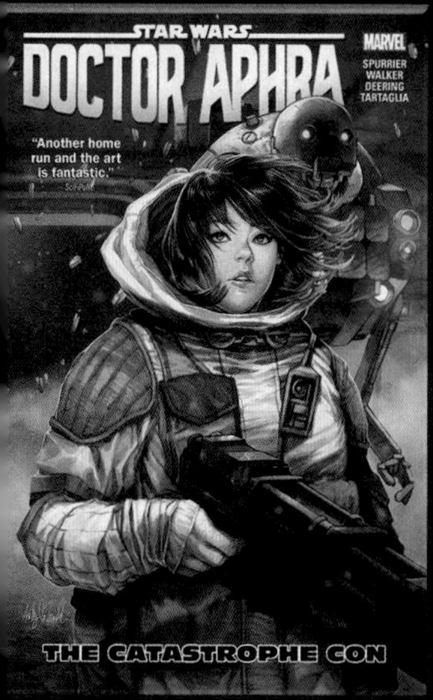
STAR WARS
DOCTOR APHRA
MARVEL
SPURRIER
WALKER
DEERING
TARTAGLIA
"Another home run and the art is fantastic."
THE CATASTROPHE CON

STAR WARS: DOCTOR APHRA VOL. 4 – THE CATASTROPHE CON TPB

ISBN: 978-1302911539

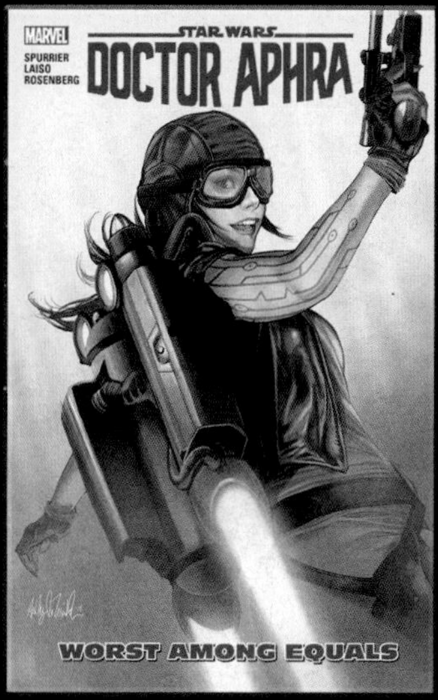
MARVEL
SPURRIER
LAISO
ROSENBERG
STAR WARS
DOCTOR APHRA
WORST AMONG EQUALS

STAR WARS: DOCTOR APHRA VOL. 5 – WORST AMONG EQUALS TPB

ISBN: 978-1302914875

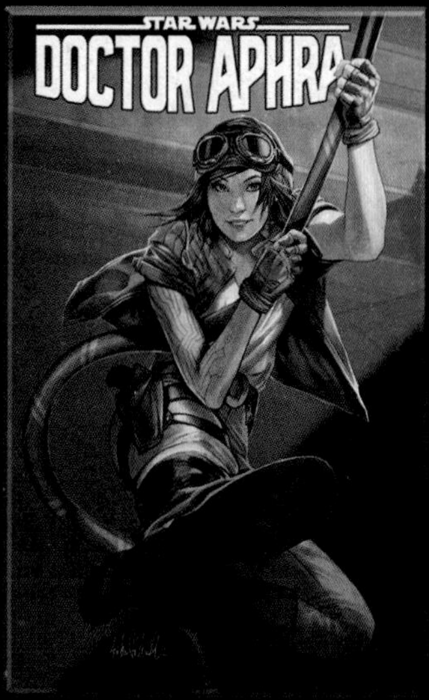
STAR WARS
DOCTOR APHRA

STAR WARS: DOCTOR APHRA VOL. 6 – UNSPEAKABLE REBEL SUPERWEAPON TPB

ISBN: 978-1302914882

ON SALE NOW

VAILABLE IN PRINT AND DIGITAL

TO FIND A COMIC SHOP NEAR YOU,

STAR WARS™

THERE ARE HEROES — AND VILLAINS — ON BOTH SIDES!

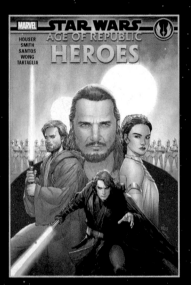

MARVEL
STAR WARS
AGE OF REPUBLIC
HEROES
HOUSER
SMITH
SANTOS
WONG
TARTAGLIA

STAR WARS: AGE OF REPUBLIC – HEROES TPB
ISBN: 978-1302917104
ON SALE NOW!

MARVEL
STAR WARS
AGE OF REBELLION
HEROES
PAK
SPROUSE
STORY
BONVILLAIN

STAR WARS: AGE OF REBELLION – HEROES TPB
ISBN: 978-1302917081
ON SALE NOW!

MARVEL
STAR WARS
AGE OF RESISTANCE
HEROES
TAYLOR
ROSANAS
GURU e-FX

STAR WARS: AGE OF RESISTANCE – HEROES TPB
ISBN: 978-1302917128
NOVEMBER 2019

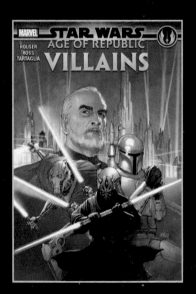

MARVEL
STAR WARS
AGE OF REPUBLIC
VILLAINS
HOUSER
ROSS
TARTAGLIA

STAR WARS: AGE OF REPUBLIC – VILLAINS TPB
ISBN: 978-1302917296
ON SALE NOW!

MARVEL
STAR WARS
AGE OF REBELLION
VILLAINS
PAK
LAMING
BOYD

STAR WARS: AGE OF REBELLION – VILLAINS TPB
ISBN: 978-1302917296
ON SALE NOW!

MARVEL
STAR WARS
AGE OF RESISTANCE
VILLAINS
TAYLOR
KIRK
HAMSCHER
GURU-EFX

STAR WARS: AGE OF RESISTANCE – VILLAINS TPB
ISBN: 978-1302917302
NOVEMBER 2019

IN PRINT AND DIGITAL WHEREVER BOOKS ARE SOLD.
TO FIND A COMIC SHOP NEAR YOU, **VISIT COMICSHOPLOCATOR.COM.**

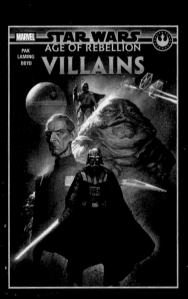

THE ORIGIN OF EVERYONE'S FAVORITE SPACE FARING SCOUNDREL!

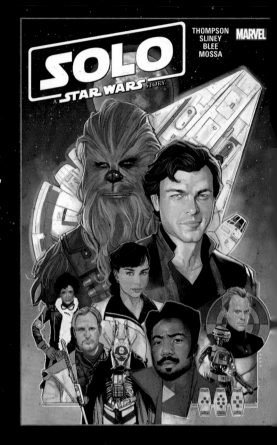
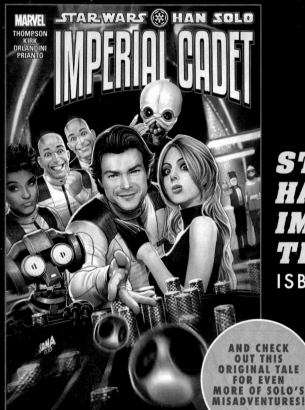